Translation & Adaptation,
Retouch, Lettering and Design -
Kitty Media

© MOTONI MODORU 2005
Originally published in Japan in 2005 by HOUBUNSHA, Tokyo.
English translation rights arranged with HOUBUNSHA, Tokyo,
through TOHAN CORPORATION, Tokyo. Kitty Media office of
publication 519 8th Avenue, 14th floor, New York, NY 10018.

Kitty Press
Office of publication 519 8th Avenue, 14th floor
New York, NY 10018.

ISBN: 1-59883-012-0

Printed in Canada.

OTONI   MODORU

POISON • CHERRY • DRIVE

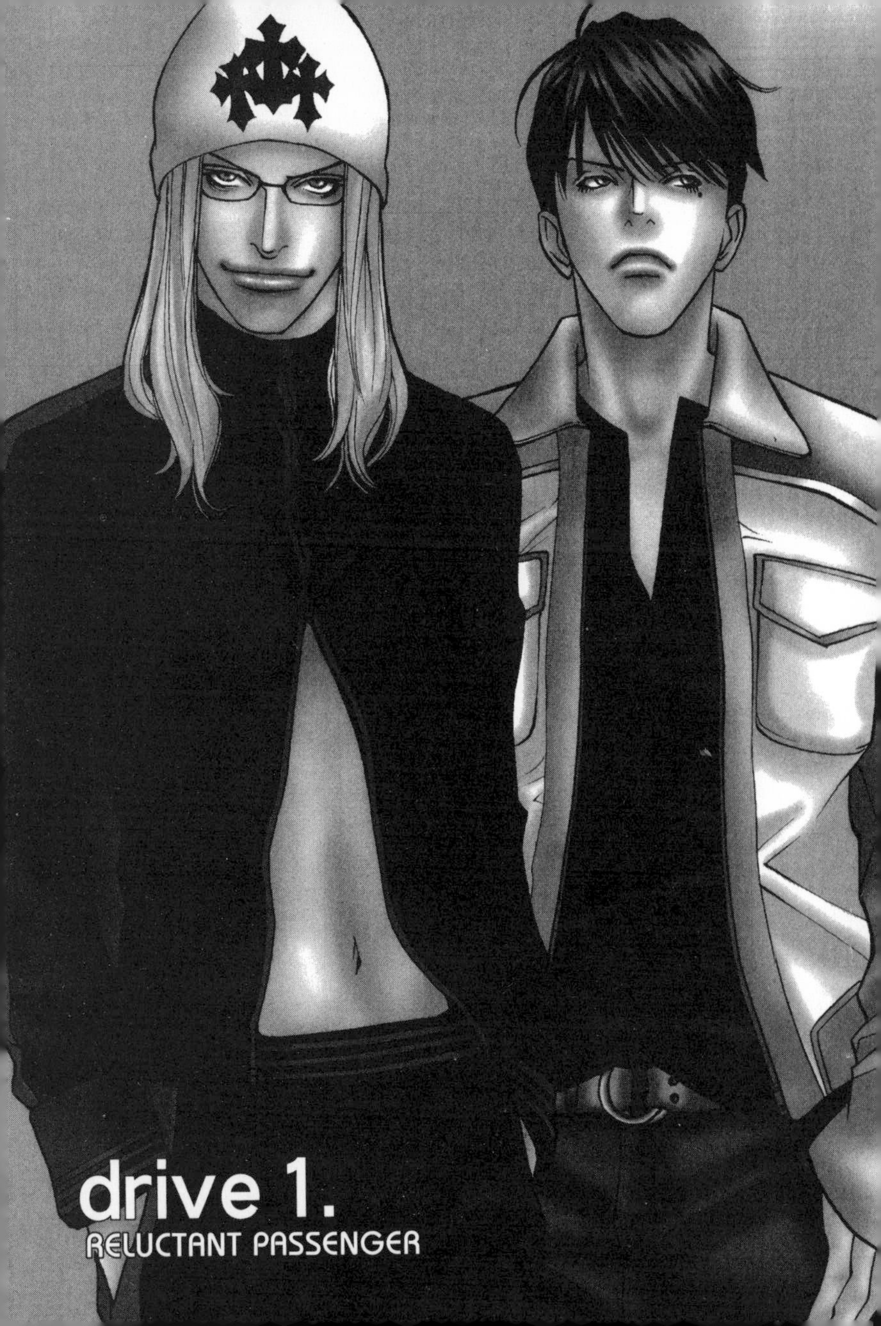

drive 1.
RELUCTANT PASSENGER

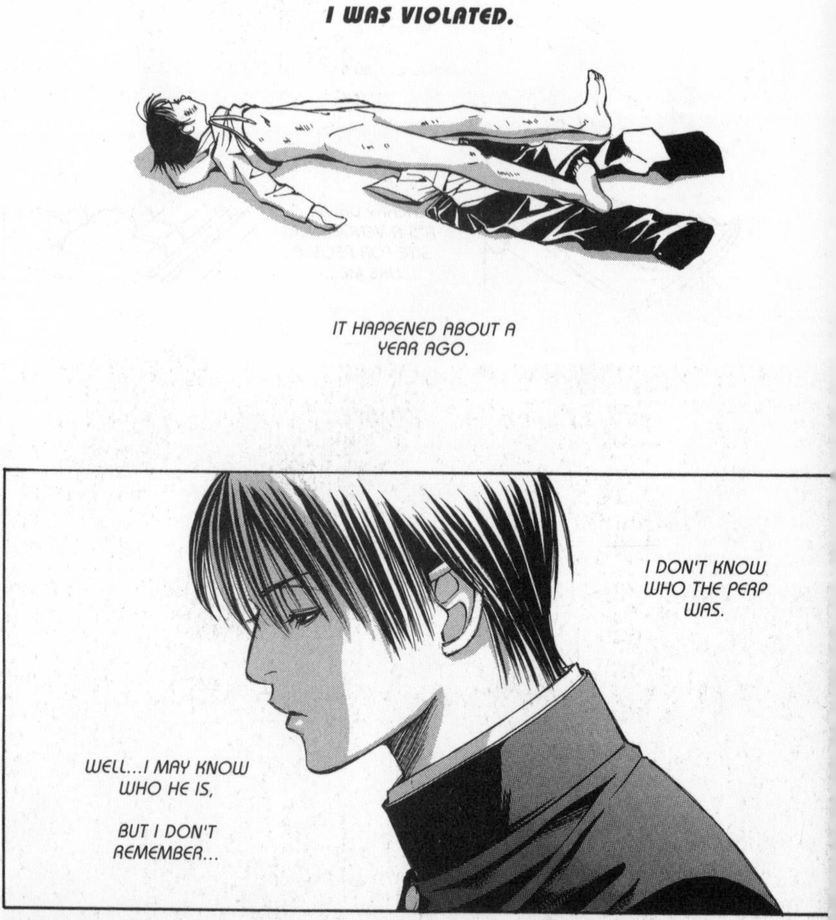
I WAS VIOLATED.
IT HAPPENED ABOUT A YEAR AGO.
I DON'T KNOW WHO THE PERP WAS.
WELL...I MAY KNOW WHO HE IS,
BUT I DON'T REMEMBER...

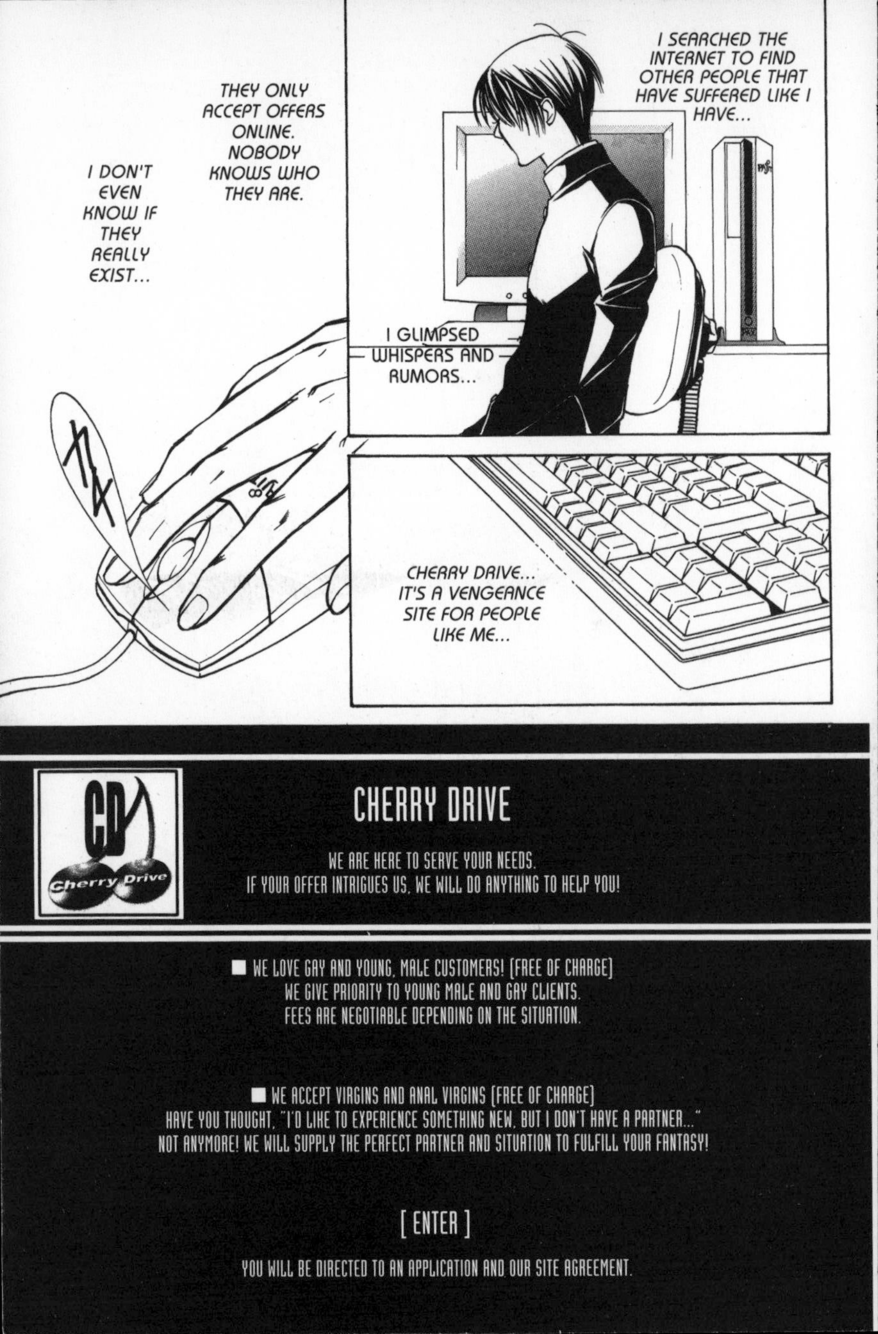
I SEARCHED THE INTERNET TO FIND OTHER PEOPLE THAT HAVE SUFFERED LIKE I HAVE...
I GLIMPSED WHISPERS AND RUMORS...
THEY ONLY ACCEPT OFFERS ONLINE. NOBODY KNOWS WHO THEY ARE.
I DON'T EVEN KNOW IF THEY REALLY EXIST...
CHERRY DRIVE... IT'S A VENGEANCE SITE FOR PEOPLE LIKE ME...
CD
Cherry Drive
CHERRY DRIVE
WE ARE HERE TO SERVE YOUR NEEDS.
IF YOUR OFFER INTRIGUES US, WE WILL DO ANYTHING TO HELP YOU!
WE LOVE GAY AND YOUNG, MALE CUSTOMERS! [FREE OF CHARGE]
WE GIVE PRIORITY TO YOUNG MALE AND GAY CLIENTS.
FEES ARE NEGOTIABLE DEPENDING ON THE SITUATION.
WE ACCEPT VIRGINS AND ANAL VIRGINS [FREE OF CHARGE]
HAVE YOU THOUGHT, "I'D LIKE TO EXPERIENCE SOMETHING NEW, BUT I DON'T HAVE A PARTNER..."
NOT ANYMORE! WE WILL SUPPLY THE PERFECT PARTNER AND SITUATION TO FULFILL YOUR FANTASY!
[ENTER]
YOU WILL BE DIRECTED TO AN APPLICATION AND OUR SITE AGREEMENT.

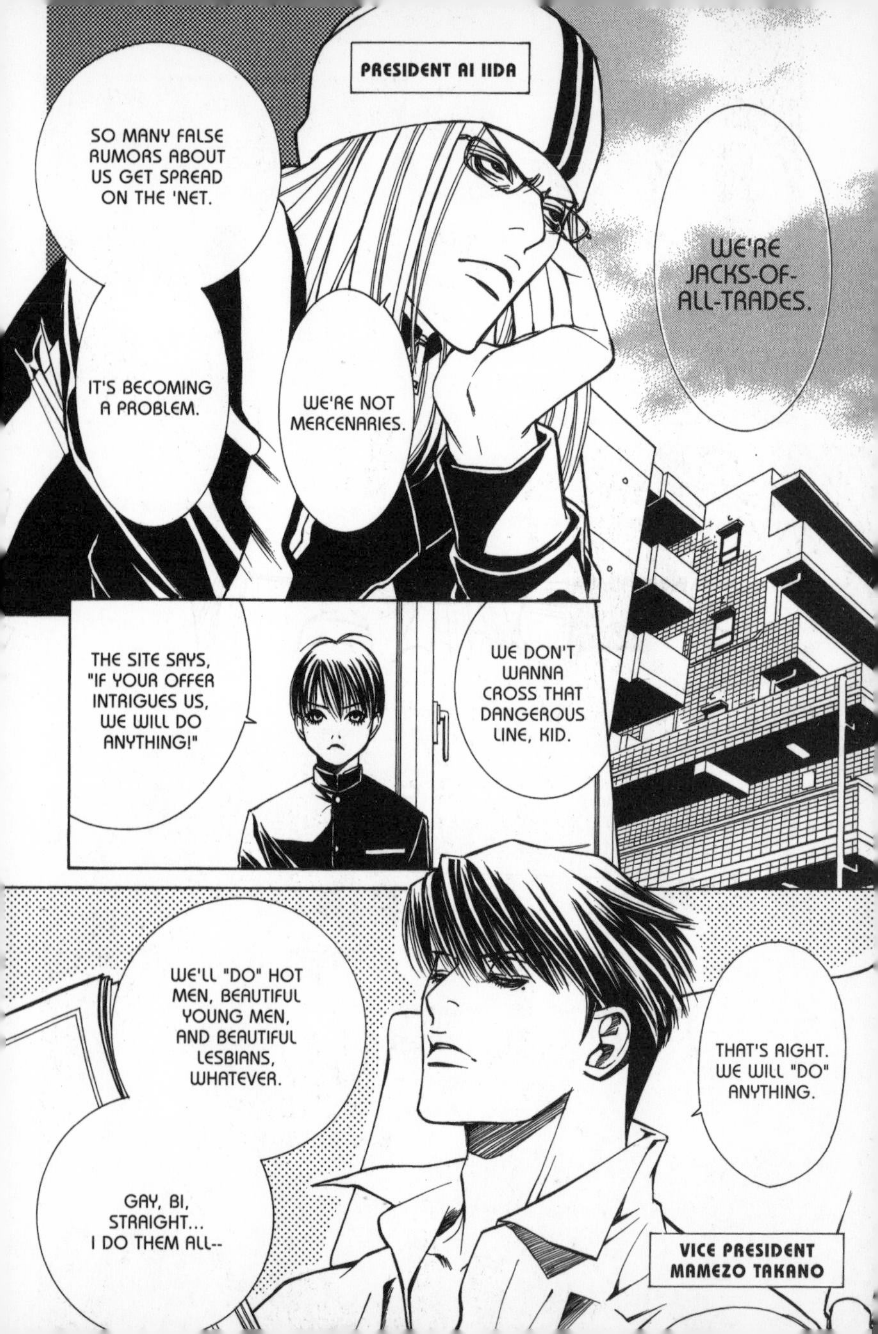
PRESIDENT AI IIDA
WE'RE JACKS-OF-ALL-TRADES.
WE'RE NOT MERCENARIES.
SO MANY FALSE RUMORS ABOUT US GET SPREAD ON THE 'NET.
IT'S BECOMING A PROBLEM.
WE DON'T WANNA CROSS THAT DANGEROUS LINE, KID.
THE SITE SAYS, "IF YOUR OFFER INTRIGUES US, WE WILL DO ANYTHING!"
THAT'S RIGHT. WE WILL "DO" ANYTHING.
WE'LL "DO" HOT MEN, BEAUTIFUL YOUNG MEN, AND BEAUTIFUL LESBIANS, WHATEVER.
GAY, BI, STRAIGHT... I DO THEM ALL--
VICE PRESIDENT MAMEZO TAKANO

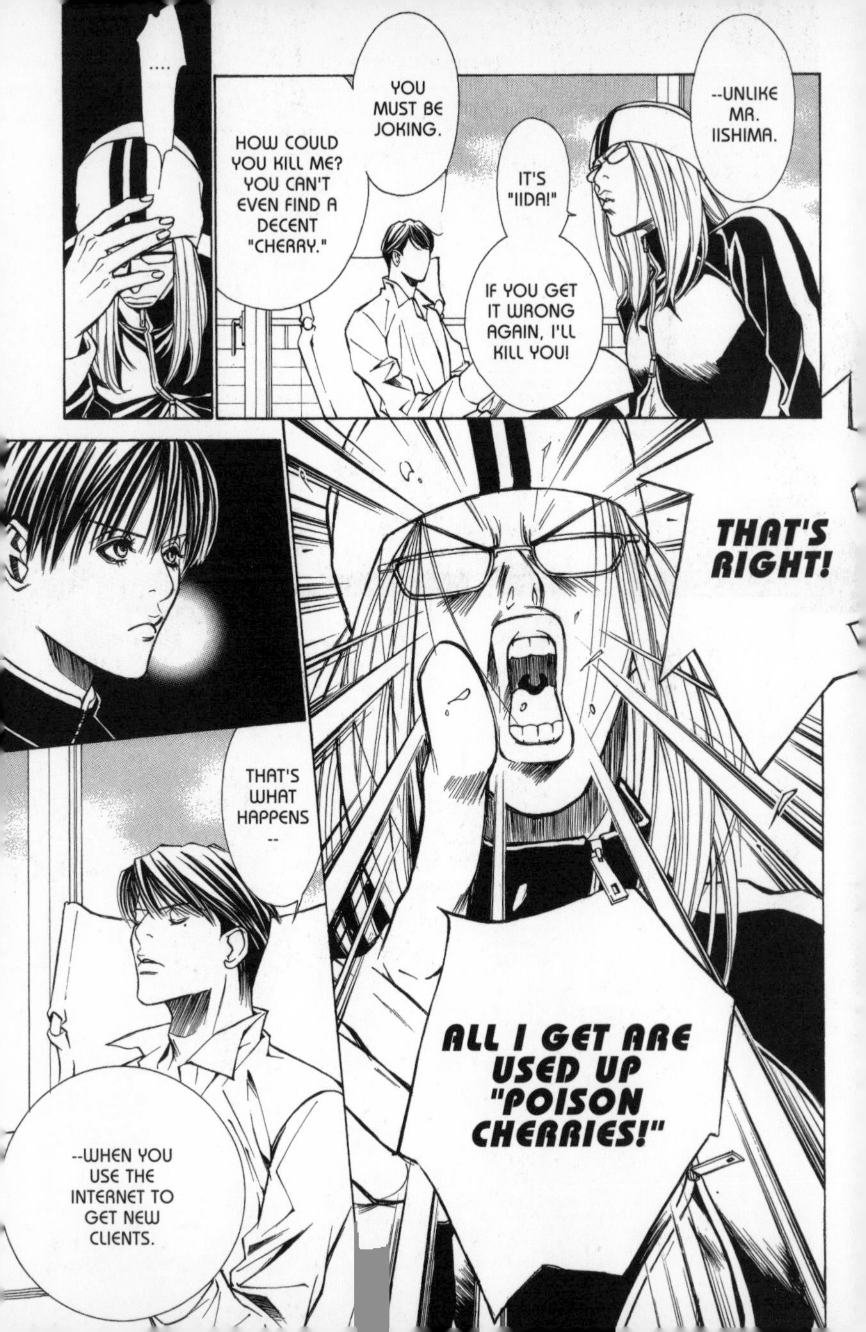

--UNLIKE MR. IISHIMA.
IT'S "IIDA!"
IF YOU GET IT WRONG AGAIN, I'LL KILL YOU!
YOU MUST BE JOKING.
HOW COULD YOU KILL ME? YOU CAN'T EVEN FIND A DECENT "CHERRY."
....
THAT'S RIGHT!
ALL I GET ARE USED UP "POISON CHERRIES!"
THAT'S WHAT HAPPENS --
--WHEN YOU USE THE INTERNET TO GET NEW CLIENTS.

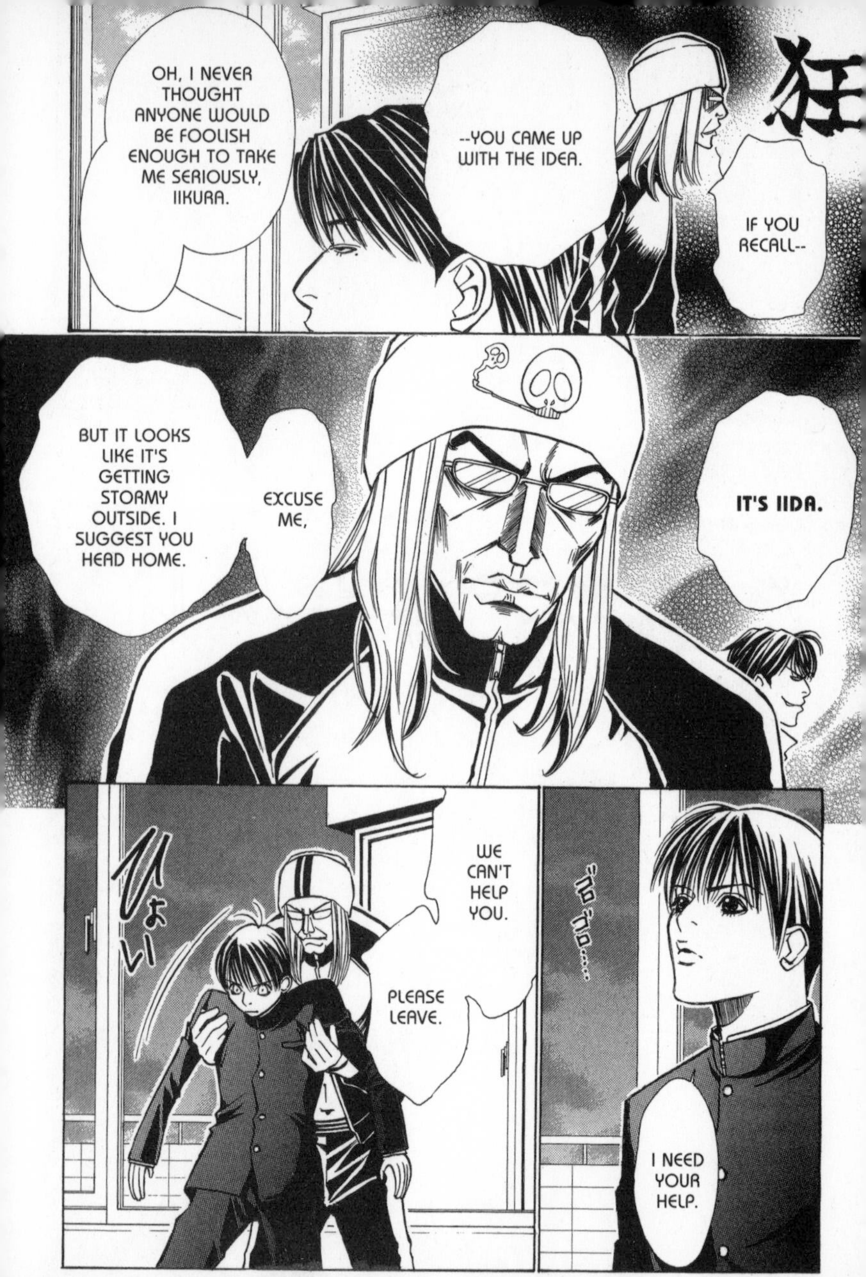

狂
IF YOU RECALL--
--YOU CAME UP WITH THE IDEA.
OH, I NEVER THOUGHT ANYONE WOULD BE FOOLISH ENOUGH TO TAKE ME SERIOUSLY, IIKURA.
IT'S IIDA.
EXCUSE ME,
BUT IT LOOKS LIKE IT'S GETTING STORMY OUTSIDE. I SUGGEST YOU HEAD HOME.
ゴロゴロ……
I NEED YOUR HELP.
ひょい
WE CAN'T HELP YOU.
PLEASE LEAVE.

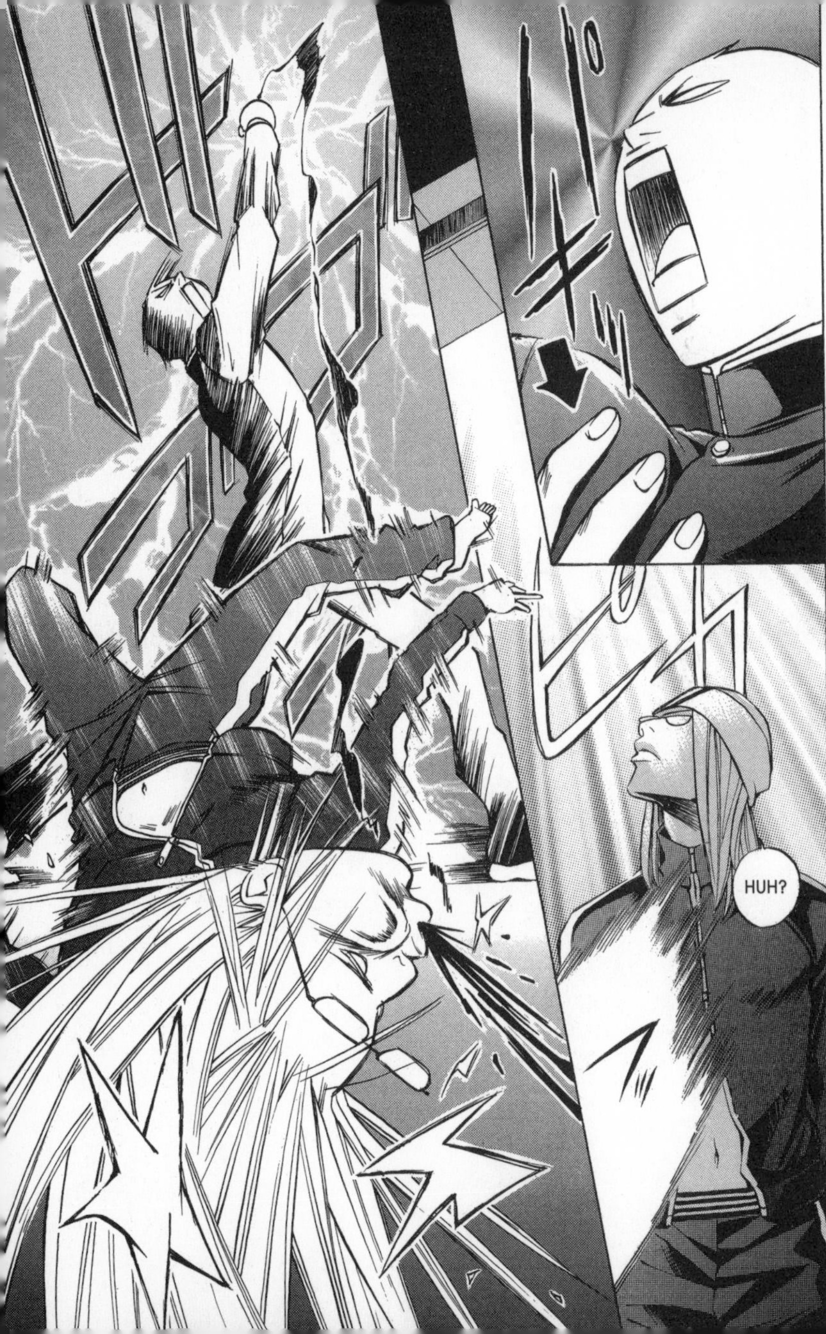
HUH?

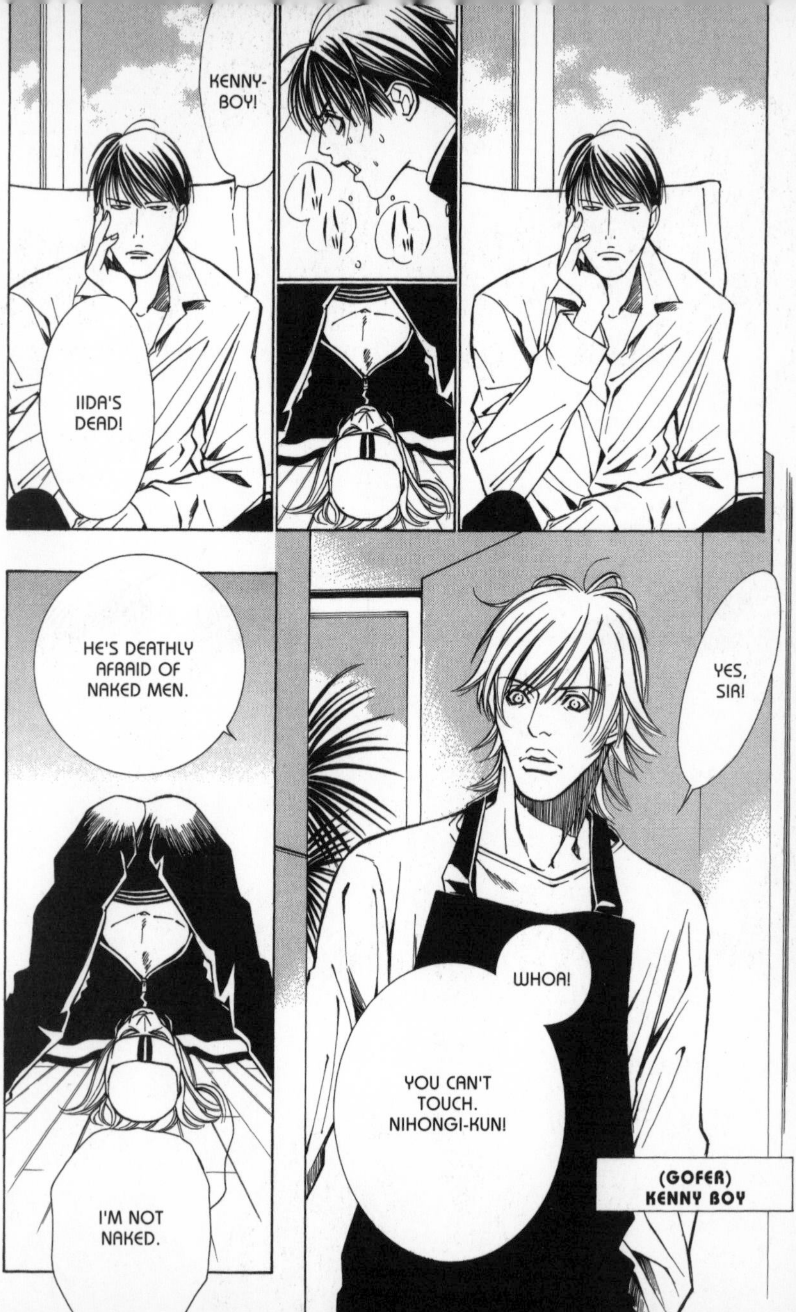
KENNY-BOY!
IIDA'S DEAD!
YES, SIR!
WHOA!
YOU CAN'T TOUCH. NIHONGI-KUN!
(GOFER) KENNY BOY
HE'S DEATHLY AFRAID OF NAKED MEN.
I'M NOT NAKED.

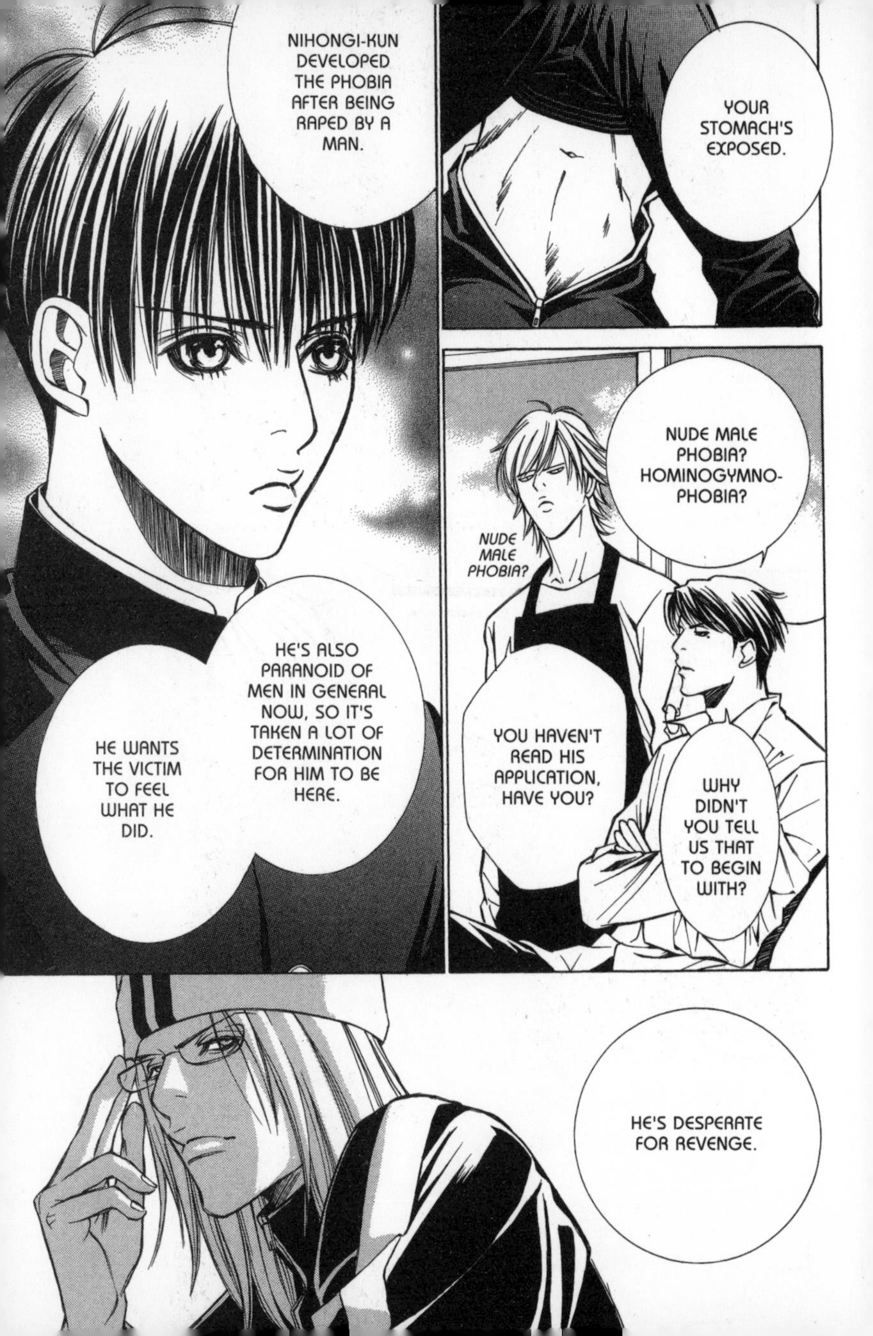
YOUR STOMACH'S EXPOSED.
NUDE MALE PHOBIA? HOMINOGYMNO-PHOBIA?
NUDE MALE PHOBIA?
WHY DIDN'T YOU TELL US THAT TO BEGIN WITH?
YOU HAVEN'T READ HIS APPLICATION, HAVE YOU?
NIHONGI-KUN DEVELOPED THE PHOBIA AFTER BEING RAPED BY A MAN.
HE'S ALSO PARANOID OF MEN IN GENERAL NOW, SO IT'S TAKEN A LOT OF DETERMINATION FOR HIM TO BE HERE.
HE WANTS THE VICTIM TO FEEL WHAT HE DID.
HE'S DESPERATE FOR REVENGE.

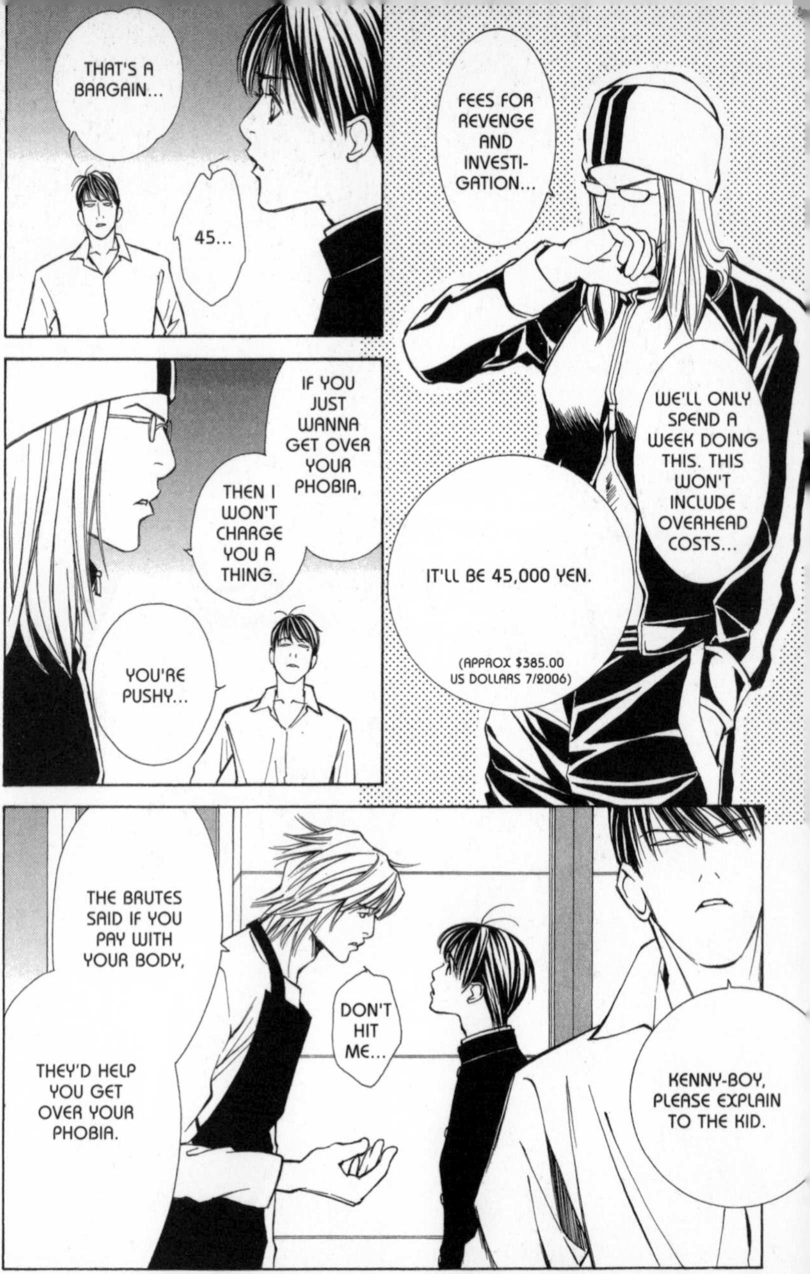
FEES FOR REVENGE AND INVESTI-GATION...
WE'LL ONLY SPEND A WEEK DOING THIS. THIS WON'T INCLUDE OVERHEAD COSTS...
IT'LL BE 45,000 YEN.
(APPROX $385.00 US DOLLARS 7/2006)
45...
THAT'S A BARGAIN...
IF YOU JUST WANNA GET OVER YOUR PHOBIA,
THEN I WON'T CHARGE YOU A THING.
YOU'RE PUSHY...
KENNY-BOY, PLEASE EXPLAIN TO THE KID.
DON'T HIT ME...
THE BRUTES SAID IF YOU PAY WITH YOUR BODY,
THEY'D HELP YOU GET OVER YOUR PHOBIA.

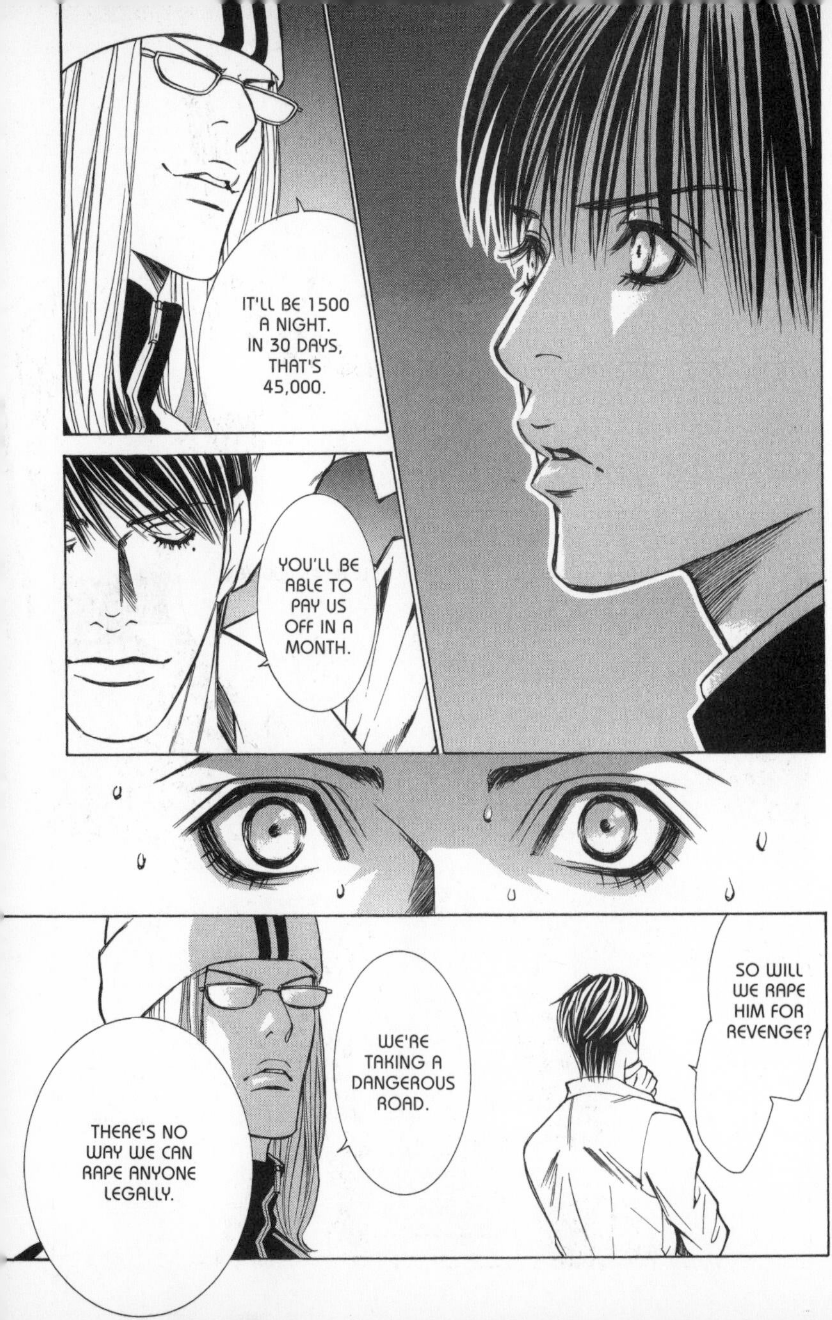
IT'LL BE 1500 A NIGHT. IN 30 DAYS, THAT'S 45,000.
YOU'LL BE ABLE TO PAY US OFF IN A MONTH.
SO WILL WE RAPE HIM FOR REVENGE?
WE'RE TAKING A DANGEROUS ROAD.
THERE'S NO WAY WE CAN RAPE ANYONE LEGALLY.

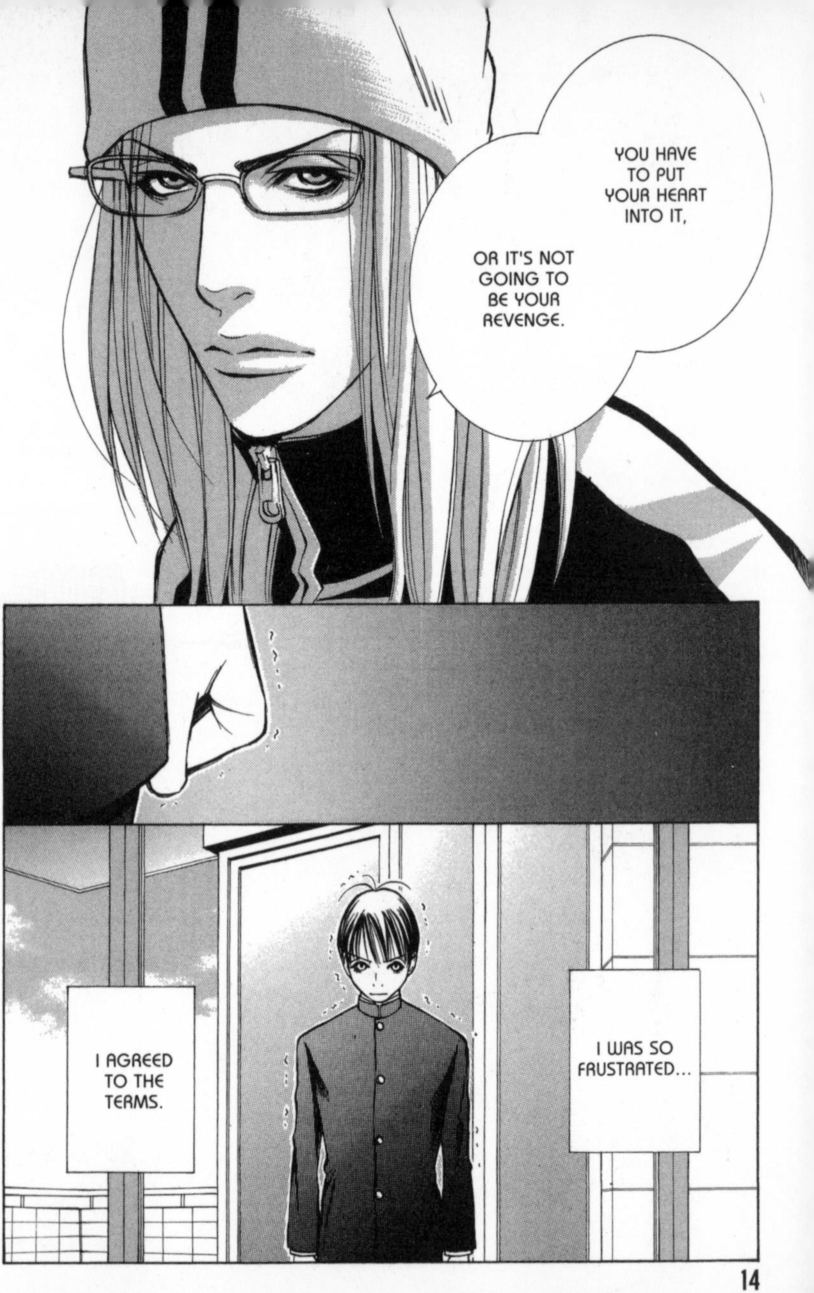
YOU HAVE TO PUT YOUR HEART INTO IT,
OR IT'S NOT GOING TO BE YOUR REVENGE.
I WAS SO FRUSTRATED...
I AGREED TO THE TERMS.

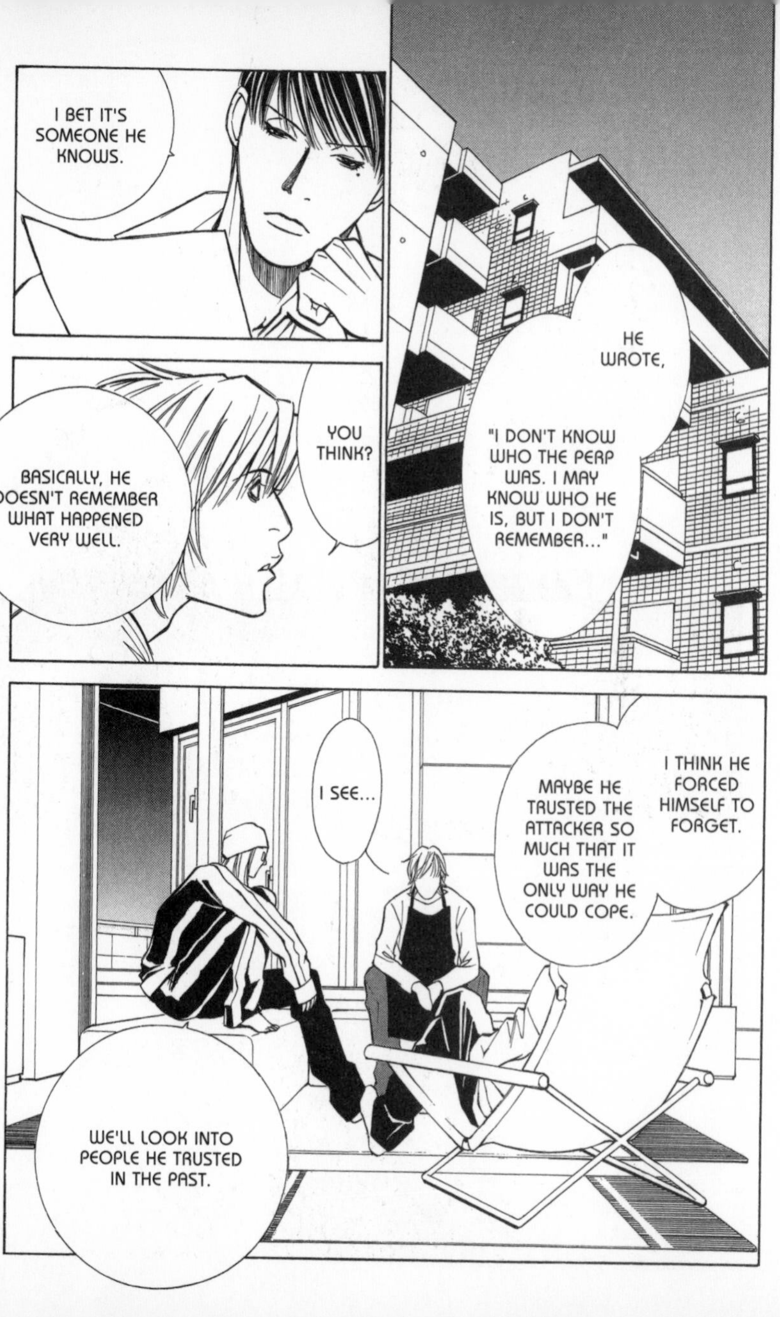
HE WROTE,
"I DON'T KNOW WHO THE PERP WAS. I MAY KNOW WHO HE IS, BUT I DON'T REMEMBER..."
I BET IT'S SOMEONE HE KNOWS.
YOU THINK?
BASICALLY, HE DOESN'T REMEMBER WHAT HAPPENED VERY WELL.
I THINK HE FORCED HIMSELF TO FORGET.
MAYBE HE TRUSTED THE ATTACKER SO MUCH THAT IT WAS THE ONLY WAY HE COULD COPE.
I SEE...
WE'LL LOOK INTO PEOPLE HE TRUSTED IN THE PAST.

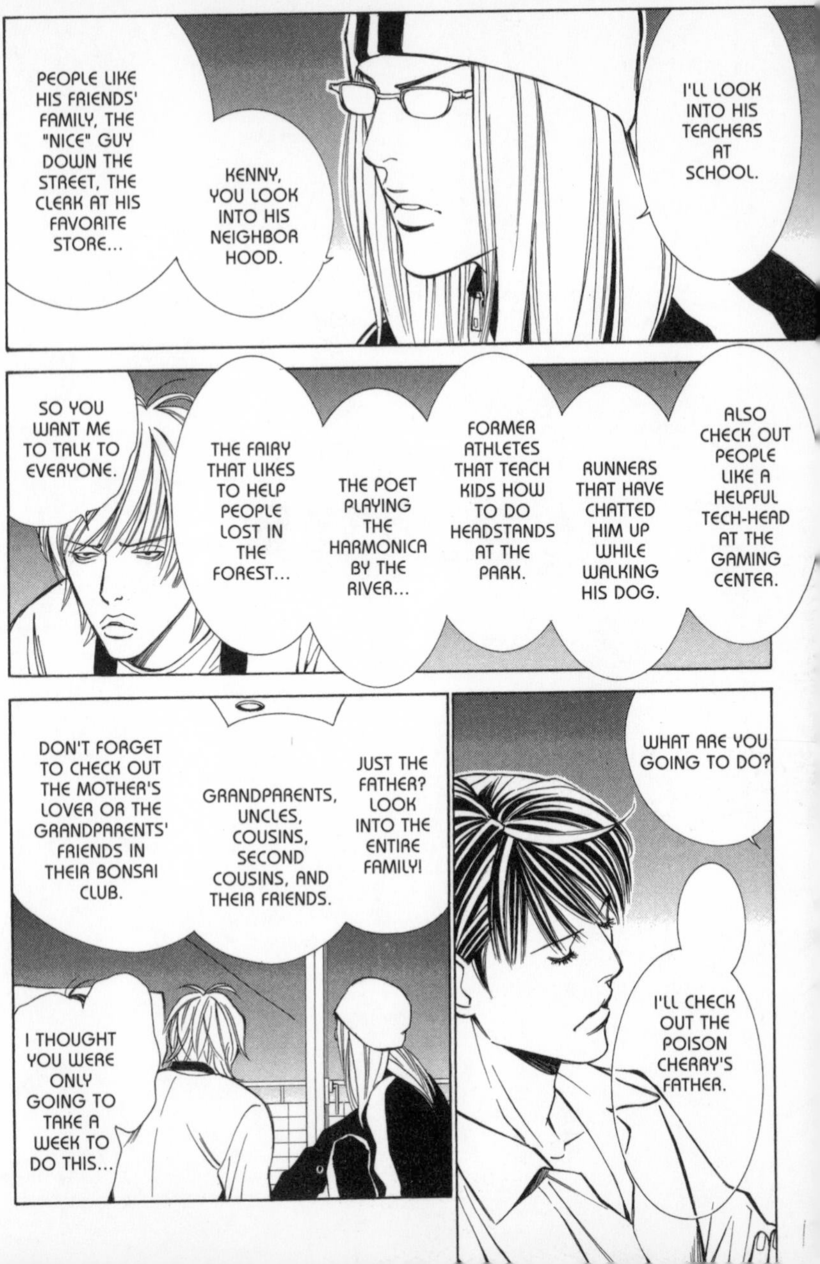
I'LL LOOK INTO HIS TEACHERS AT SCHOOL.
KENNY, YOU LOOK INTO HIS NEIGHBOR HOOD.
PEOPLE LIKE HIS FRIENDS' FAMILY, THE "NICE" GUY DOWN THE STREET, THE CLERK AT HIS FAVORITE STORE...
ALSO CHECK OUT PEOPLE LIKE A HELPFUL TECH-HEAD AT THE GAMING CENTER.
RUNNERS THAT HAVE CHATTED HIM UP WHILE WALKING HIS DOG.
FORMER ATHLETES THAT TEACH KIDS HOW TO DO HEADSTANDS AT THE PARK.
THE POET PLAYING THE HARMONICA BY THE RIVER...
THE FAIRY THAT LIKES TO HELP PEOPLE LOST IN THE FOREST...
SO YOU WANT ME TO TALK TO EVERYONE.
WHAT ARE YOU GOING TO DO?
I'LL CHECK OUT THE POISON CHERRY'S FATHER.
JUST THE FATHER? LOOK INTO THE ENTIRE FAMILY!
GRANDPARENTS, UNCLES, COUSINS, SECOND COUSINS, AND THEIR FRIENDS.
DON'T FORGET TO CHECK OUT THE MOTHER'S LOVER OR THE GRANDPARENTS' FRIENDS IN THEIR BONSAI CLUB.
I THOUGHT YOU WERE ONLY GOING TO TAKE A WEEK TO DO THIS...

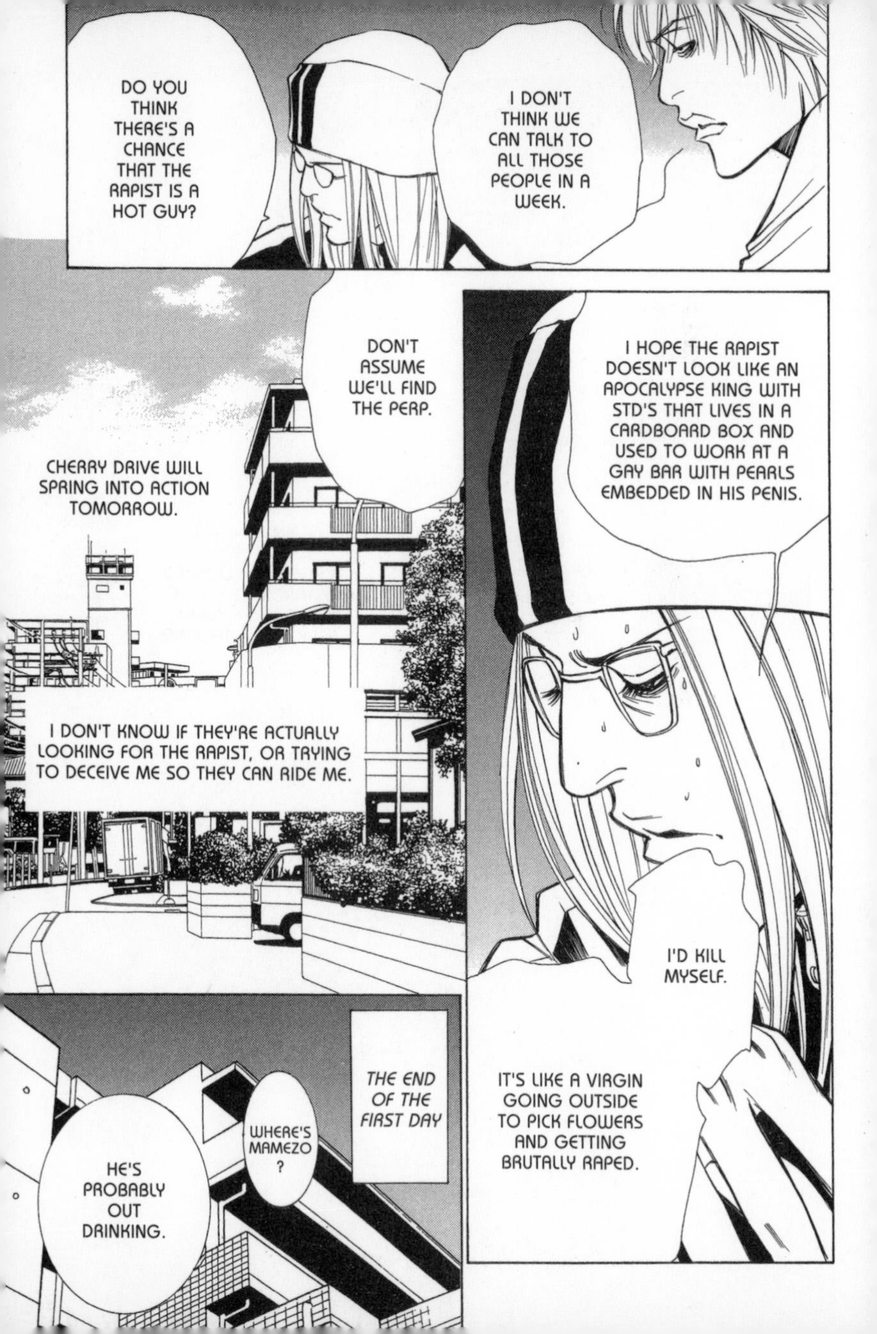
I DON'T THINK WE CAN TALK TO ALL THOSE PEOPLE IN A WEEK.
DO YOU THINK THERE'S A CHANCE THAT THE RAPIST IS A HOT GUY?
DON'T ASSUME WE'LL FIND THE PERP.
I HOPE THE RAPIST DOESN'T LOOK LIKE AN APOCALYPSE KING WITH STD'S THAT LIVES IN A CARDBOARD BOX AND USED TO WORK AT A GAY BAR WITH PEARLS EMBEDDED IN HIS PENIS.
I'D KILL MYSELF.
IT'S LIKE A VIRGIN GOING OUTSIDE TO PICK FLOWERS AND GETTING BRUTALLY RAPED.
CHERRY DRIVE WILL SPRING INTO ACTION TOMORROW.
I DON'T KNOW IF THEY'RE ACTUALLY LOOKING FOR THE RAPIST, OR TRYING TO DECEIVE ME SO THEY CAN RIDE ME.
THE END OF THE FIRST DAY
WHERE'S MAMEZO ?
HE'S PROBABLY OUT DRINKING.

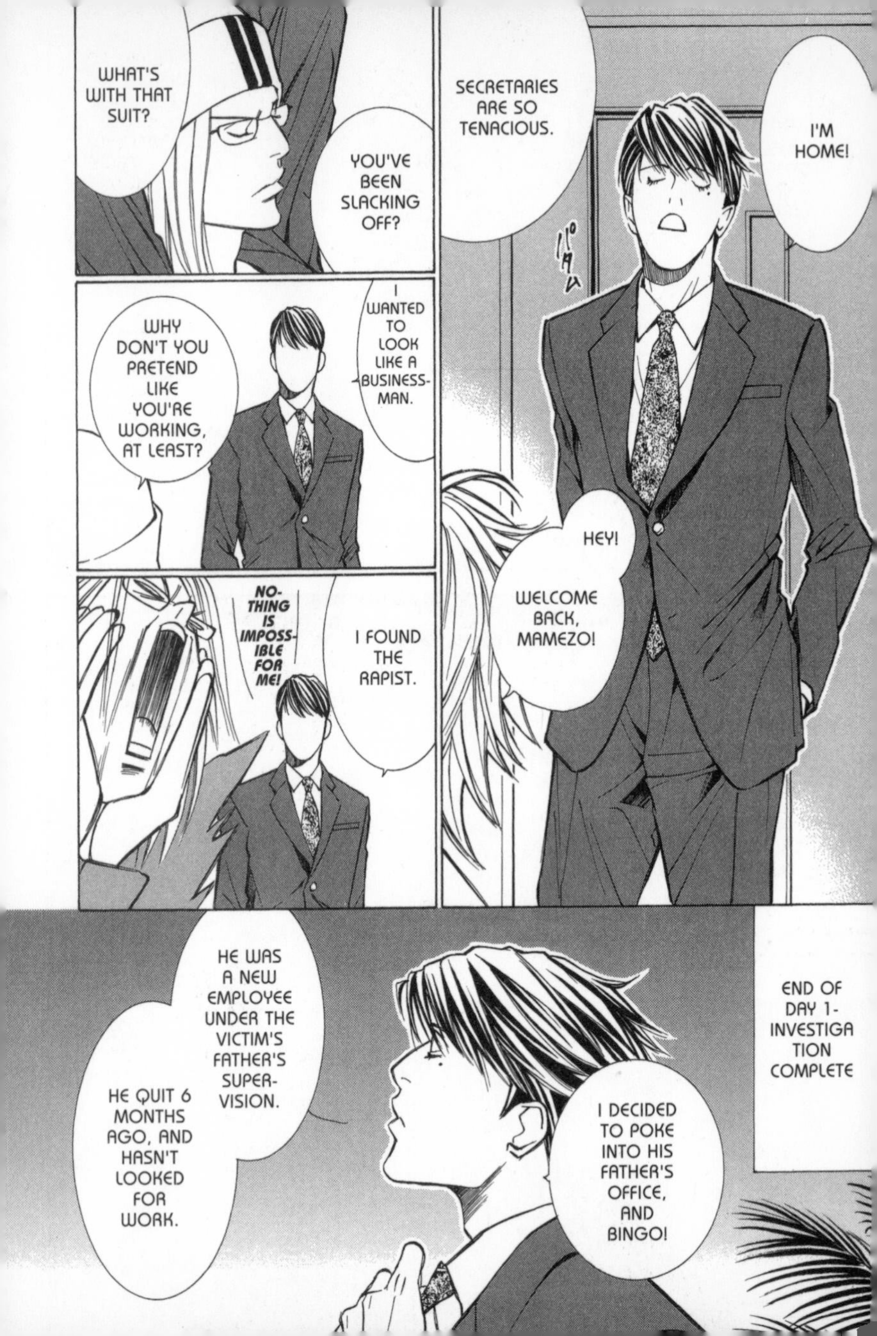
I'M HOME!
パタム
SECRETARIES ARE SO TENACIOUS.
HEY! WELCOME BACK, MAMEZO!
WHAT'S WITH THAT SUIT?
YOU'VE BEEN SLACKING OFF?
I WANTED TO LOOK LIKE A BUSINESS-MAN.
WHY DON'T YOU PRETEND LIKE YOU'RE WORKING, AT LEAST?
I FOUND THE RAPIST.
NO-THING IS IMPOSS-IBLE FOR ME!
END OF DAY 1- INVESTIGA TION COMPLETE
I DECIDED TO POKE INTO HIS FATHER'S OFFICE, AND BINGO!
HE WAS A NEW EMPLOYEE UNDER THE VICTIM'S FATHER'S SUPER-VISION.
HE QUIT 6 MONTHS AGO, AND HASN'T LOOKED FOR WORK.

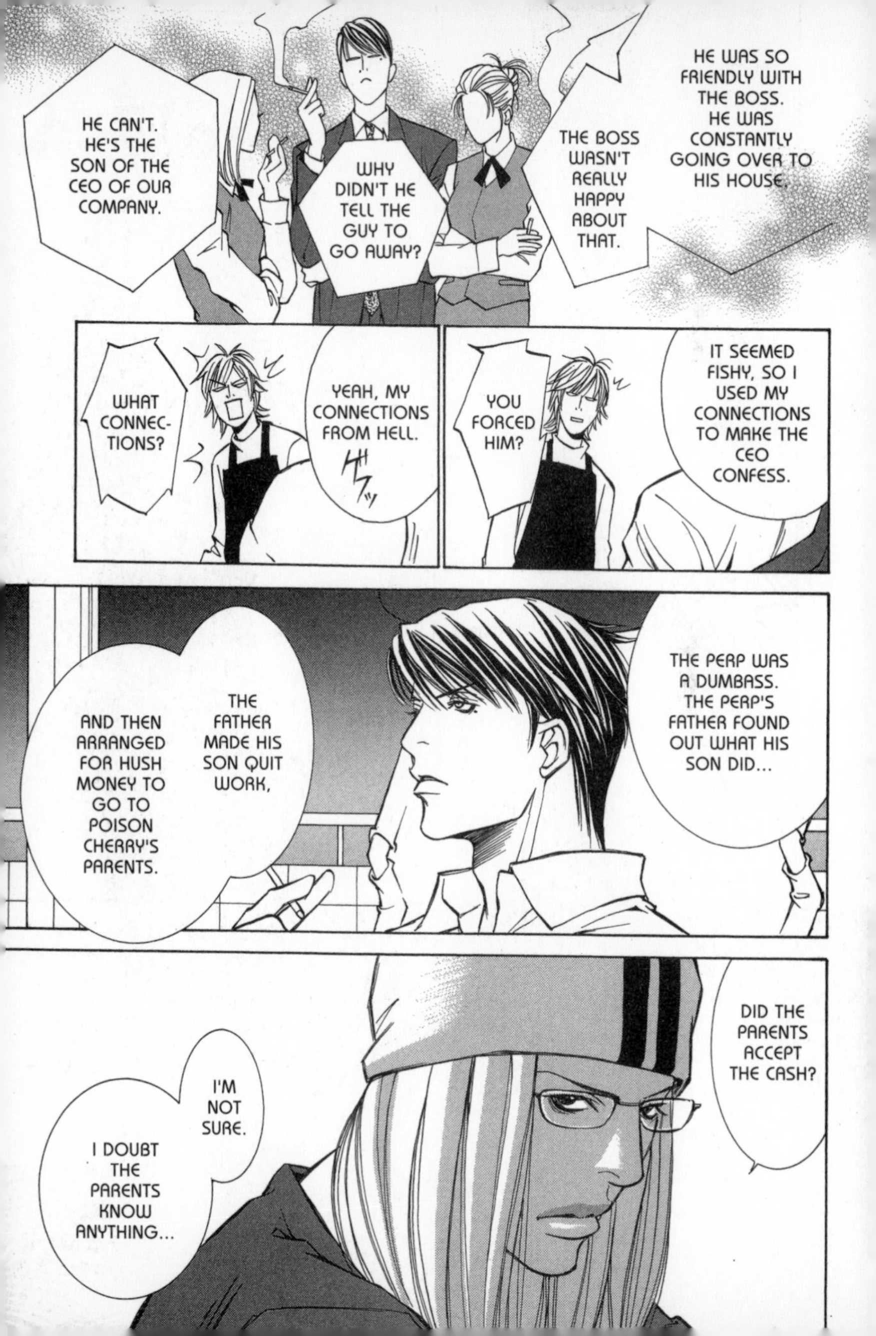
HE WAS SO FRIENDLY WITH THE BOSS. HE WAS CONSTANTLY GOING OVER TO HIS HOUSE.
THE BOSS WASN'T REALLY HAPPY ABOUT THAT.
WHY DIDN'T HE TELL THE GUY TO GO AWAY?
HE CAN'T. HE'S THE SON OF THE CEO OF OUR COMPANY.
IT SEEMED FISHY, SO I USED MY CONNECTIONS TO MAKE THE CEO CONFESS.
YOU FORCED HIM?
YEAH, MY CONNECTIONS FROM HELL.
WHAT CONNEC-TIONS?
THE PERP WAS A DUMBASS. THE PERP'S FATHER FOUND OUT WHAT HIS SON DID...
THE FATHER MADE HIS SON QUIT WORK,
AND THEN ARRANGED FOR HUSH MONEY TO GO TO POISON CHERRY'S PARENTS.
DID THE PARENTS ACCEPT THE CASH?
I'M NOT SURE.
I DOUBT THE PARENTS KNOW ANYTHING...

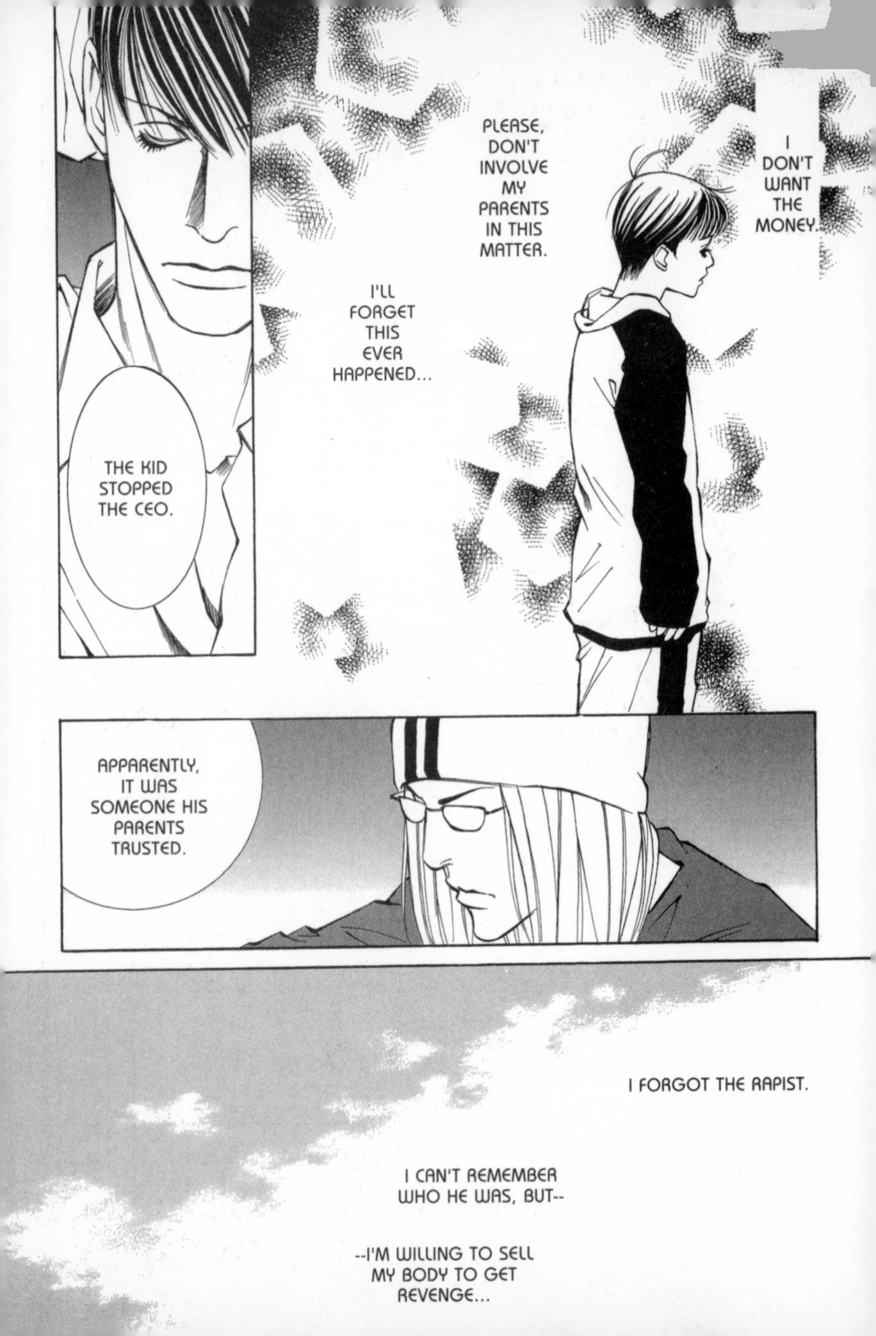
I DON'T WANT THE MONEY.
PLEASE, DON'T INVOLVE MY PARENTS IN THIS MATTER.
I'LL FORGET THIS EVER HAPPENED...
THE KID STOPPED THE CEO.
APPARENTLY, IT WAS SOMEONE HIS PARENTS TRUSTED.
I FORGOT THE RAPIST.
I CAN'T REMEMBER WHO HE WAS, BUT--
--I'M WILLING TO SELL MY BODY TO GET REVENGE...

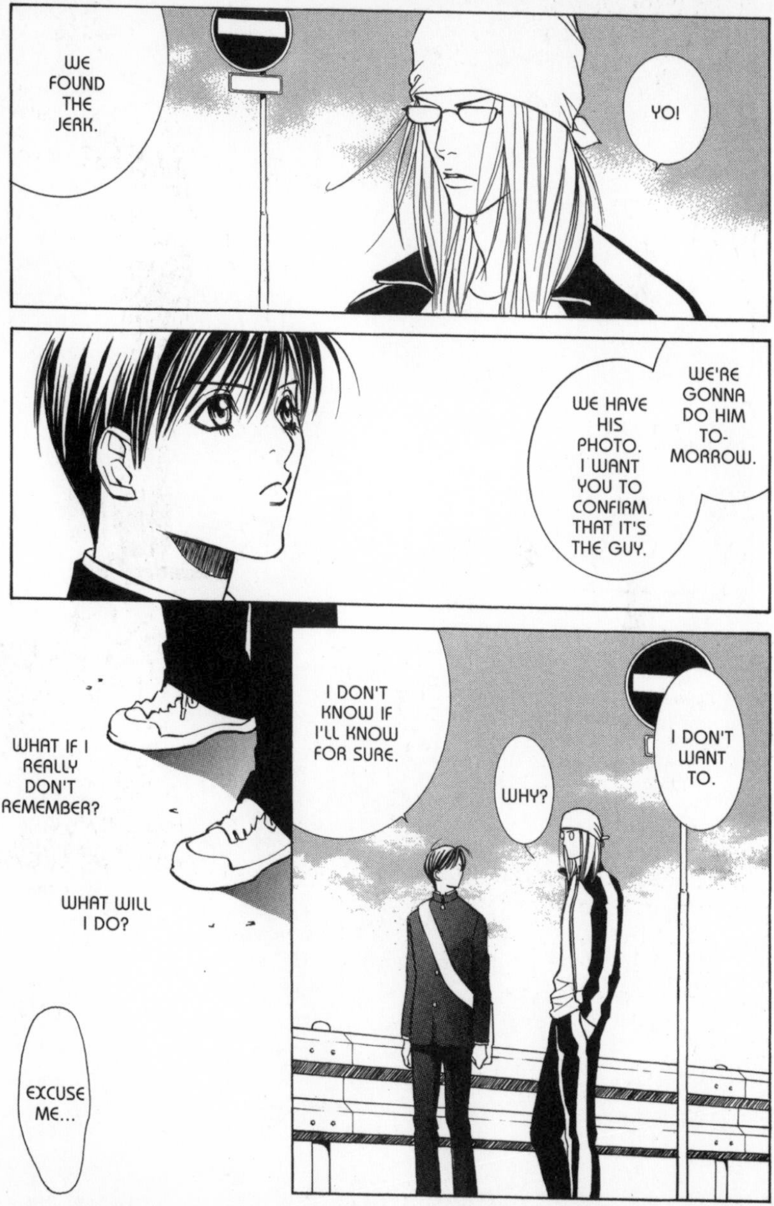
YO!
WE FOUND THE JERK.
WE'RE GONNA DO HIM TO-MORROW.
WE HAVE HIS PHOTO. I WANT YOU TO CONFIRM THAT IT'S THE GUY.
I DON'T WANT TO.
WHY?
I DON'T KNOW IF I'LL KNOW FOR SURE.
WHAT IF I REALLY DON'T REMEMBER?
WHAT WILL I DO?
EXCUSE ME...

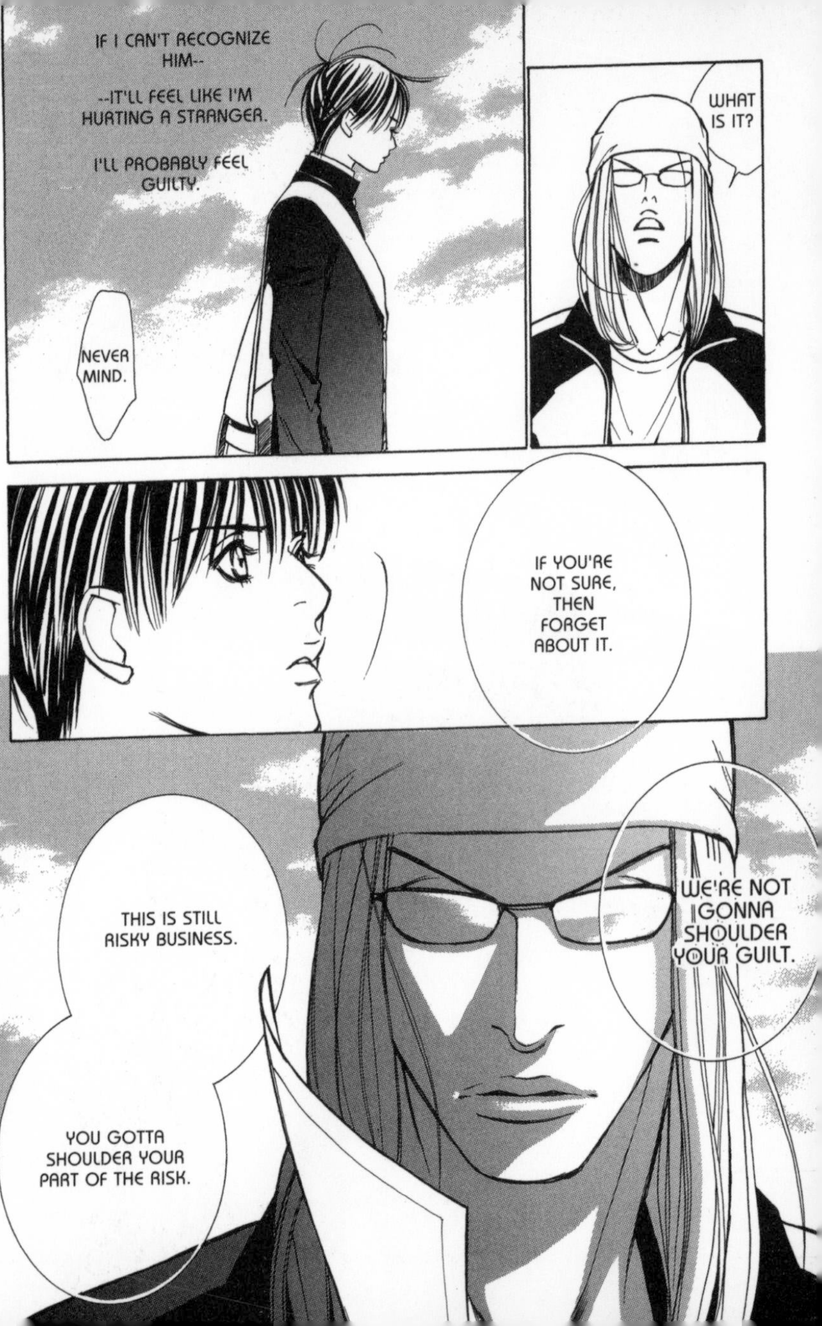
WHAT IS IT?
IF I CAN'T RECOGNIZE HIM--
--IT'LL FEEL LIKE I'M HURTING A STRANGER.
I'LL PROBABLY FEEL GUILTY.
NEVER MIND.
IF YOU'RE NOT SURE, THEN FORGET ABOUT IT.
WE'RE NOT GONNA SHOULDER YOUR GUILT.
THIS IS STILL RISKY BUSINESS.
YOU GOTTA SHOULDER YOUR PART OF THE RISK.

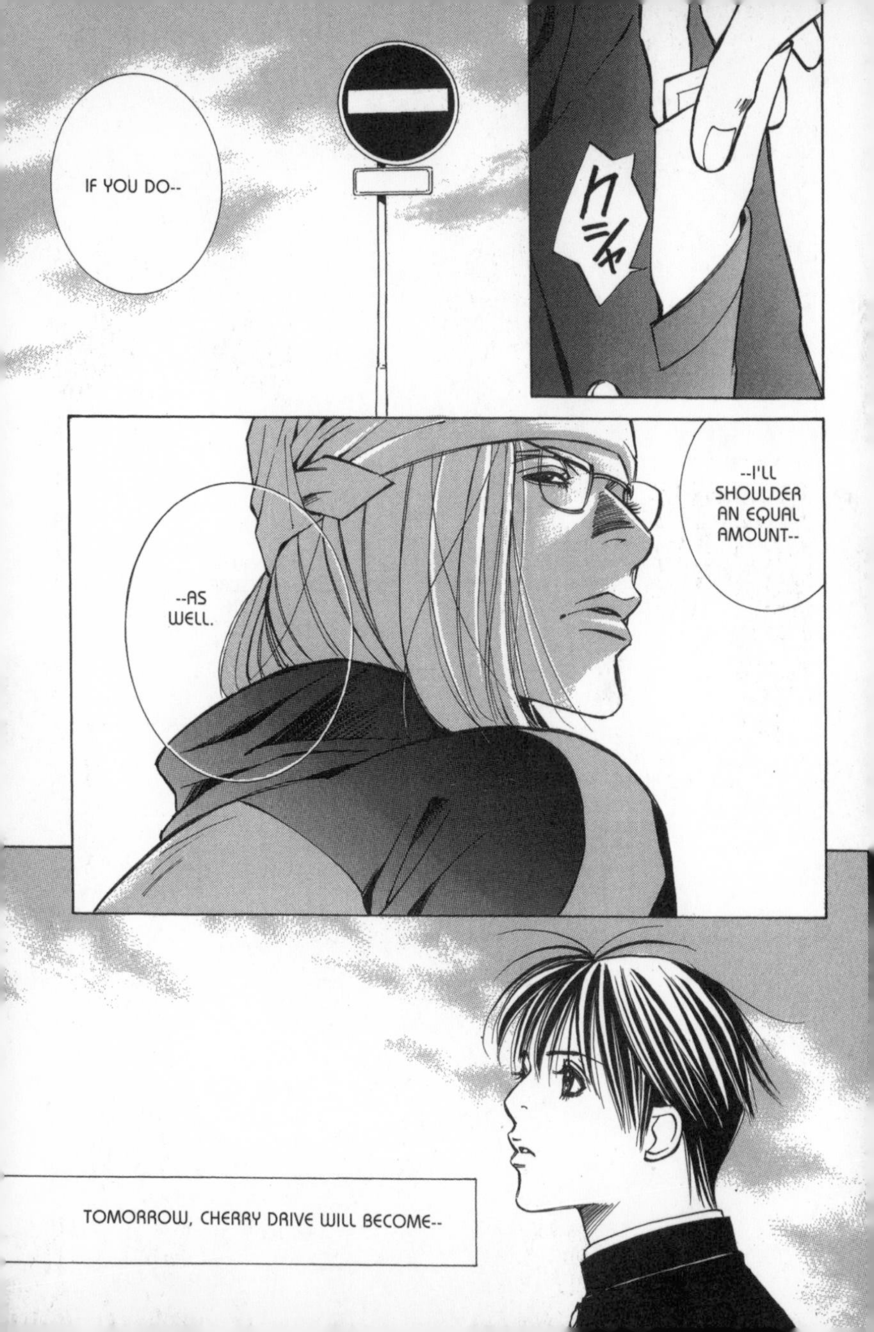
カシャ
IF YOU DO--
--I'LL SHOULDER AN EQUAL AMOUNT--
--AS WELL.
TOMORROW, CHERRY DRIVE WILL BECOME--

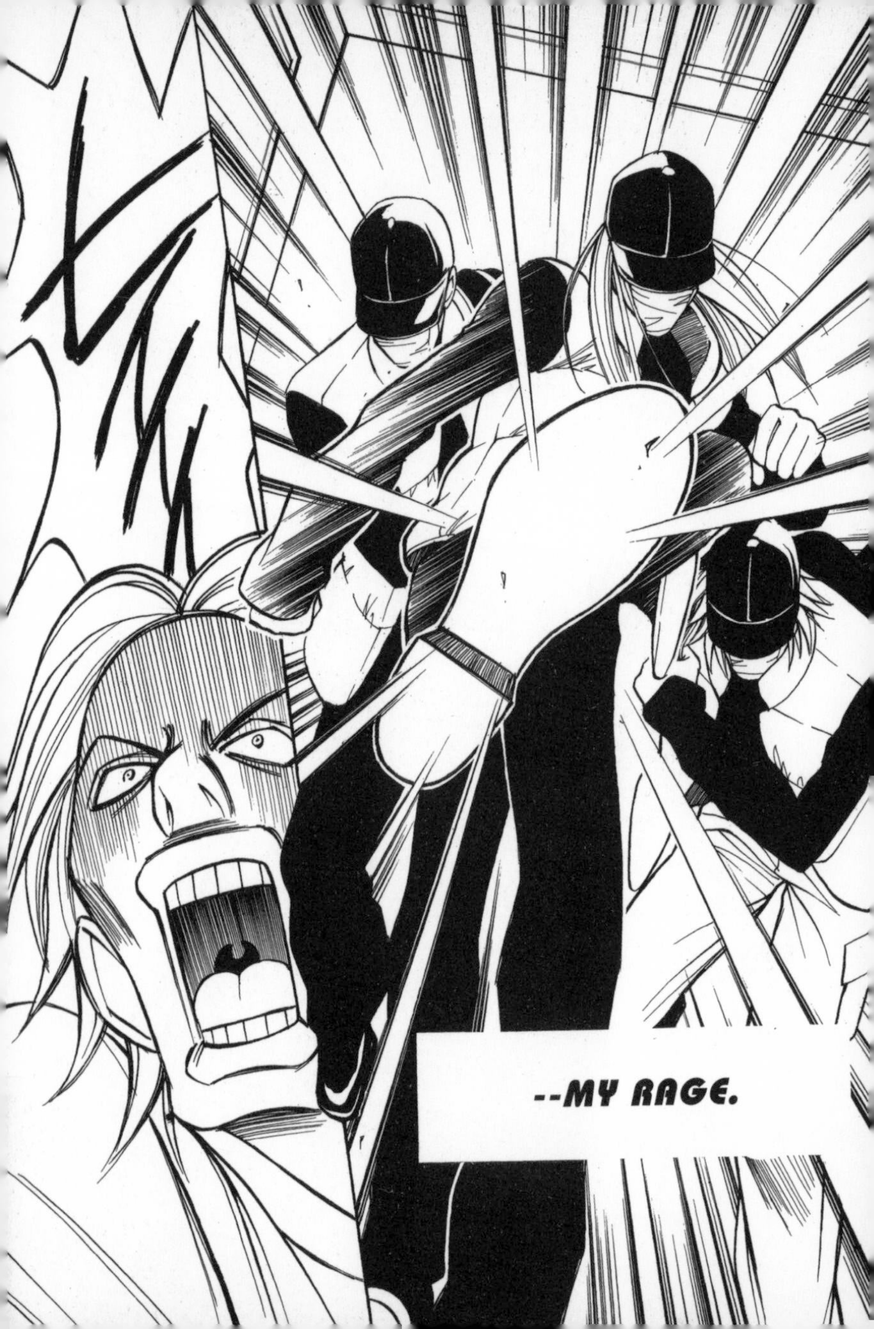
--MY RAGE.

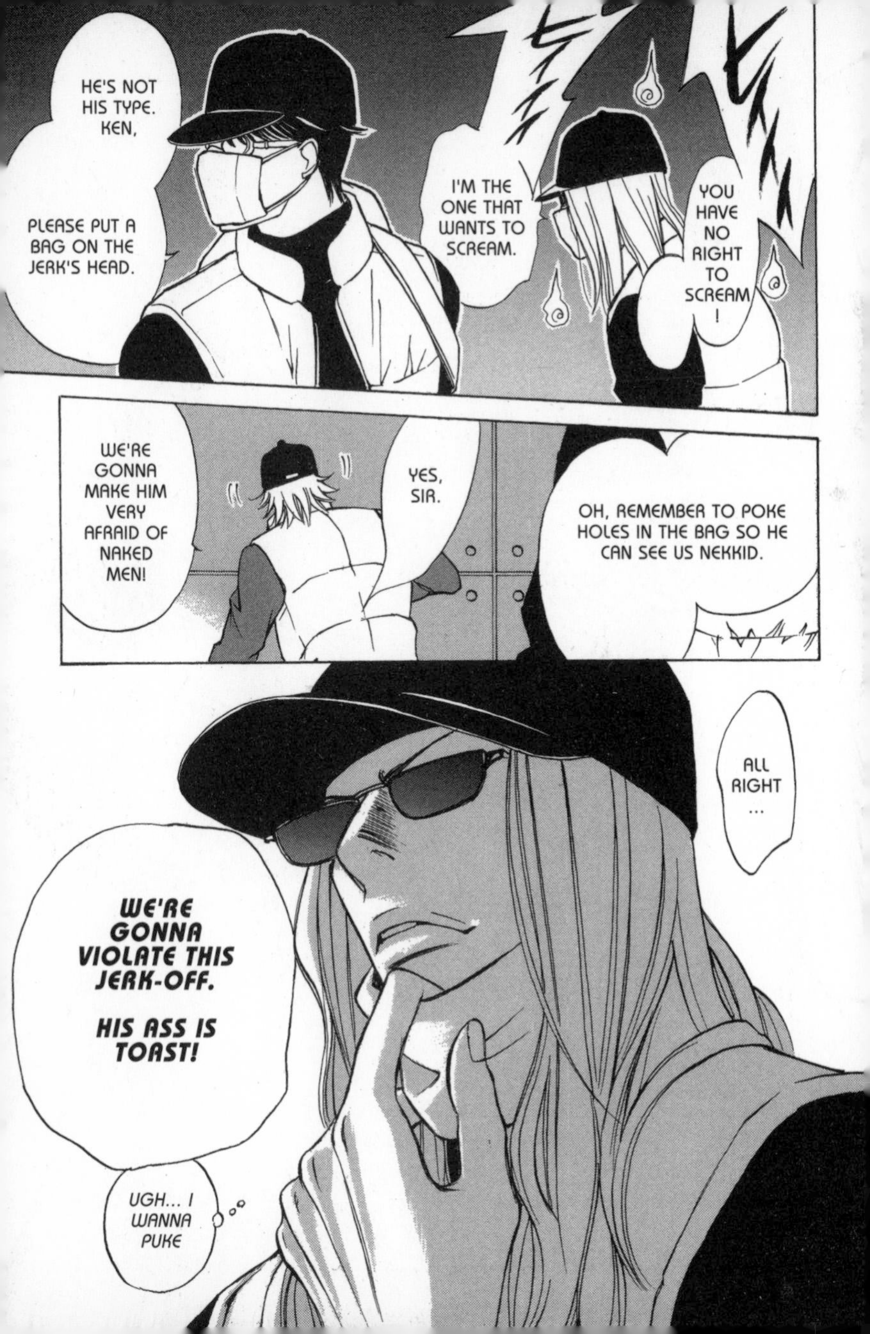
YOU HAVE NO RIGHT TO SCREAM!
I'M THE ONE THAT WANTS TO SCREAM.
HE'S NOT HIS TYPE. KEN,
PLEASE PUT A BAG ON THE JERK'S HEAD.
OH, REMEMBER TO POKE HOLES IN THE BAG SO HE CAN SEE US NEKKID.
YES, SIR.
WE'RE GONNA MAKE HIM VERY AFRAID OF NAKED MEN!
ALL RIGHT ...
WE'RE GONNA VIOLATE THIS JERK-OFF.
HIS ASS IS TOAST!
UGH... I WANNA PUKE

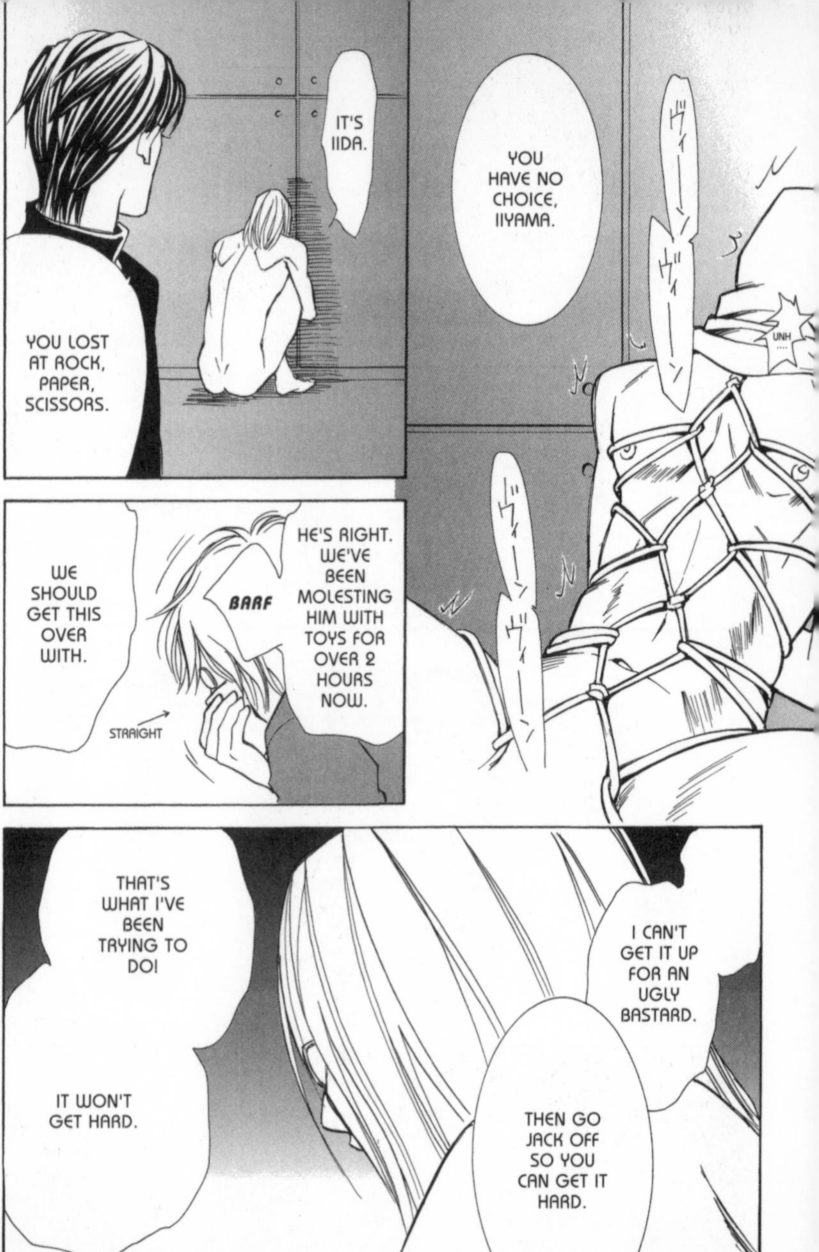
YOU HAVE NO CHOICE, IIYAMA.
ヴィー ヴィー
UNH....
ヴィー ヴィー
IT'S IIDA.
YOU LOST AT ROCK, PAPER, SCISSORS.
HE'S RIGHT. WE'VE BEEN MOLESTING HIM WITH TOYS FOR OVER 2 HOURS NOW.
BARF
WE SHOULD GET THIS OVER WITH.
STRAIGHT
I CAN'T GET IT UP FOR AN UGLY BASTARD.
THEN GO JACK OFF SO YOU CAN GET IT HARD.
THAT'S WHAT I'VE BEEN TRYING TO DO!
IT WON'T GET HARD.

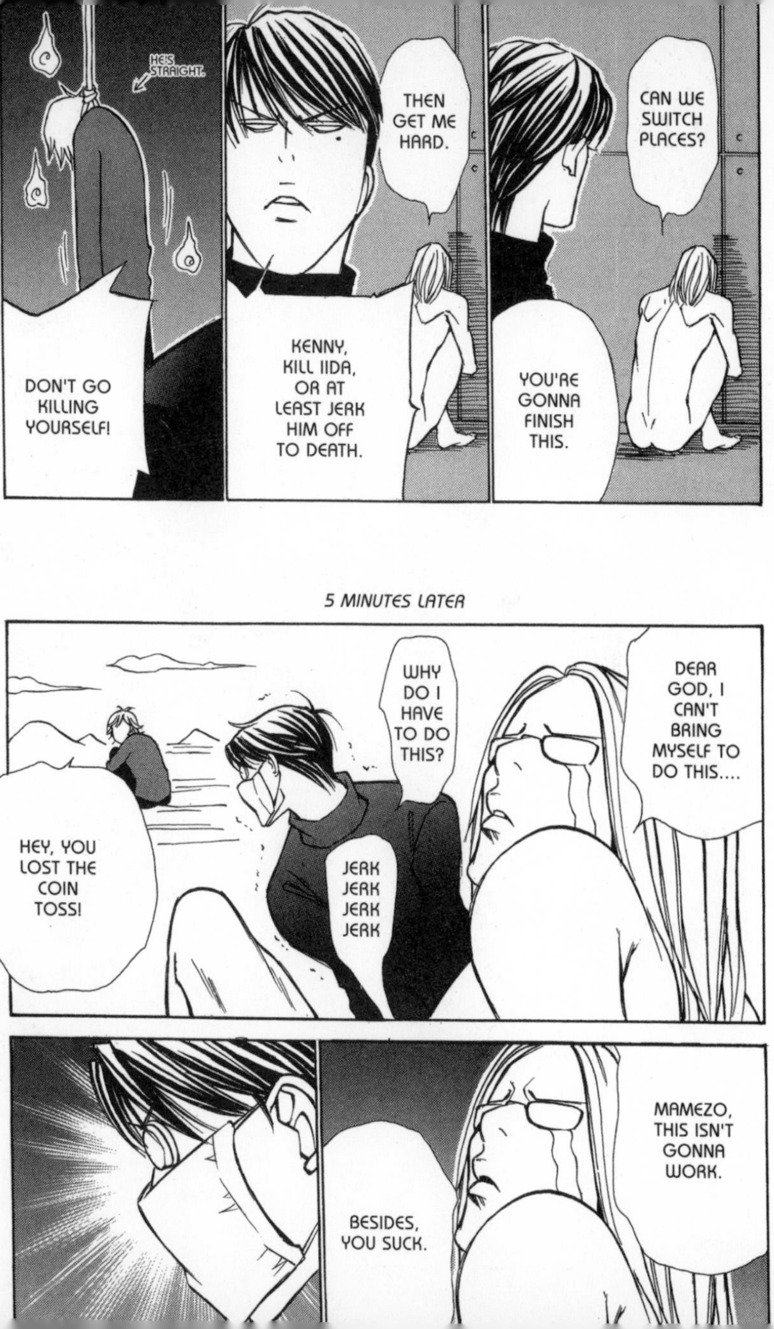
CAN WE SWITCH PLACES?
YOU'RE GONNA FINISH THIS.
THEN GET ME HARD.
KENNY, KILL IIDA, OR AT LEAST JERK HIM OFF TO DEATH.
HE'S STRAIGHT.
DON'T GO KILLING YOURSELF!
5 MINUTES LATER
DEAR GOD, I CAN'T BRING MYSELF TO DO THIS....
WHY DO I HAVE TO DO THIS?
JERK JERK JERK JERK
HEY, YOU LOST THE COIN TOSS!
MAMEZO, THIS ISN'T GONNA WORK.
BESIDES, YOU SUCK.

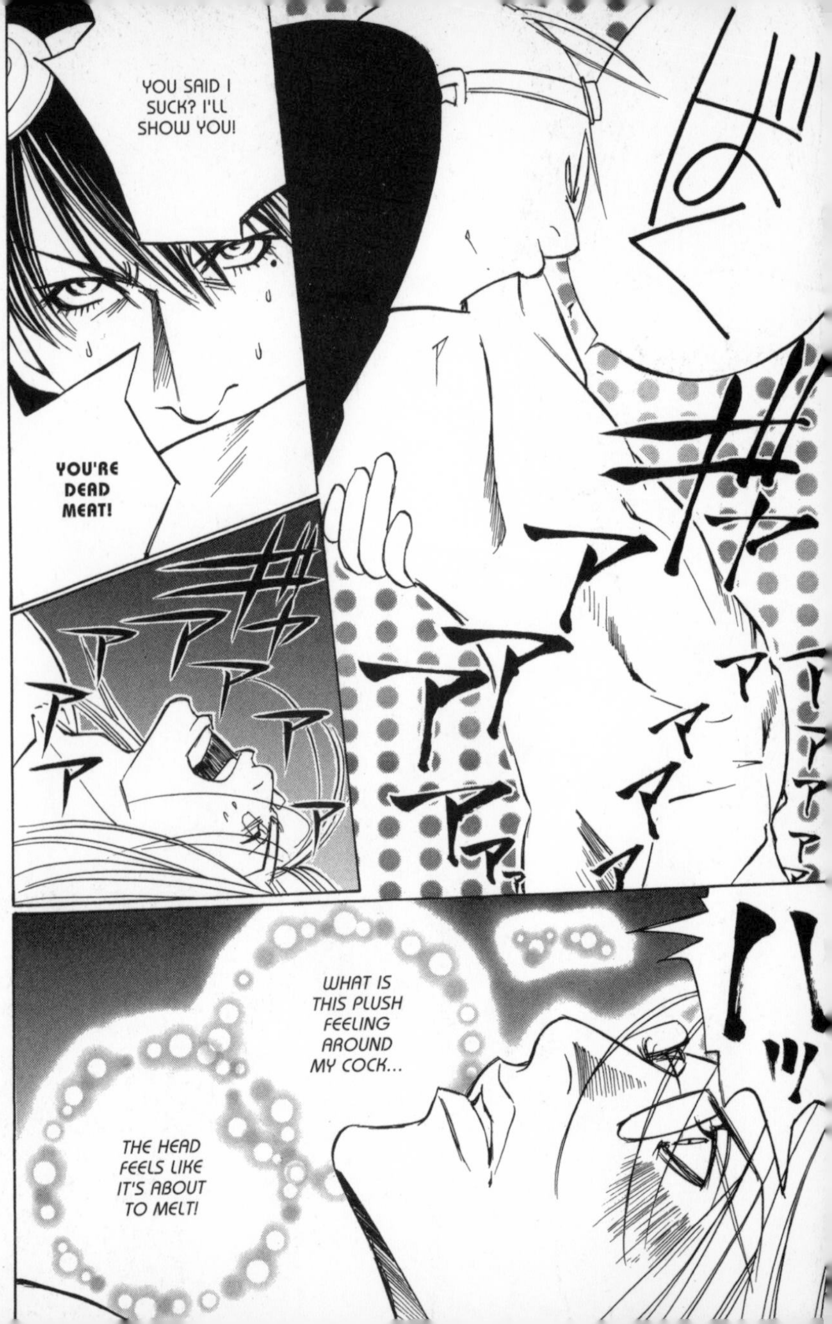
YOU SAID I SUCK? I'LL SHOW YOU!
YOU'RE DEAD MEAT!
WHAT IS THIS PLUSH FEELING AROUND MY COCK...
THE HEAD FEELS LIKE IT'S ABOUT TO MELT!

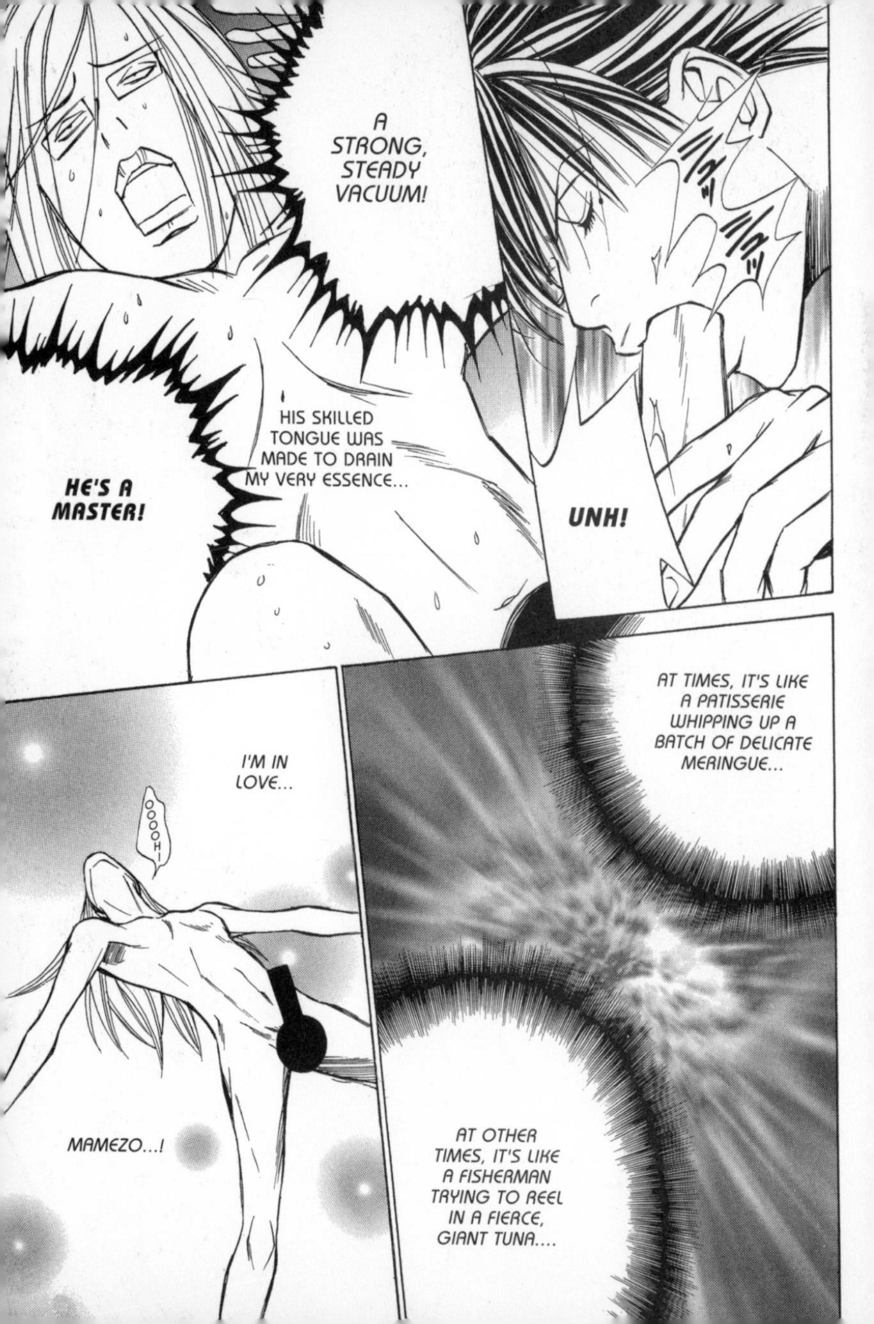
A STRONG, STEADY VACUUM!
UNH!
HIS SKILLED TONGUE WAS MADE TO DRAIN MY VERY ESSENCE...
HE'S A MASTER!
AT TIMES, IT'S LIKE A PATISSERIE WHIPPING UP A BATCH OF DELICATE MERINGUE...
AT OTHER TIMES, IT'S LIKE A FISHERMAN TRYING TO REEL IN A FIERCE, GIANT TUNA....
I'M IN LOVE...
OOOOH!
MAMEZO...!

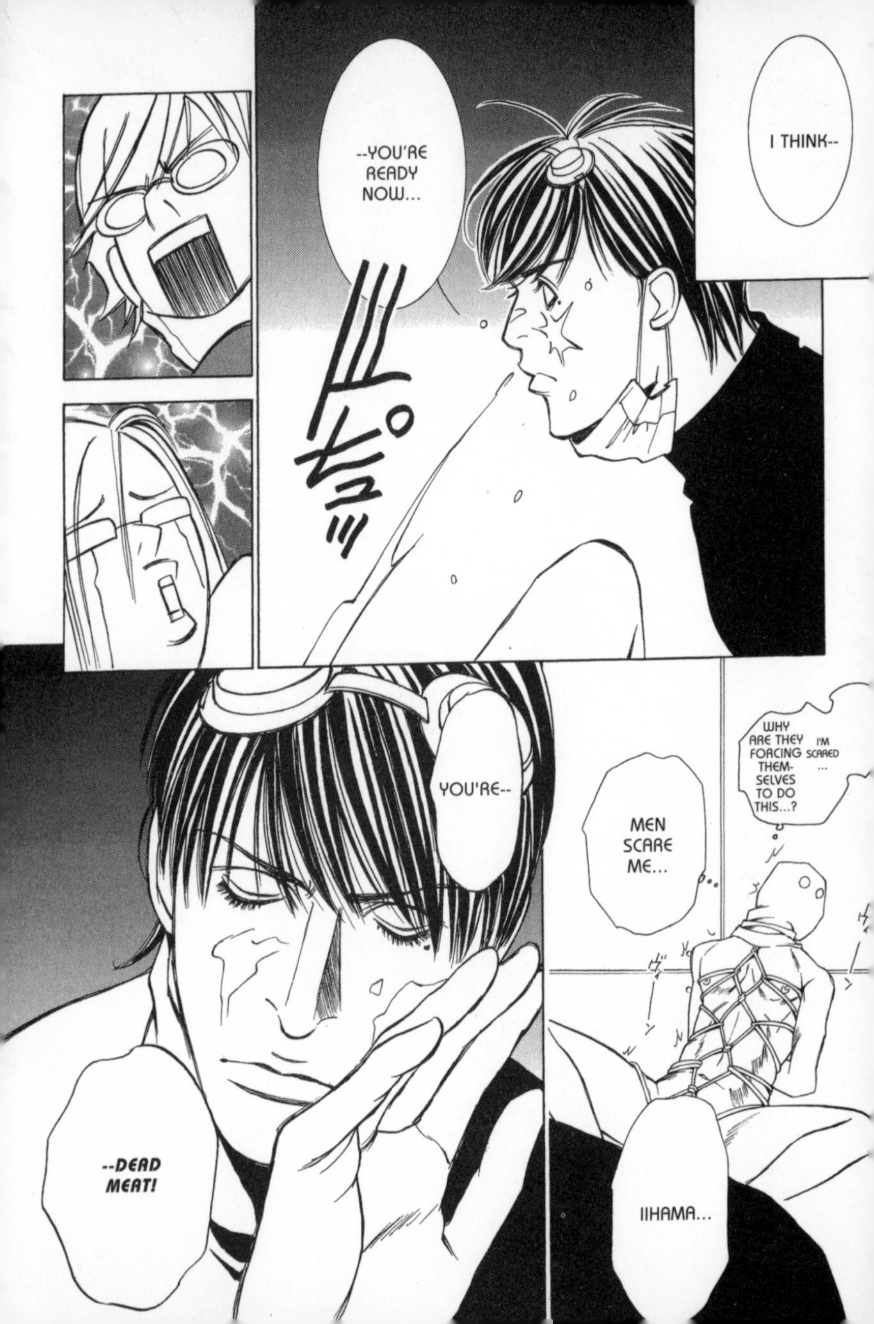

I THINK--
--YOU'RE READY NOW...
MEN SCARE ME...
WHY ARE THEY FORCING THEMSELVES TO DO THIS...?
I'M SCARED...
IIHAMA...
YOU'RE--
--DEAD MEAT!

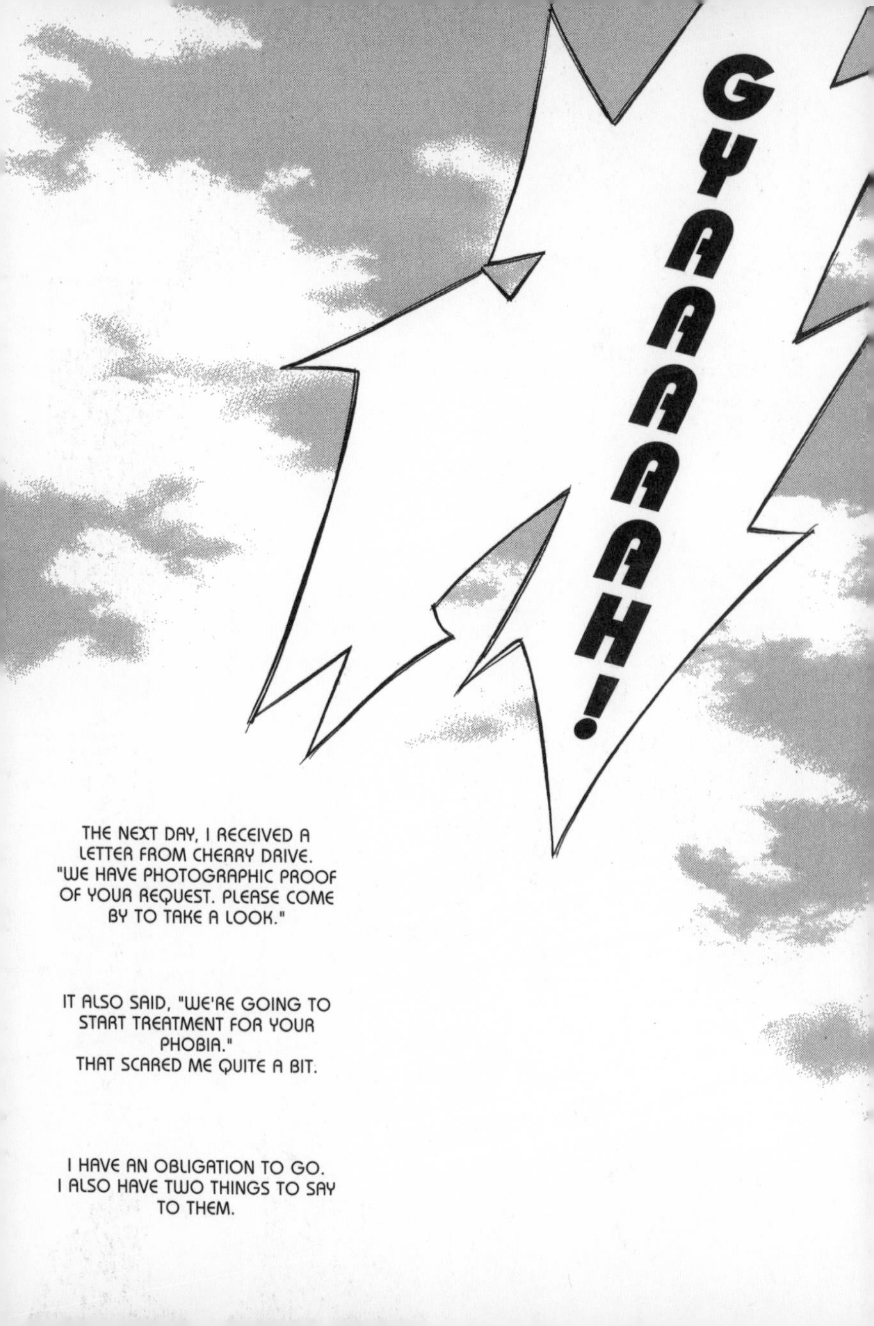
GYAAAAAH!
THE NEXT DAY, I RECEIVED A LETTER FROM CHERRY DRIVE. "WE HAVE PHOTOGRAPHIC PROOF OF YOUR REQUEST. PLEASE COME BY TO TAKE A LOOK."
IT ALSO SAID, "WE'RE GOING TO START TREATMENT FOR YOUR PHOBIA." THAT SCARED ME QUITE A BIT.
I HAVE AN OBLIGATION TO GO. I ALSO HAVE TWO THINGS TO SAY TO THEM.

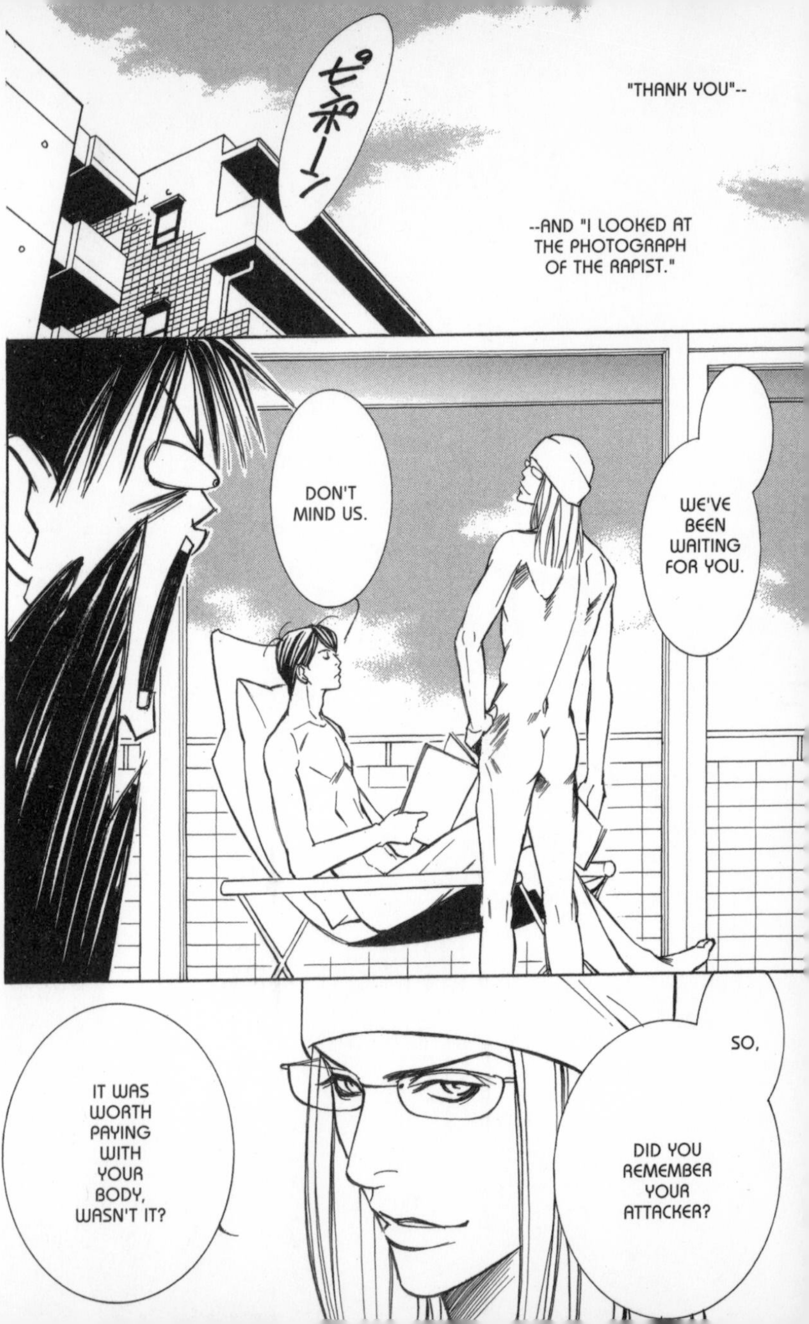
ピポーン
"THANK YOU"--
--AND "I LOOKED AT THE PHOTOGRAPH OF THE RAPIST."
WE'VE BEEN WAITING FOR YOU.
DON'T MIND US.
SO,
DID YOU REMEMBER YOUR ATTACKER?
IT WAS WORTH PAYING WITH YOUR BODY, WASN'T IT?

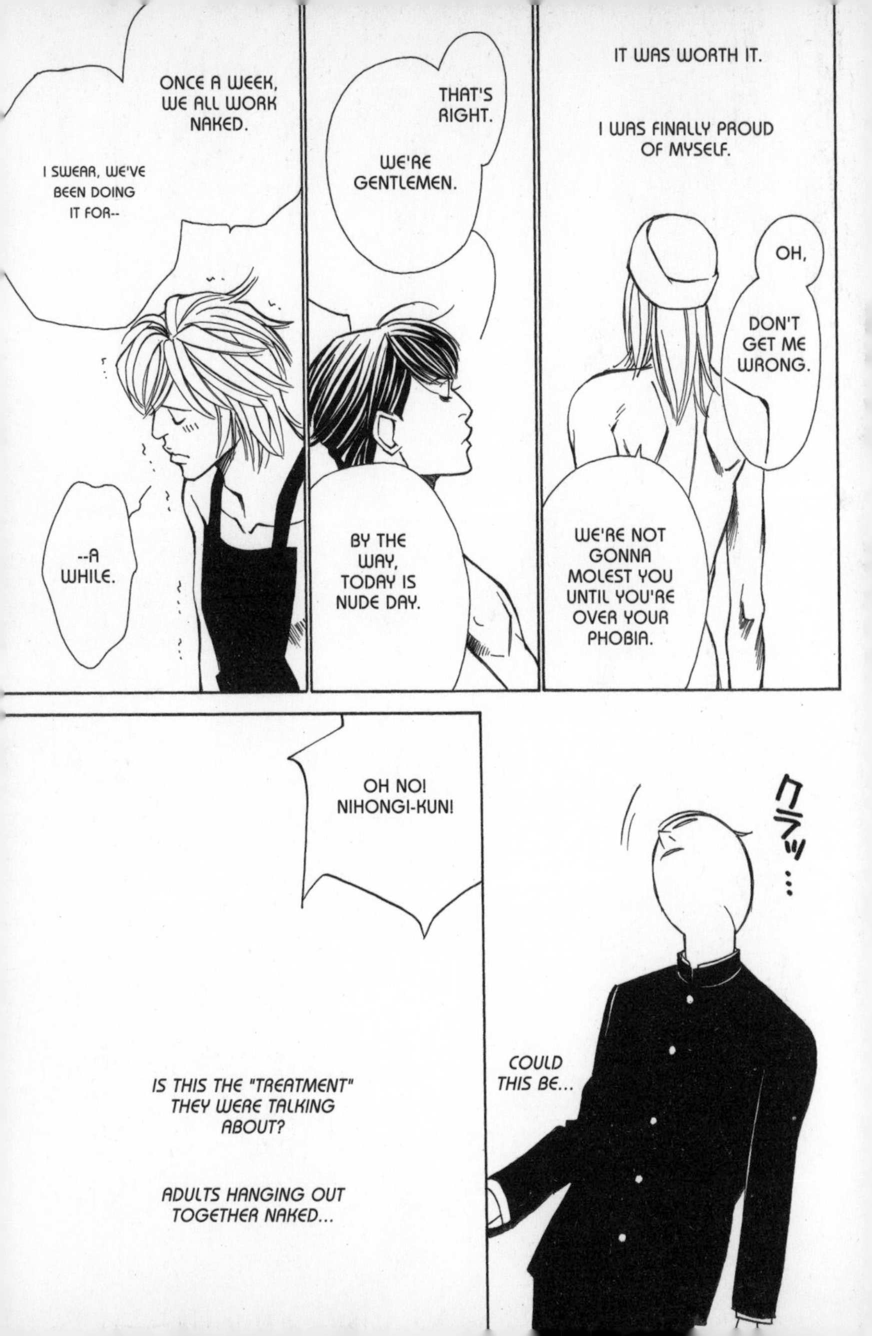
IT WAS WORTH IT.
I WAS FINALLY PROUD OF MYSELF.
OH,
DON'T GET ME WRONG.
WE'RE NOT GONNA MOLEST YOU UNTIL YOU'RE OVER YOUR PHOBIA.
THAT'S RIGHT.
WE'RE GENTLEMEN.
BY THE WAY, TODAY IS NUDE DAY.
ONCE A WEEK, WE ALL WORK NAKED.
I SWEAR, WE'VE BEEN DOING IT FOR--
--A WHILE.
クラッ…
COULD THIS BE...
OH NO! NIHONGI-KUN!
IS THIS THE "TREATMENT" THEY WERE TALKING ABOUT?
ADULTS HANGING OUT TOGETHER NAKED...

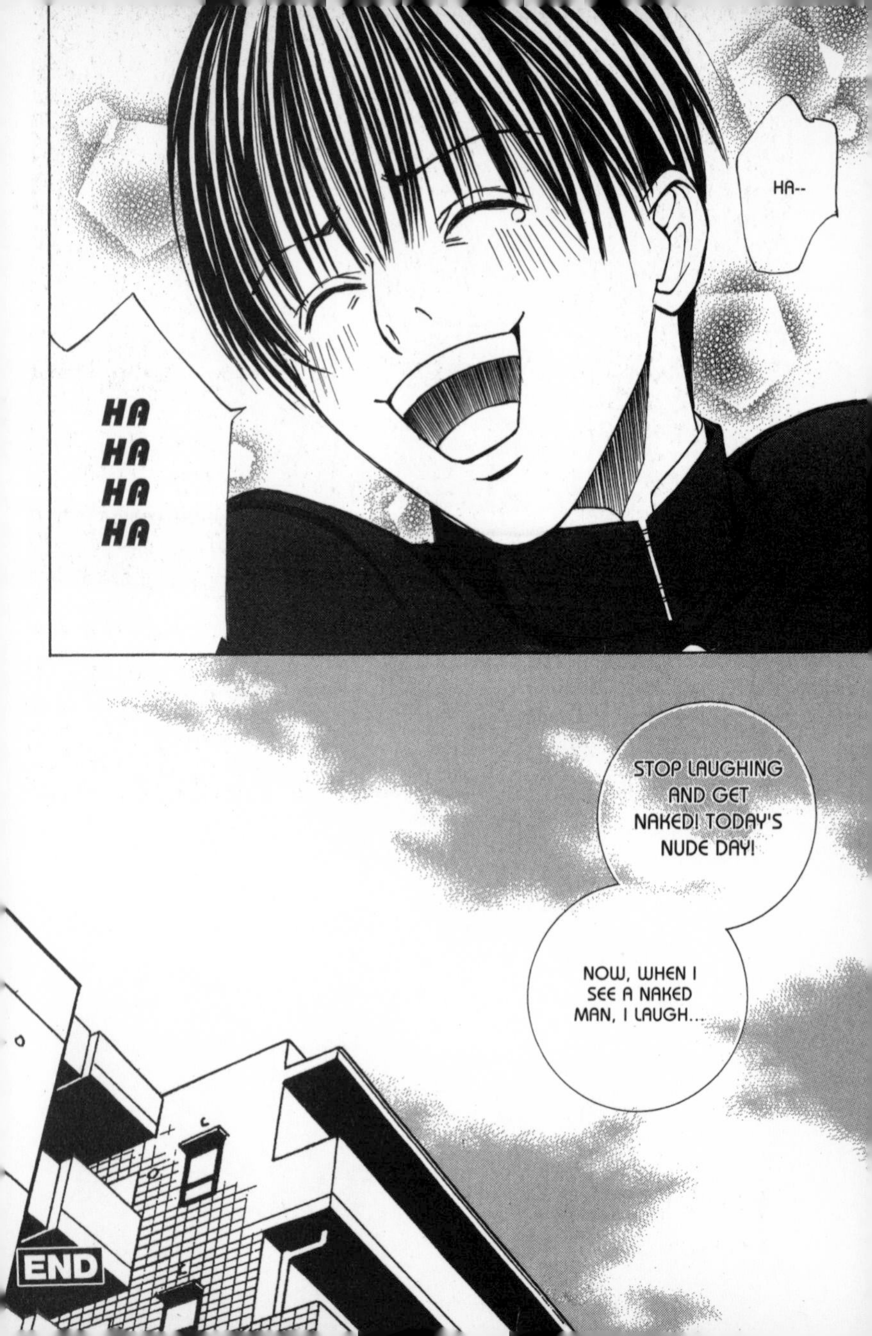
HA--
HA HA HA HA
STOP LAUGHING AND GET NAKED! TODAY'S NUDE DAY!
NOW, WHEN I SEE A NAKED MAN, I LAUGH...
END

A MYSTERIOUS, GAY SITE THAT HELPS PEOPLE GET REVENGE FOR A RAPE, OR RAVISH A WARM BODY FOR THE NIGHT...
THEY ACCEPT ALL KINDS OF OFFERS TO PLEASE THEIR CLIENTS...

drive2.
PASSIONATE DRIVER

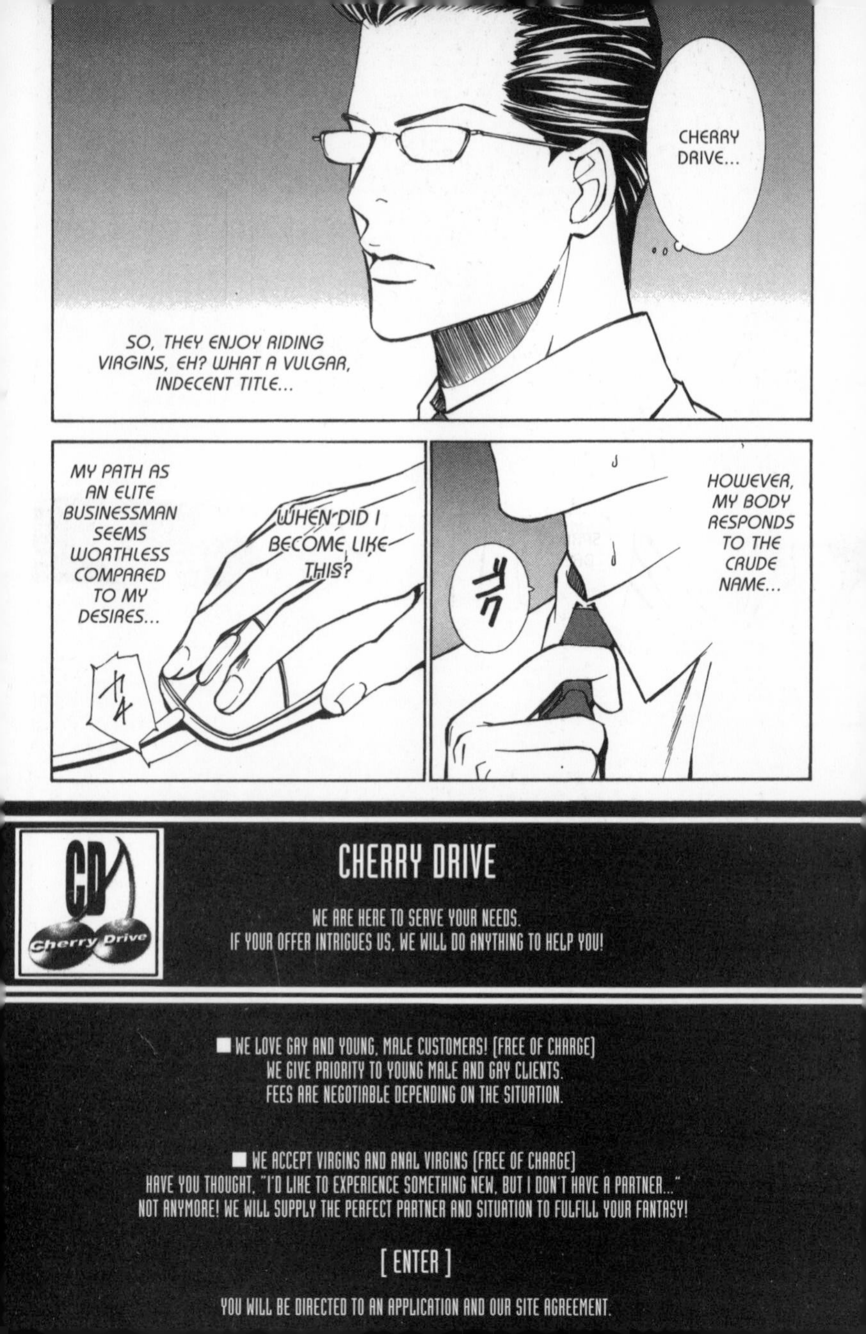
CHERRY DRIVE...
SO, THEY ENJOY RIDING VIRGINS, EH? WHAT A VULGAR, INDECENT TITLE...
HOWEVER, MY BODY RESPONDS TO THE CRUDE NAME...
ゴク
MY PATH AS AN ELITE BUSINESSMAN SEEMS WORTHLESS COMPARED TO MY DESIRES...
WHEN DID I BECOME LIKE THIS?
カチ
CD
Cherry Drive
CHERRY DRIVE
WE ARE HERE TO SERVE YOUR NEEDS.
IF YOUR OFFER INTRIGUES US, WE WILL DO ANYTHING TO HELP YOU!
■ WE LOVE GAY AND YOUNG, MALE CUSTOMERS! [FREE OF CHARGE]
WE GIVE PRIORITY TO YOUNG MALE AND GAY CLIENTS.
FEES ARE NEGOTIABLE DEPENDING ON THE SITUATION.
■ WE ACCEPT VIRGINS AND ANAL VIRGINS [FREE OF CHARGE]
HAVE YOU THOUGHT, "I'D LIKE TO EXPERIENCE SOMETHING NEW, BUT I DON'T HAVE A PARTNER..."
NOT ANYMORE! WE WILL SUPPLY THE PERFECT PARTNER AND SITUATION TO FULFILL YOUR FANTASY!
[ENTER]
YOU WILL BE DIRECTED TO AN APPLICATION AND OUR SITE AGREEMENT.

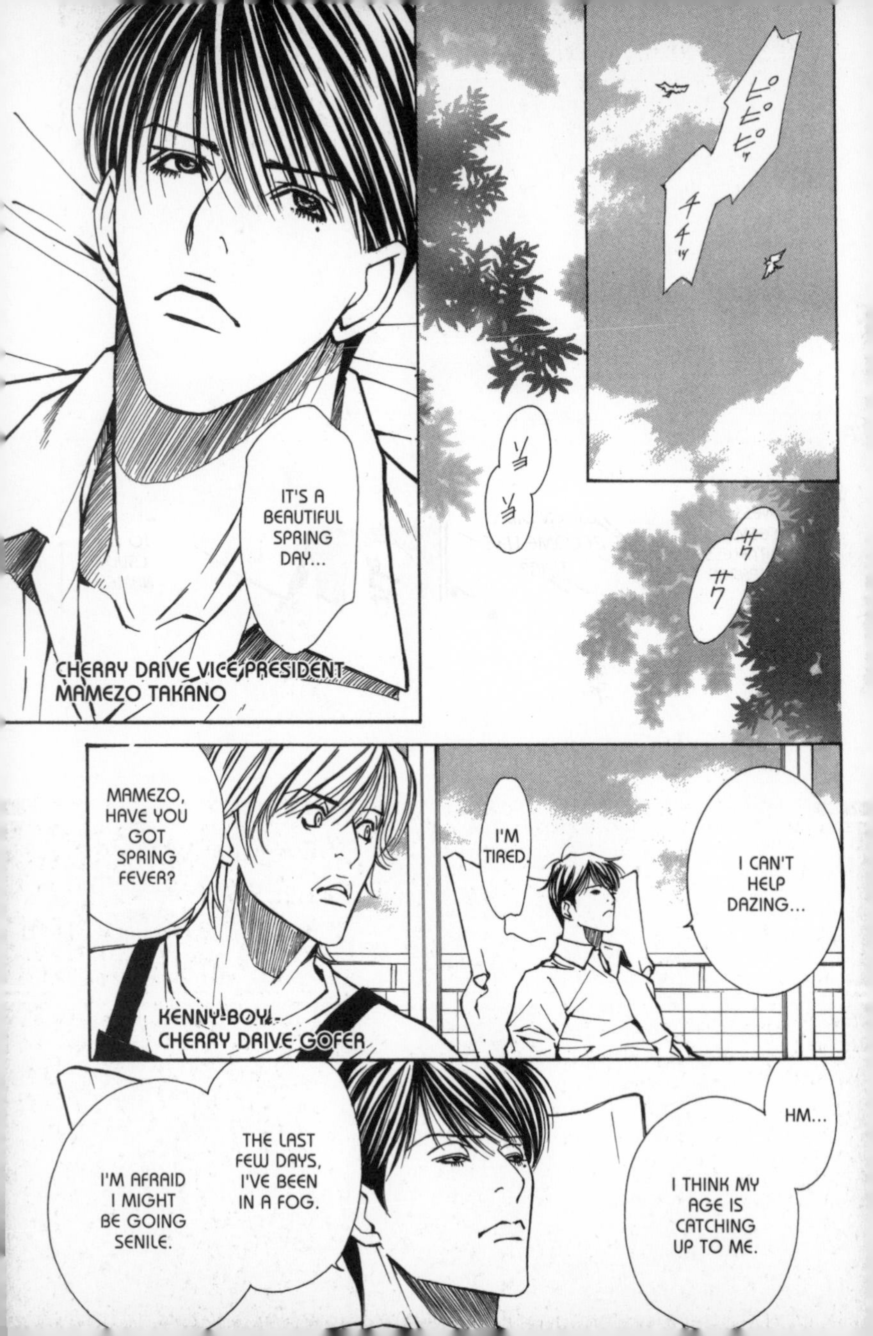

ピピピッ
チチッ
サワ サワ
IT'S A BEAUTIFUL SPRING DAY...
CHERRY DRIVE VICE PRESIDENT MAMEZO TAKANO
I CAN'T HELP DAZING...
I'M TIRED.
MAMEZO, HAVE YOU GOT SPRING FEVER?
KENNY-BOY- CHERRY DRIVE GOFER
HM...
I THINK MY AGE IS CATCHING UP TO ME.
THE LAST FEW DAYS, I'VE BEEN IN A FOG.
I'M AFRAID I MIGHT BE GOING SENILE.

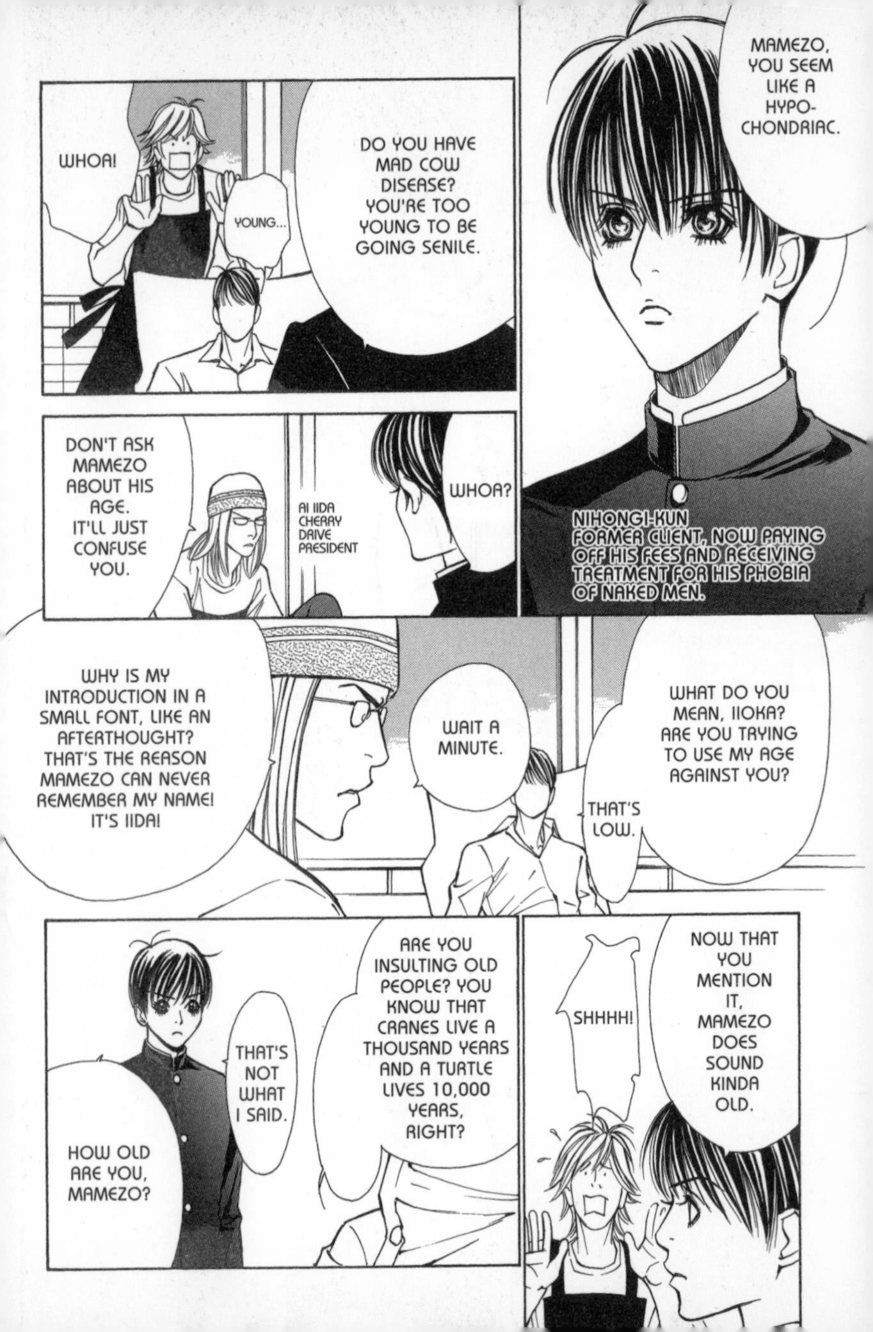
MAMEZO, YOU SEEM LIKE A HYPO-CHONDRIAC.
NIHONGI-KUN FORMER CLIENT, NOW PAYING OFF HIS FEES AND RECEIVING TREATMENT FOR HIS PHOBIA OF NAKED MEN.
DO YOU HAVE MAD COW DISEASE? YOU'RE TOO YOUNG TO BE GOING SENILE.
YOUNG...
WHOA!
WHOA?
AI IIDA CHERRY DRIVE PRESIDENT
DON'T ASK MAMEZO ABOUT HIS AGE. IT'LL JUST CONFUSE YOU.
WHAT DO YOU MEAN, IIOKA? ARE YOU TRYING TO USE MY AGE AGAINST YOU?
THAT'S LOW.
WAIT A MINUTE.
WHY IS MY INTRODUCTION IN A SMALL FONT, LIKE AN AFTERTHOUGHT? THAT'S THE REASON MAMEZO CAN NEVER REMEMBER MY NAME! IT'S IIDA!
NOW THAT YOU MENTION IT, MAMEZO DOES SOUND KINDA OLD.
SHHHH!
ARE YOU INSULTING OLD PEOPLE? YOU KNOW THAT CRANES LIVE A THOUSAND YEARS AND A TURTLE LIVES 10,000 YEARS, RIGHT?
THAT'S NOT WHAT I SAID.
HOW OLD ARE YOU, MAMEZO?

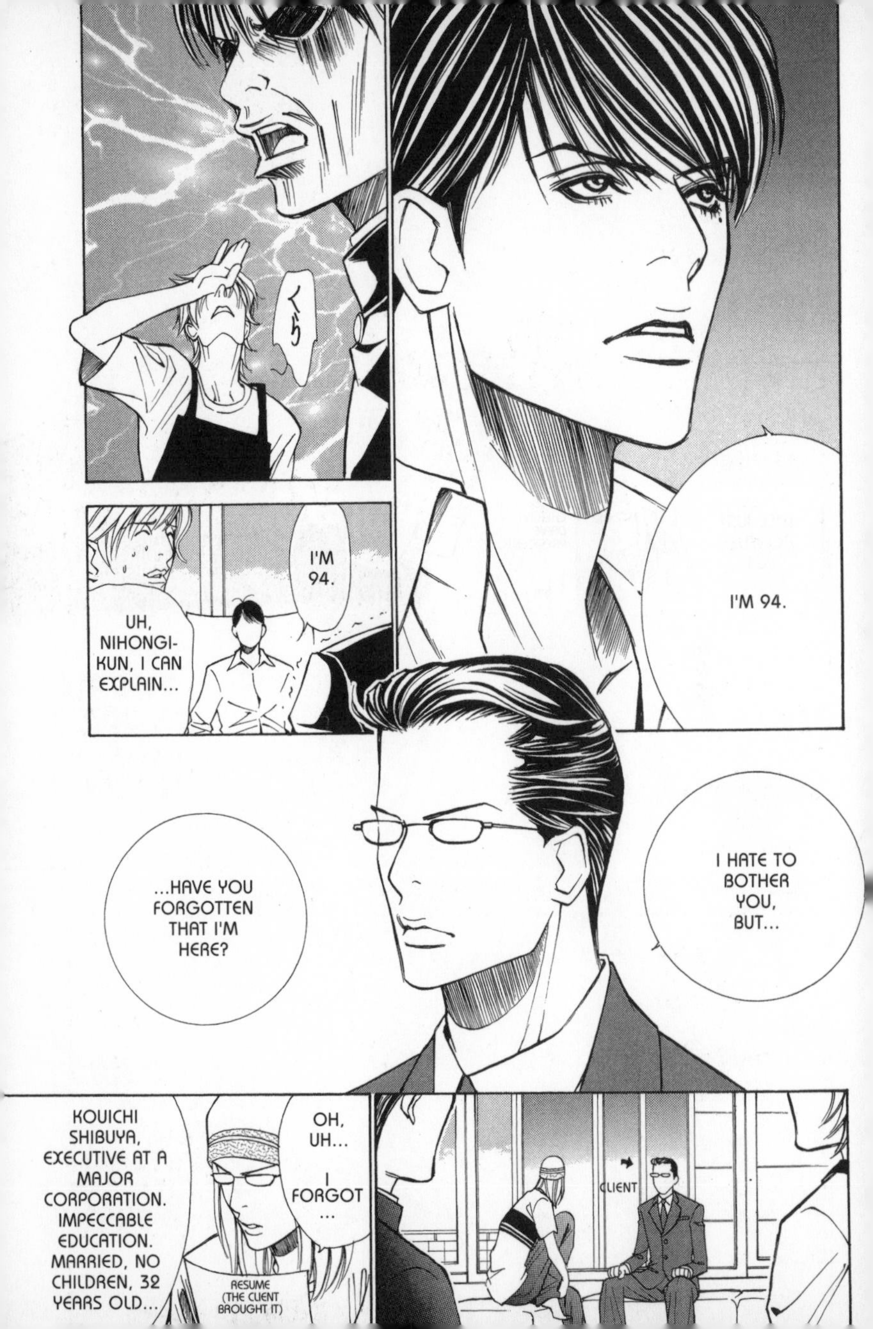
I'M 94.
くら
I'M 94.
UH, NIHONGI-KUN, I CAN EXPLAIN...
I HATE TO BOTHER YOU, BUT...
...HAVE YOU FORGOTTEN THAT I'M HERE?
CLIENT
OH, UH...
I FORGOT...
KOUICHI SHIBUYA, EXECUTIVE AT A MAJOR CORPORATION. IMPECCABLE EDUCATION. MARRIED, NO CHILDREN, 32 YEARS OLD...
RESUME (THE CLIENT BROUGHT IT)

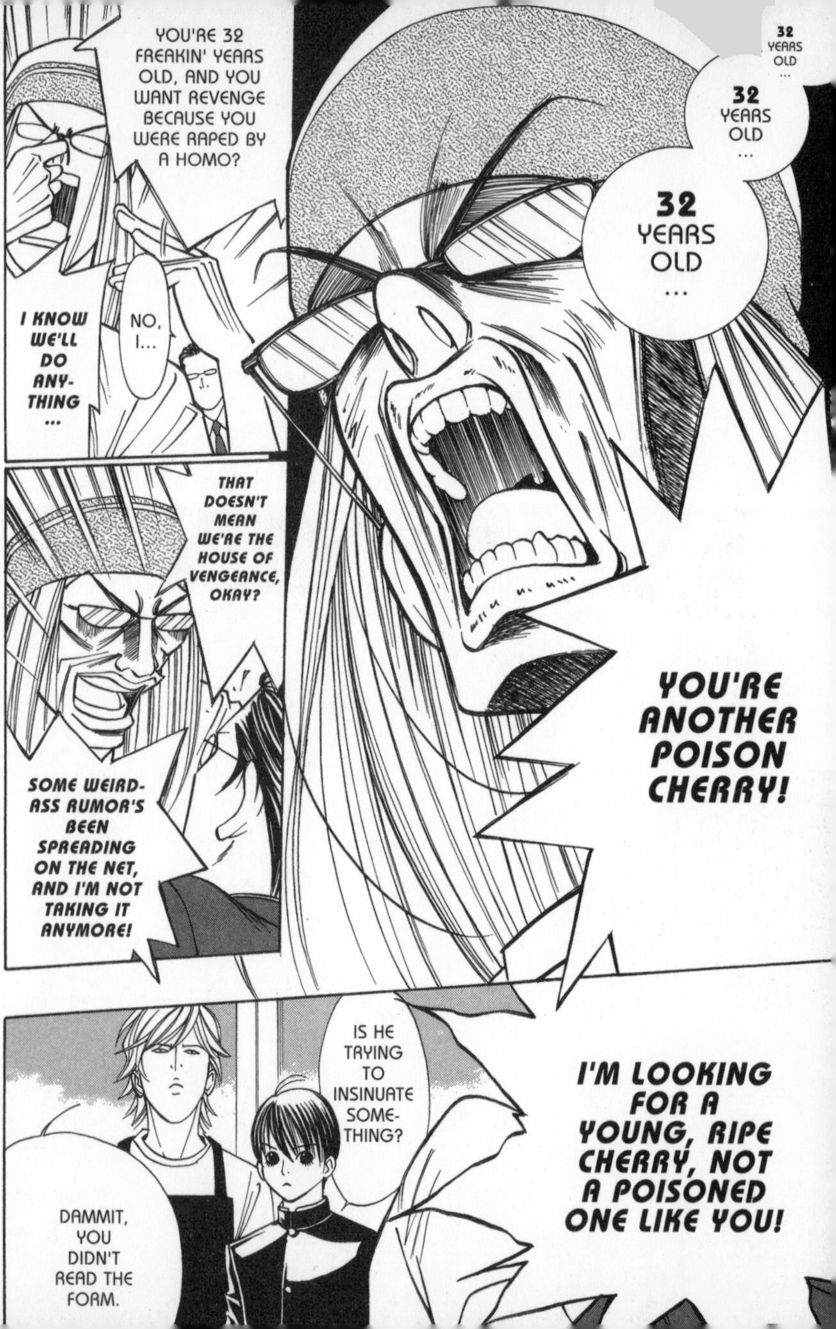
YOU'RE 32 FREAKIN' YEARS OLD, AND YOU WANT REVENGE BECAUSE YOU WERE RAPED BY A HOMO?
NO, I...
I KNOW WE'LL DO ANY-THING ...
THAT DOESN'T MEAN WE'RE THE HOUSE OF VENGEANCE, OKAY?
SOME WEIRD-ASS RUMOR'S BEEN SPREADING ON THE NET, AND I'M NOT TAKING IT ANYMORE!
32 YEARS OLD ...
32 YEARS OLD ...
32 YEARS OLD ...
YOU'RE ANOTHER POISON CHERRY!
I'M LOOKING FOR A YOUNG, RIPE CHERRY, NOT A POISONED ONE LIKE YOU!
IS HE TRYING TO INSINUATE SOME-THING?
DAMMIT, YOU DIDN'T READ THE FORM.

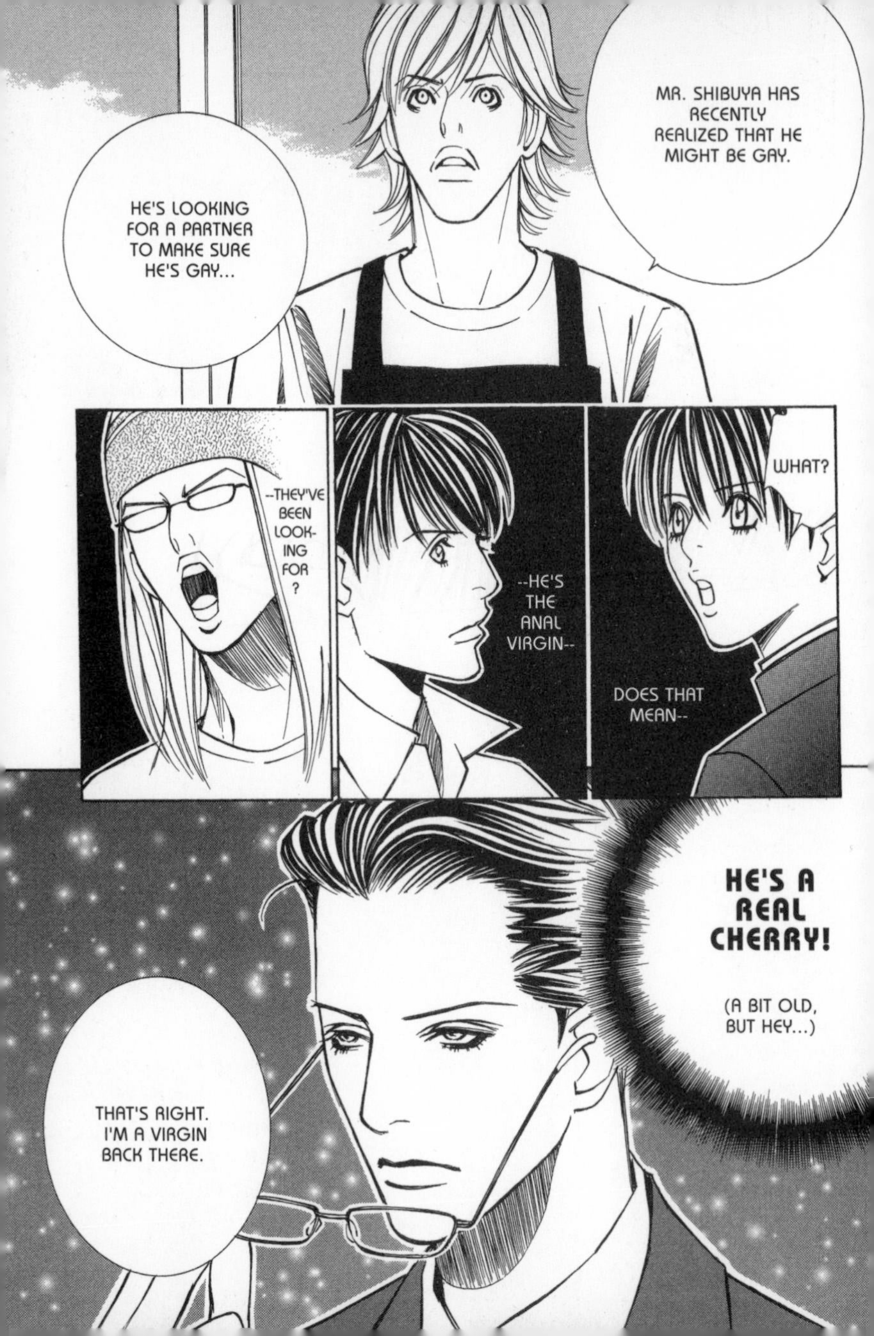
MR. SHIBUYA HAS RECENTLY REALIZED THAT HE MIGHT BE GAY.
HE'S LOOKING FOR A PARTNER TO MAKE SURE HE'S GAY...
WHAT?
DOES THAT MEAN--
--HE'S THE ANAL VIRGIN--
--THEY'VE BEEN LOOKING FOR?
HE'S A REAL CHERRY!
(A BIT OLD, BUT HEY...)
THAT'S RIGHT. I'M A VIRGIN BACK THERE.

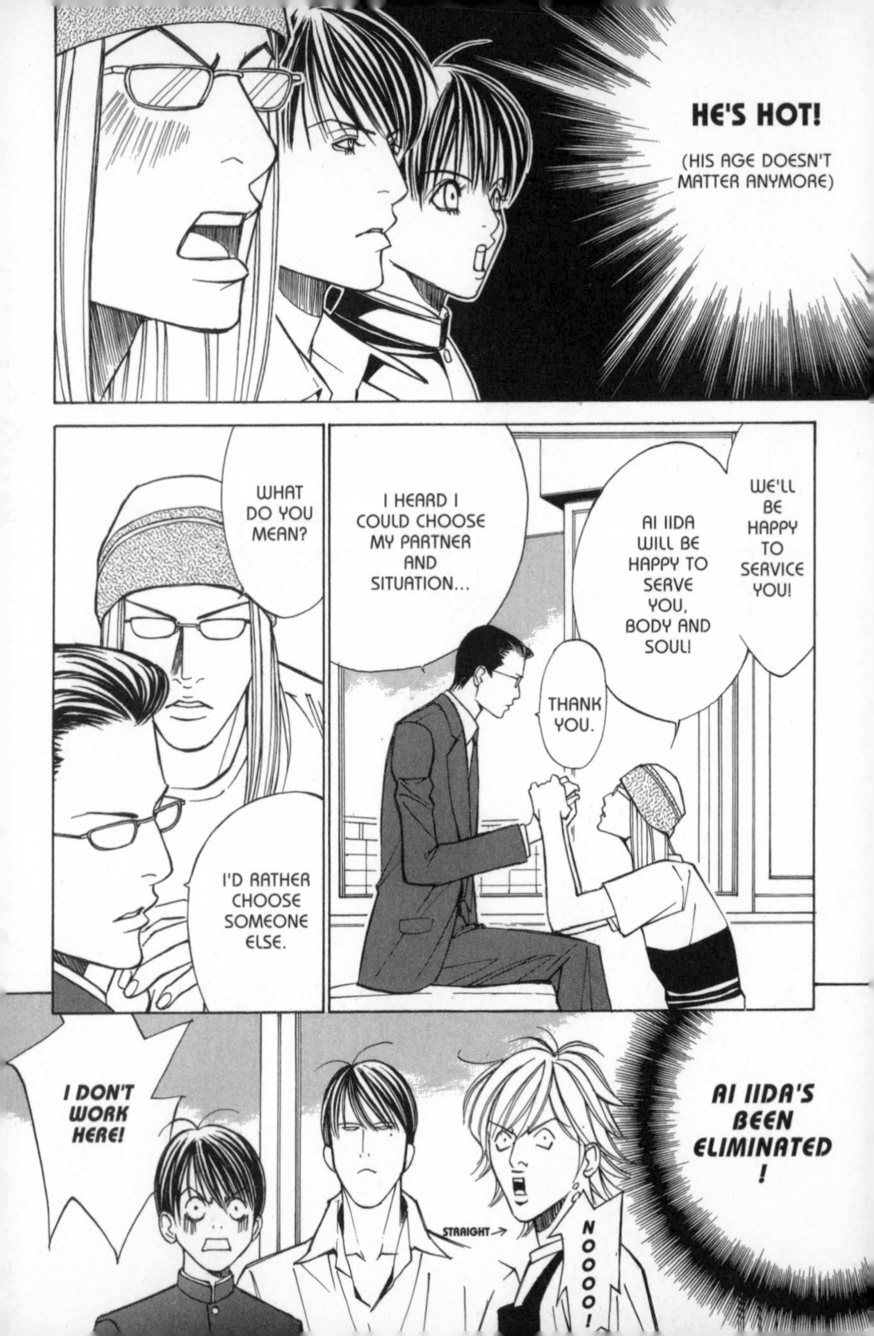
HE'S HOT!
(HIS AGE DOESN'T MATTER ANYMORE)
WE'LL BE HAPPY TO SERVICE YOU!
AI IIDA WILL BE HAPPY TO SERVE YOU, BODY AND SOUL!
THANK YOU.
I HEARD I COULD CHOOSE MY PARTNER AND SITUATION...
WHAT DO YOU MEAN?
I'D RATHER CHOOSE SOMEONE ELSE.
AI IIDA'S BEEN ELIMINATED!
NOOOOO!
STRAIGHT
I DON'T WORK HERE!

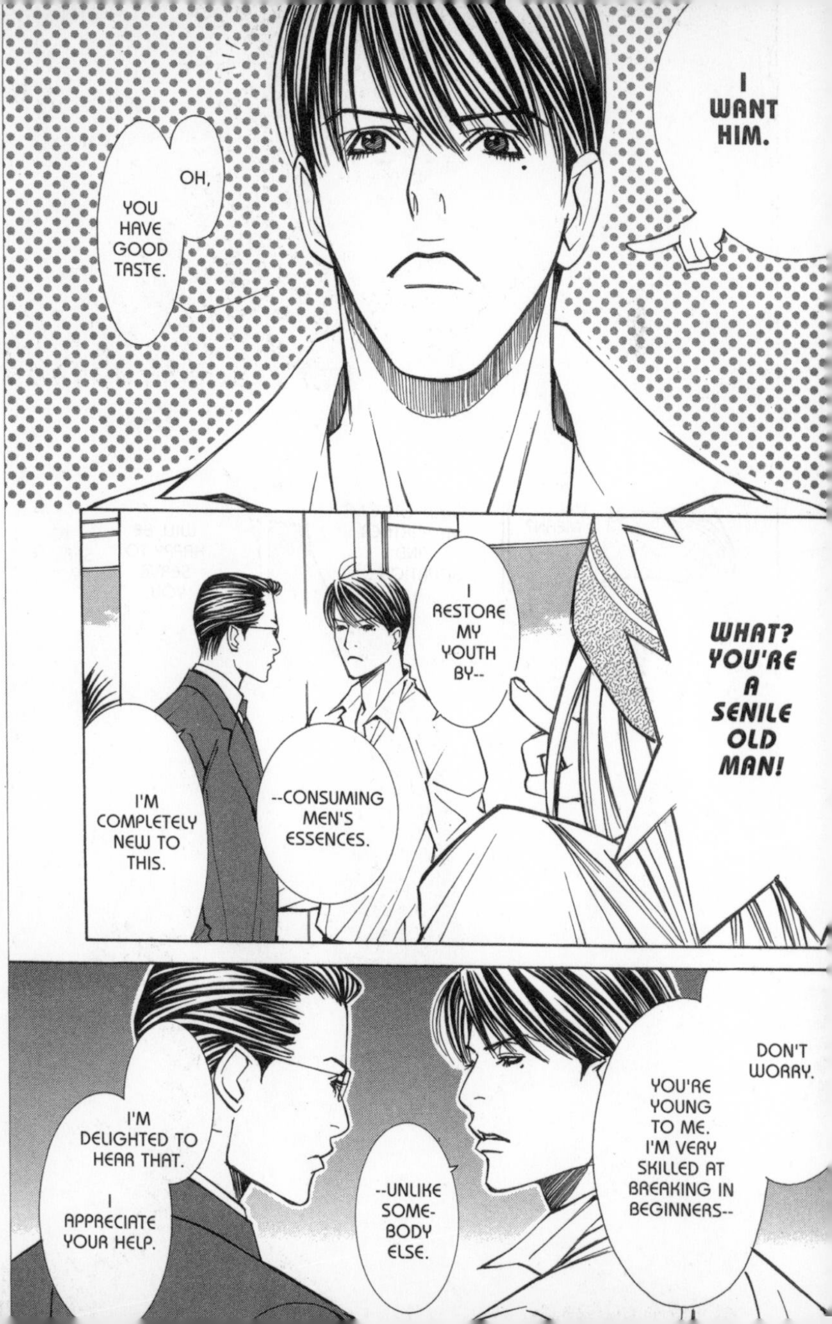
I WANT HIM.
OH, YOU HAVE GOOD TASTE.
WHAT? YOU'RE A SENILE OLD MAN!
I RESTORE MY YOUTH BY--
--CONSUMING MEN'S ESSENCES.
I'M COMPLETELY NEW TO THIS.
DON'T WORRY.
YOU'RE YOUNG TO ME. I'M VERY SKILLED AT BREAKING IN BEGINNERS--
--UNLIKE SOMEBODY ELSE.
I'M DELIGHTED TO HEAR THAT.
I APPRECIATE YOUR HELP.

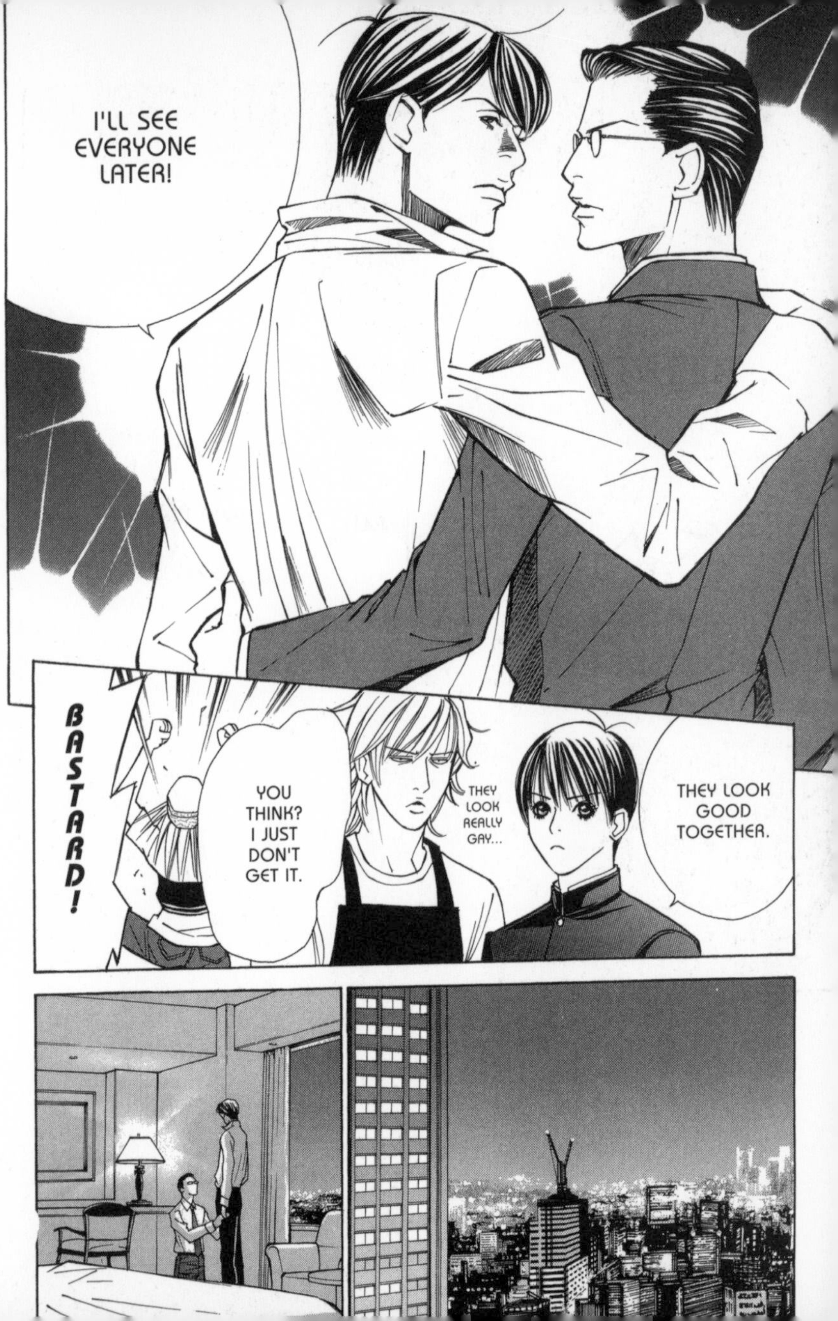
I'LL SEE EVERYONE LATER!
THEY LOOK GOOD TOGETHER.
THEY LOOK REALLY GAY...
YOU THINK? I JUST DON'T GET IT.
BASTARD!

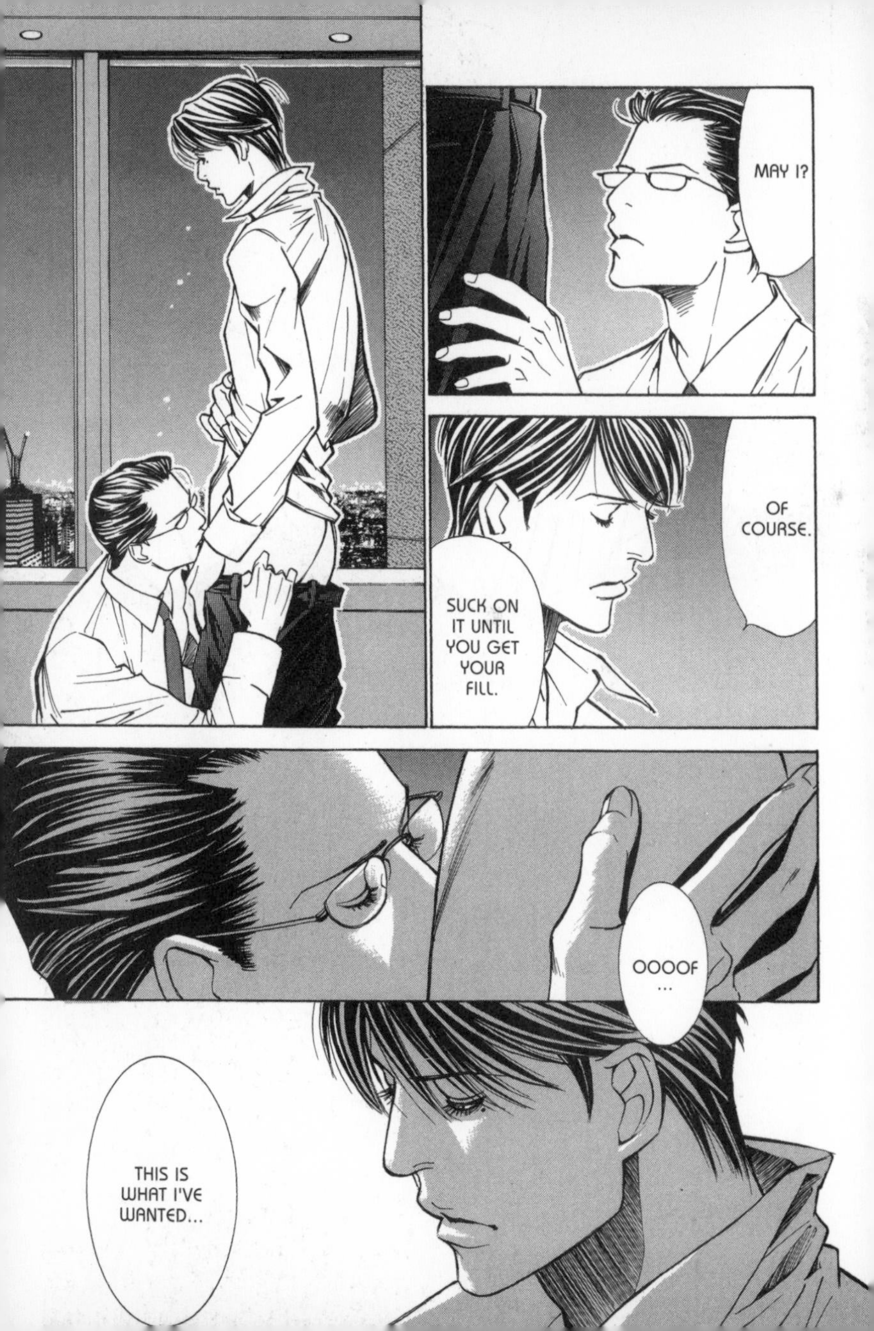
MAY I?
OF COURSE.
SUCK ON IT UNTIL YOU GET YOUR FILL.
OOOOF ...
THIS IS WHAT I'VE WANTED...

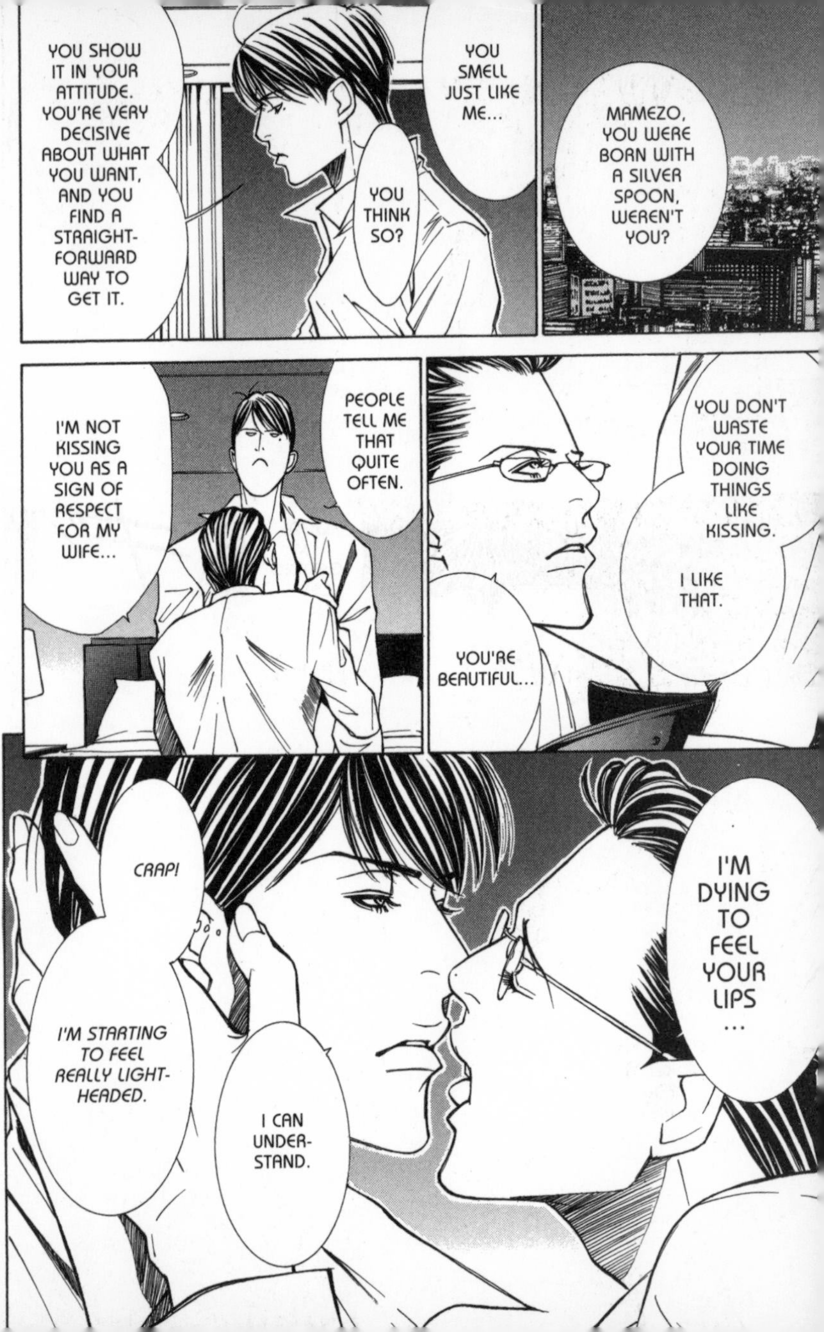
MAMEZO, YOU WERE BORN WITH A SILVER SPOON, WEREN'T YOU?
YOU SMELL JUST LIKE ME...
YOU THINK SO?
YOU SHOW IT IN YOUR ATTITUDE. YOU'RE VERY DECISIVE ABOUT WHAT YOU WANT, AND YOU FIND A STRAIGHT-FORWARD WAY TO GET IT.
YOU DON'T WASTE YOUR TIME DOING THINGS LIKE KISSING.
I LIKE THAT.
YOU'RE BEAUTIFUL...
PEOPLE TELL ME THAT QUITE OFTEN.
I'M NOT KISSING YOU AS A SIGN OF RESPECT FOR MY WIFE...
I'M DYING TO FEEL YOUR LIPS...
I CAN UNDER-STAND.
CRAP!
I'M STARTING TO FEEL REALLY LIGHT-HEADED.

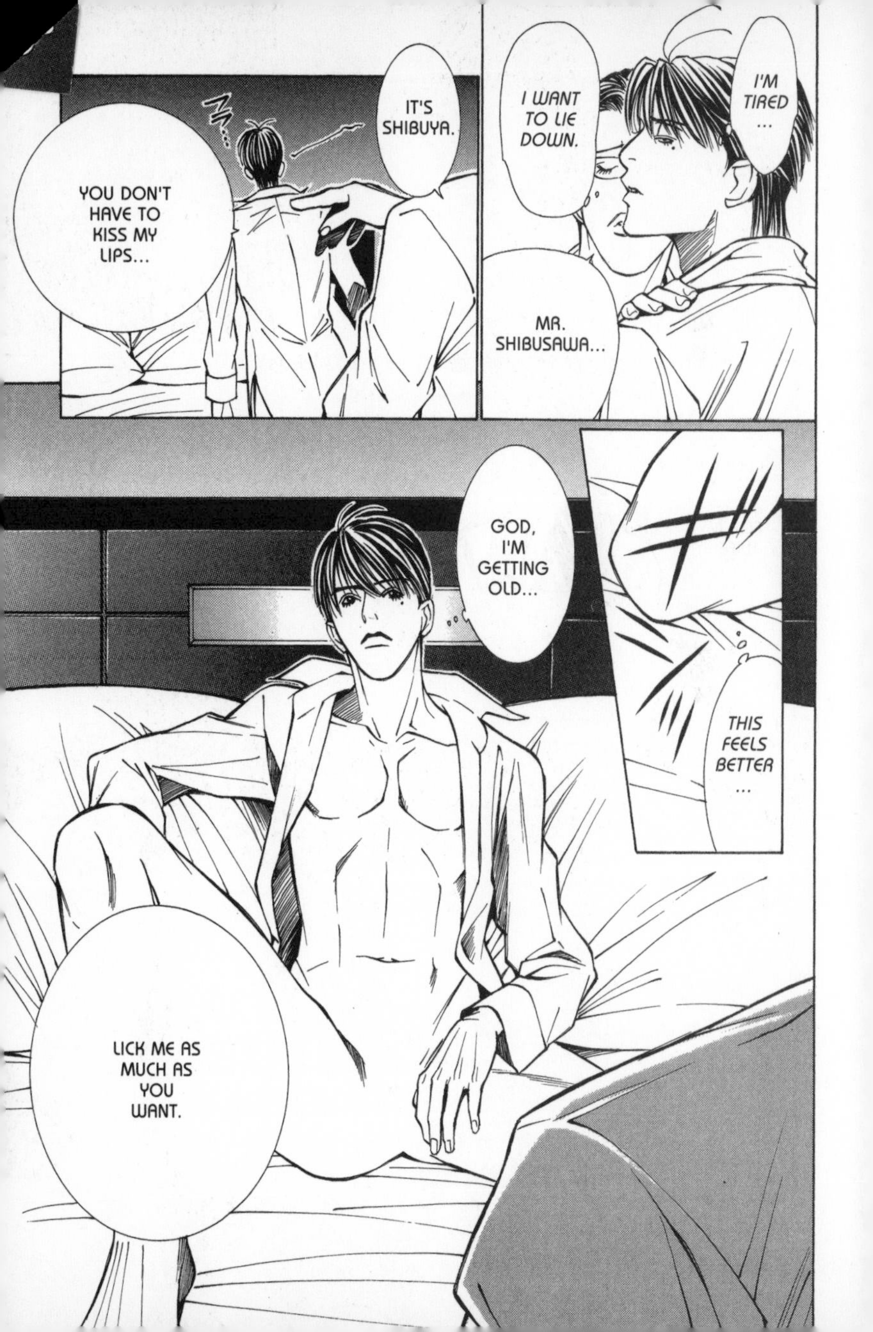
I'M TIRED...
I WANT TO LIE DOWN.
MR. SHIBUSAWA...
IT'S SHIBUYA.
YOU DON'T HAVE TO KISS MY LIPS...
THIS FEELS BETTER...
GOD, I'M GETTING OLD...
LICK ME AS MUCH AS YOU WANT.

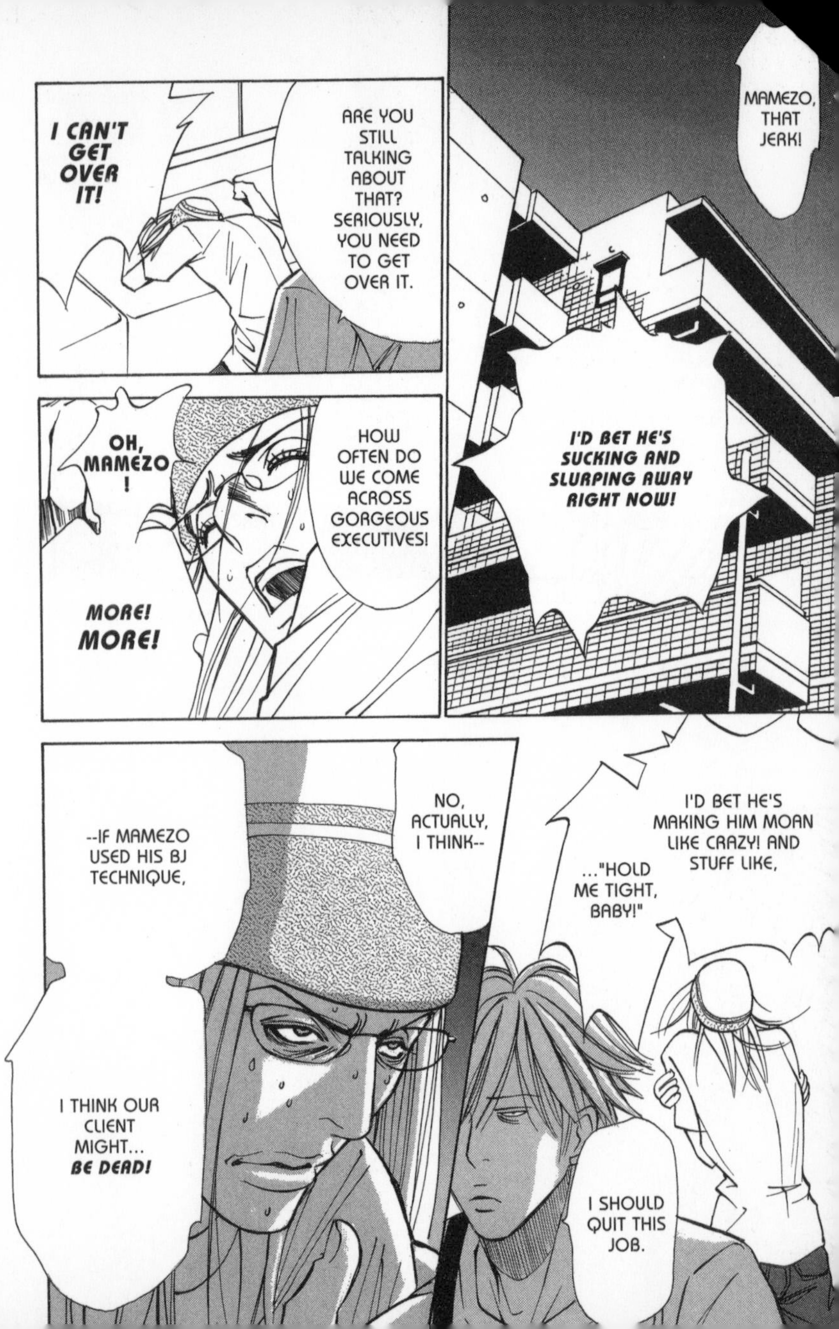
MAMEZO, THAT JERK!
I'D BET HE'S SUCKING AND SLURPING AWAY RIGHT NOW!
I CAN'T GET OVER IT!
ARE YOU STILL TALKING ABOUT THAT? SERIOUSLY, YOU NEED TO GET OVER IT.
OH, MAMEZO!
HOW OFTEN DO WE COME ACROSS GORGEOUS EXECUTIVES!
MORE! MORE!
I'D BET HE'S MAKING HIM MOAN LIKE CRAZY! AND STUFF LIKE,
..."HOLD ME TIGHT, BABY!"
NO, ACTUALLY, I THINK--
--IF MAMEZO USED HIS BJ TECHNIQUE,
I THINK OUR CLIENT MIGHT... BE DEAD!
I SHOULD QUIT THIS JOB.

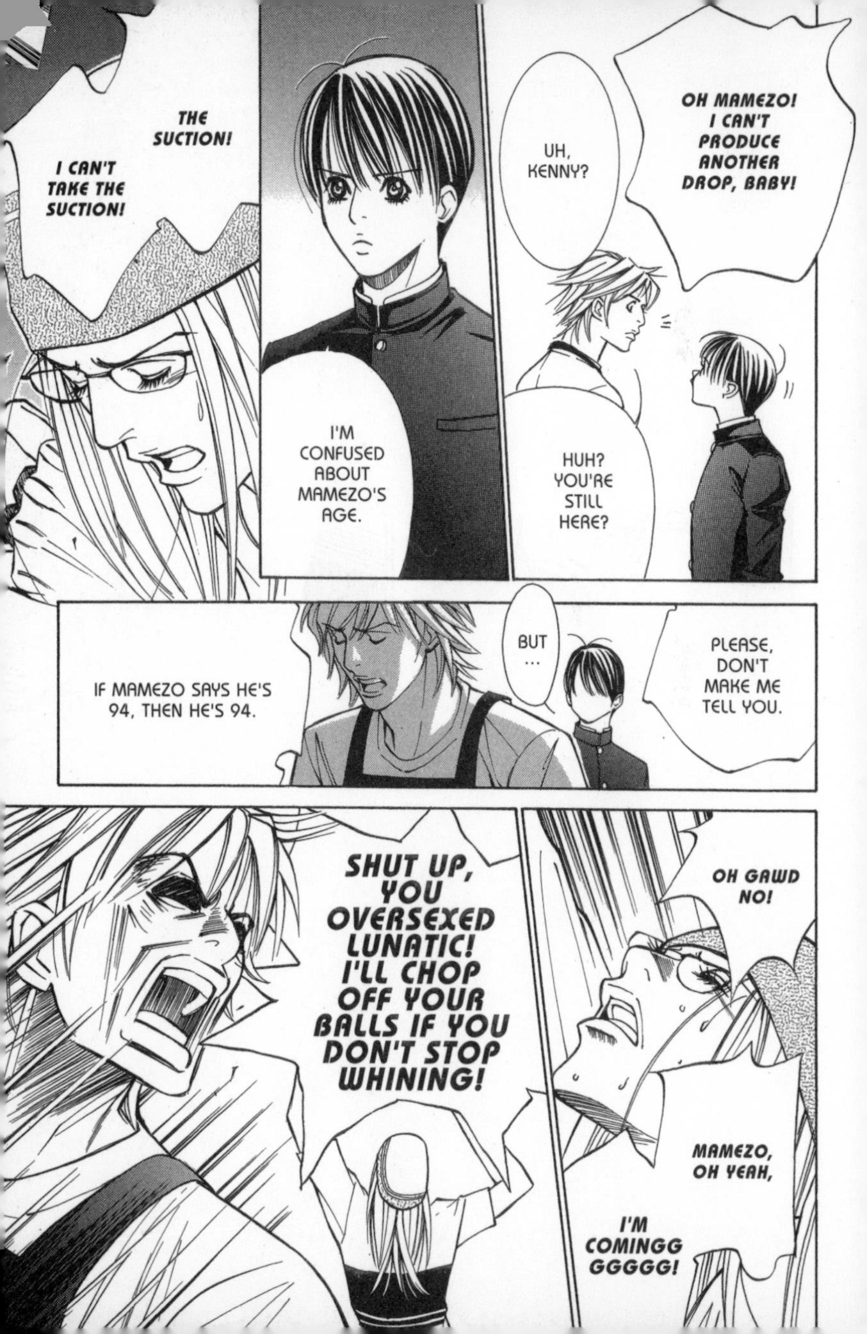
OH MAMEZO! I CAN'T PRODUCE ANOTHER DROP, BABY!
UH, KENNY?
HUH? YOU'RE STILL HERE?
I'M CONFUSED ABOUT MAMEZO'S AGE.
THE SUCTION!
I CAN'T TAKE THE SUCTION!
PLEASE, DON'T MAKE ME TELL YOU.
BUT ...
IF MAMEZO SAYS HE'S 94, THEN HE'S 94.
OH GAWD NO!
MAMEZO, OH YEAH,
I'M COMINGG GGGGG!
SHUT UP, YOU OVERSEXED LUNATIC! I'LL CHOP OFF YOUR BALLS IF YOU DON'T STOP WHINING!

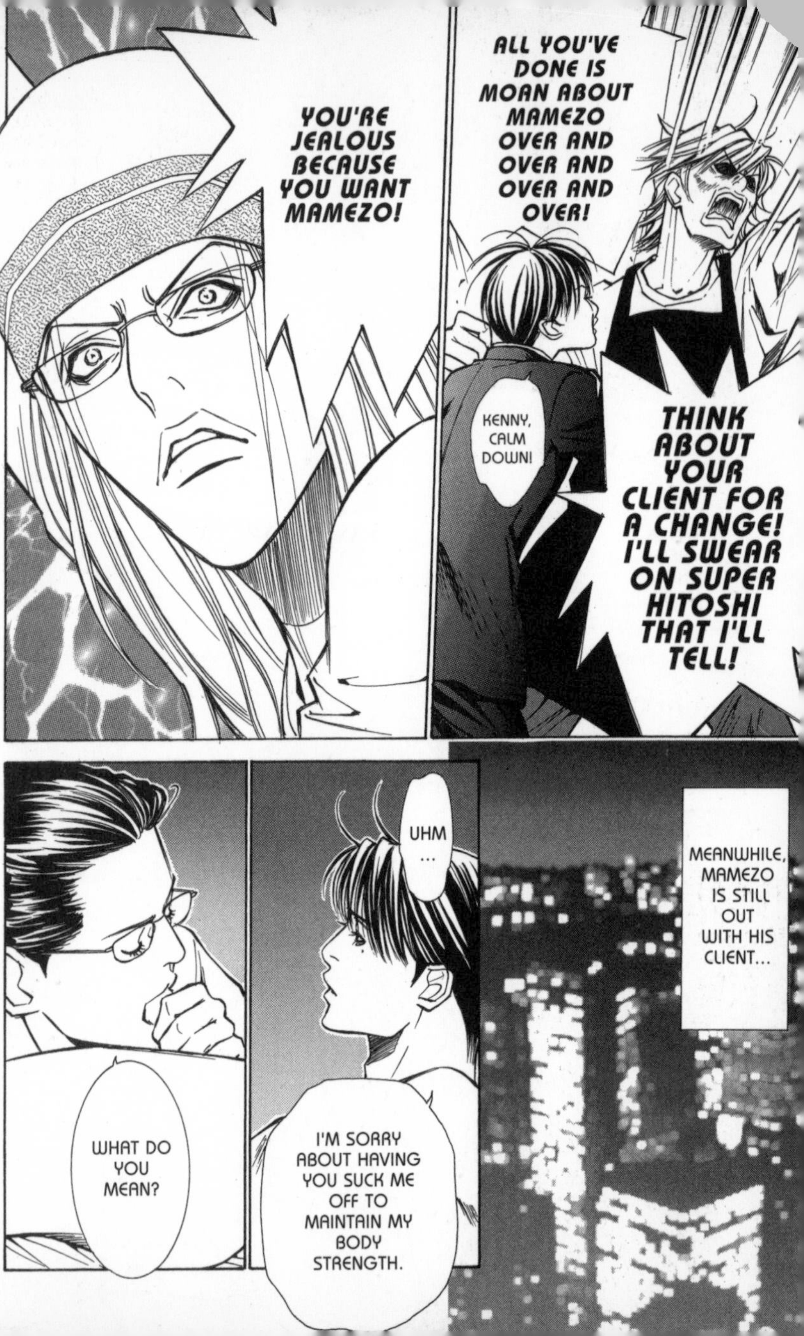
ALL YOU'VE DONE IS MOAN ABOUT MAMEZO OVER AND OVER AND OVER AND OVER!
THINK ABOUT YOUR CLIENT FOR A CHANGE! I'LL SWEAR ON SUPER HITOSHI THAT I'LL TELL!
KENNY, CALM DOWN!
YOU'RE JEALOUS BECAUSE YOU WANT MAMEZO!
MEANWHILE, MAMEZO IS STILL OUT WITH HIS CLIENT...
UHM ...
I'M SORRY ABOUT HAVING YOU SUCK ME OFF TO MAINTAIN MY BODY STRENGTH.
WHAT DO YOU MEAN?

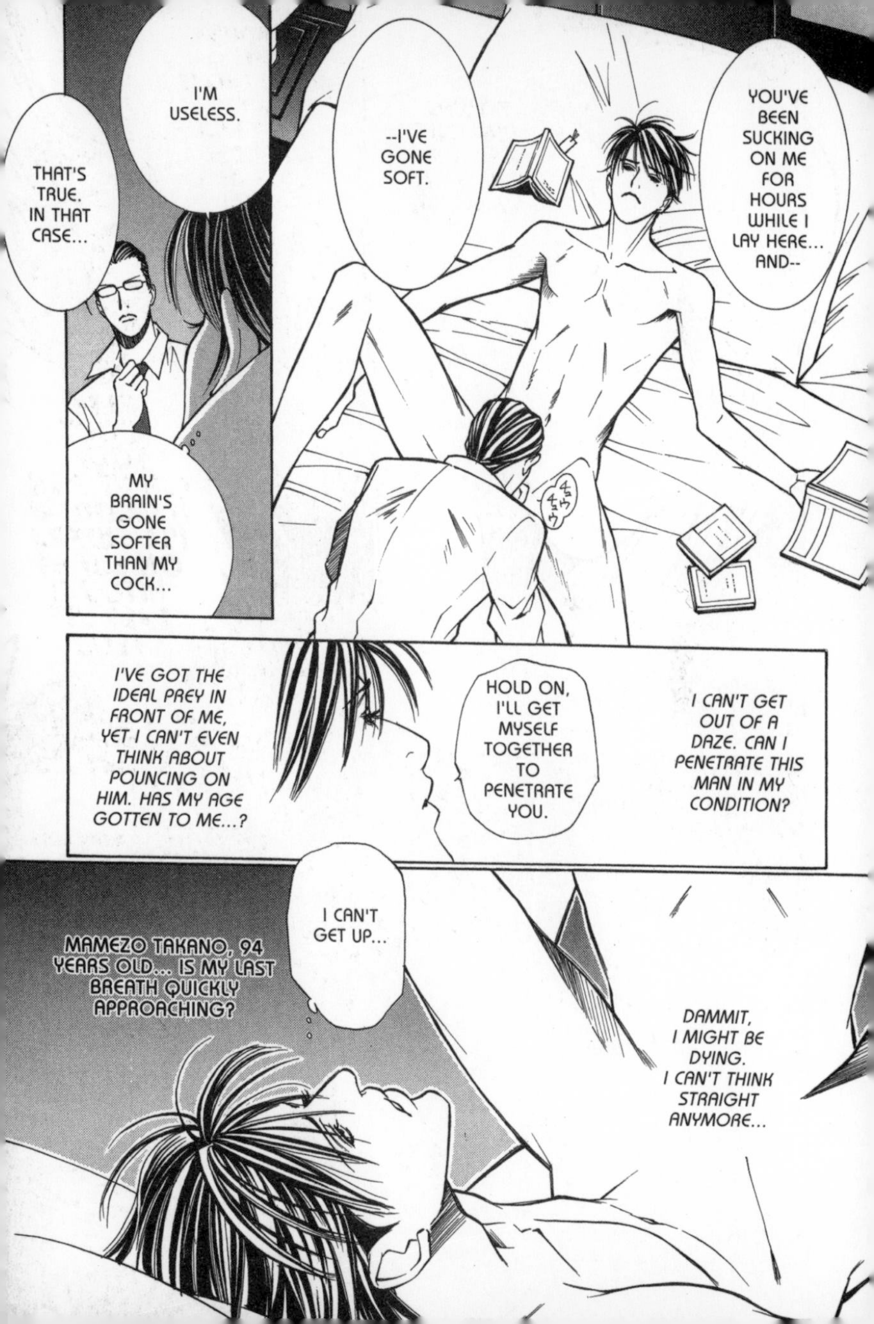
YOU'VE BEEN SUCKING ON ME FOR HOURS WHILE I LAY HERE... AND--
--I'VE GONE SOFT.
I'M USELESS.
THAT'S TRUE. IN THAT CASE...
MY BRAIN'S GONE SOFTER THAN MY COCK...
I CAN'T GET OUT OF A DAZE. CAN I PENETRATE THIS MAN IN MY CONDITION?
HOLD ON, I'LL GET MYSELF TOGETHER TO PENETRATE YOU.
I'VE GOT THE IDEAL PREY IN FRONT OF ME, YET I CAN'T EVEN THINK ABOUT POUNCING ON HIM. HAS MY AGE GOTTEN TO ME...?
DAMMIT, I MIGHT BE DYING. I CAN'T THINK STRAIGHT ANYMORE...
I CAN'T GET UP...
MAMEZO TAKANO, 94 YEARS OLD... IS MY LAST BREATH QUICKLY APPROACHING?

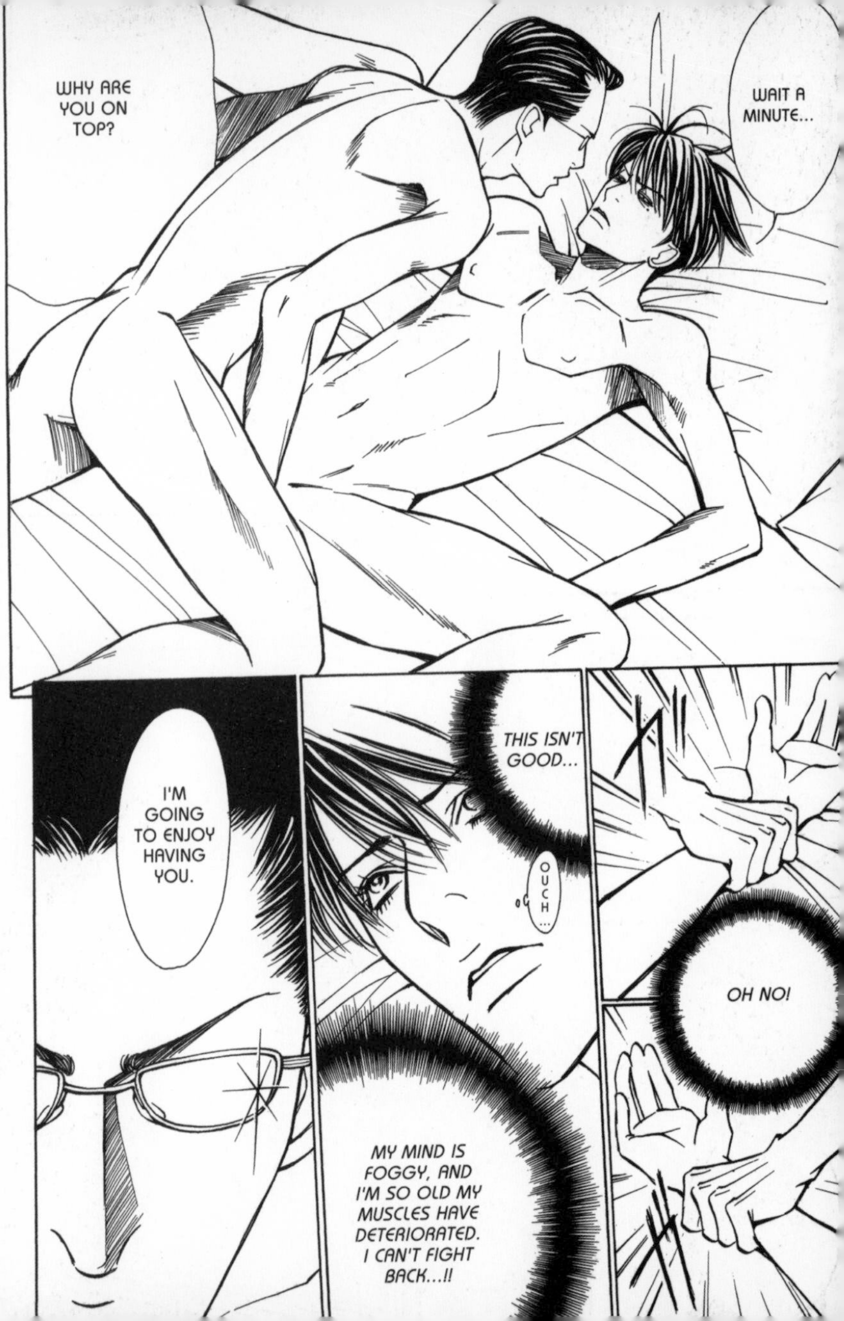
WAIT A MINUTE...
WHY ARE YOU ON TOP?
OH NO!
THIS ISN'T GOOD...
OUCH...
MY MIND IS FOGGY, AND I'M SO OLD MY MUSCLES HAVE DETERIORATED. I CAN'T FIGHT BACK...!!
I'M GOING TO ENJOY HAVING YOU.

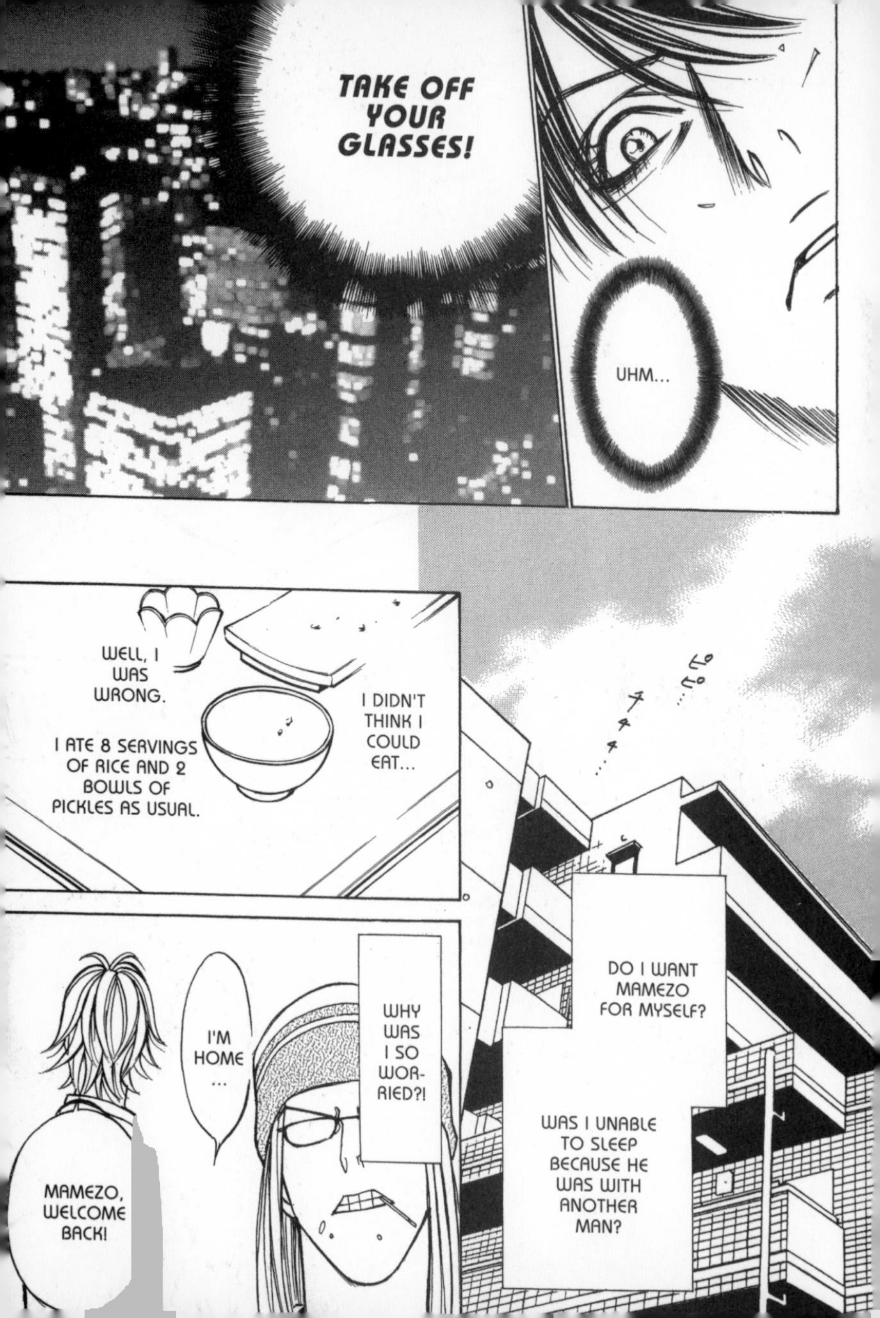
TAKE OFF YOUR GLASSES!
UHM...
DO I WANT MAMEZO FOR MYSELF?
WAS I UNABLE TO SLEEP BECAUSE HE WAS WITH ANOTHER MAN?
I DIDN'T THINK I COULD EAT...
WELL, I WAS WRONG.
I ATE 8 SERVINGS OF RICE AND 2 BOWLS OF PICKLES AS USUAL.
WHY WAS I SO WOR-RIED?!
I'M HOME ...
MAMEZO, WELCOME BACK!

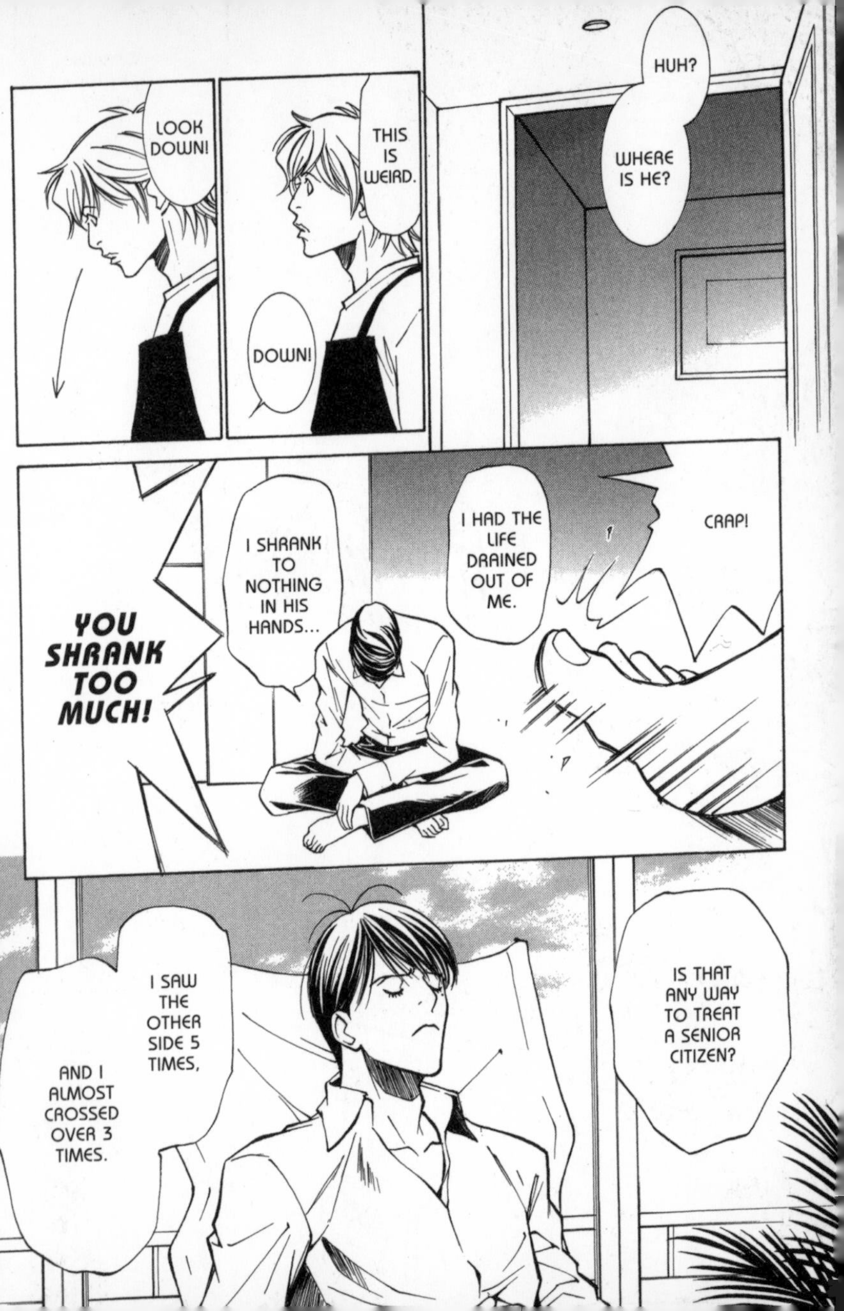
HUH?
WHERE IS HE?
THIS IS WEIRD.
DOWN!
LOOK DOWN!
CRAP!
I HAD THE LIFE DRAINED OUT OF ME.
I SHRANK TO NOTHING IN HIS HANDS...
YOU SHRANK TOO MUCH!
IS THAT ANY WAY TO TREAT A SENIOR CITIZEN?
I SAW THE OTHER SIDE 5 TIMES,
AND I ALMOST CROSSED OVER 3 TIMES.

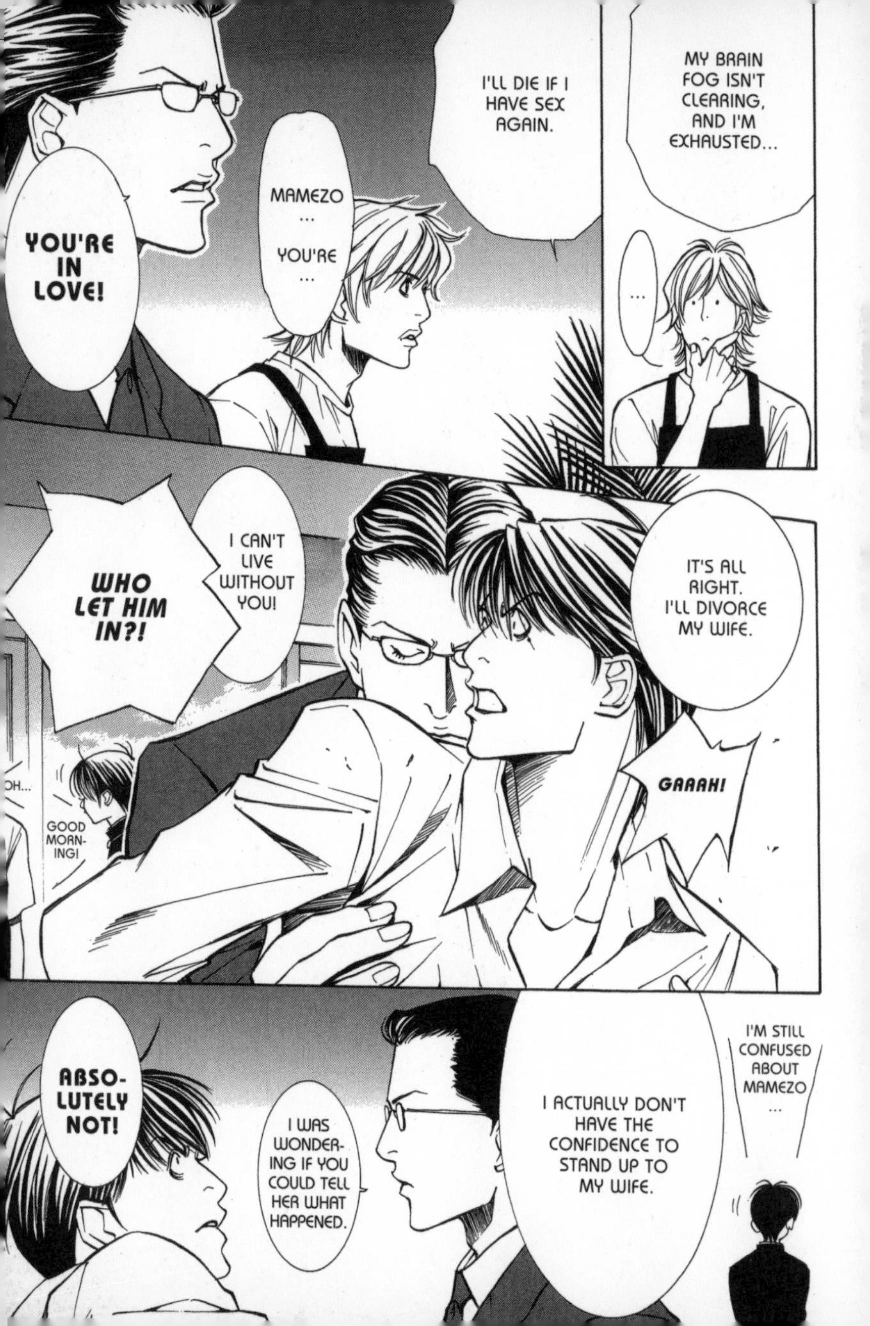
MY BRAIN FOG ISN'T CLEARING, AND I'M EXHAUSTED...
...
I'LL DIE IF I HAVE SEX AGAIN.
MAMEZO... YOU'RE...
YOU'RE IN LOVE!
IT'S ALL RIGHT. I'LL DIVORCE MY WIFE.
GAAAH!
I CAN'T LIVE WITHOUT YOU!
WHO LET HIM IN?!
OH...
GOOD MORNING!
I'M STILL CONFUSED ABOUT MAMEZO...
I ACTUALLY DON'T HAVE THE CONFIDENCE TO STAND UP TO MY WIFE.
I WAS WONDERING IF YOU COULD TELL HER WHAT HAPPENED.
ABSOLUTELY NOT!

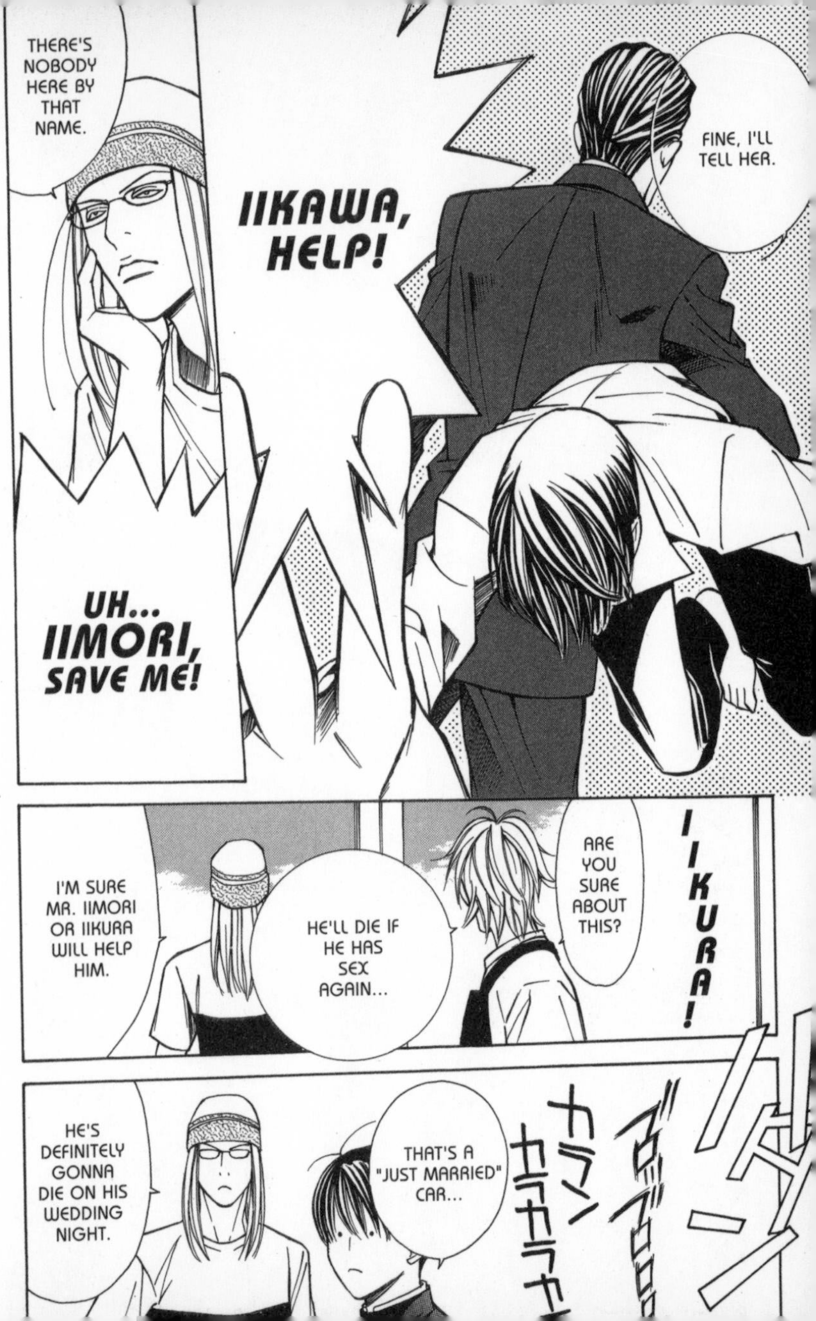
FINE, I'LL TELL HER.
IIKAWA, HELP!
THERE'S NOBODY HERE BY THAT NAME.
UH... IIMORI, SAVE ME!
IIKURA!
ARE YOU SURE ABOUT THIS?
HE'LL DIE IF HE HAS SEX AGAIN...
I'M SURE MR. IIMORI OR IIKURA WILL HELP HIM.
THAT'S A "JUST MARRIED" CAR...
HE'S DEFINITELY GONNA DIE ON HIS WEDDING NIGHT.

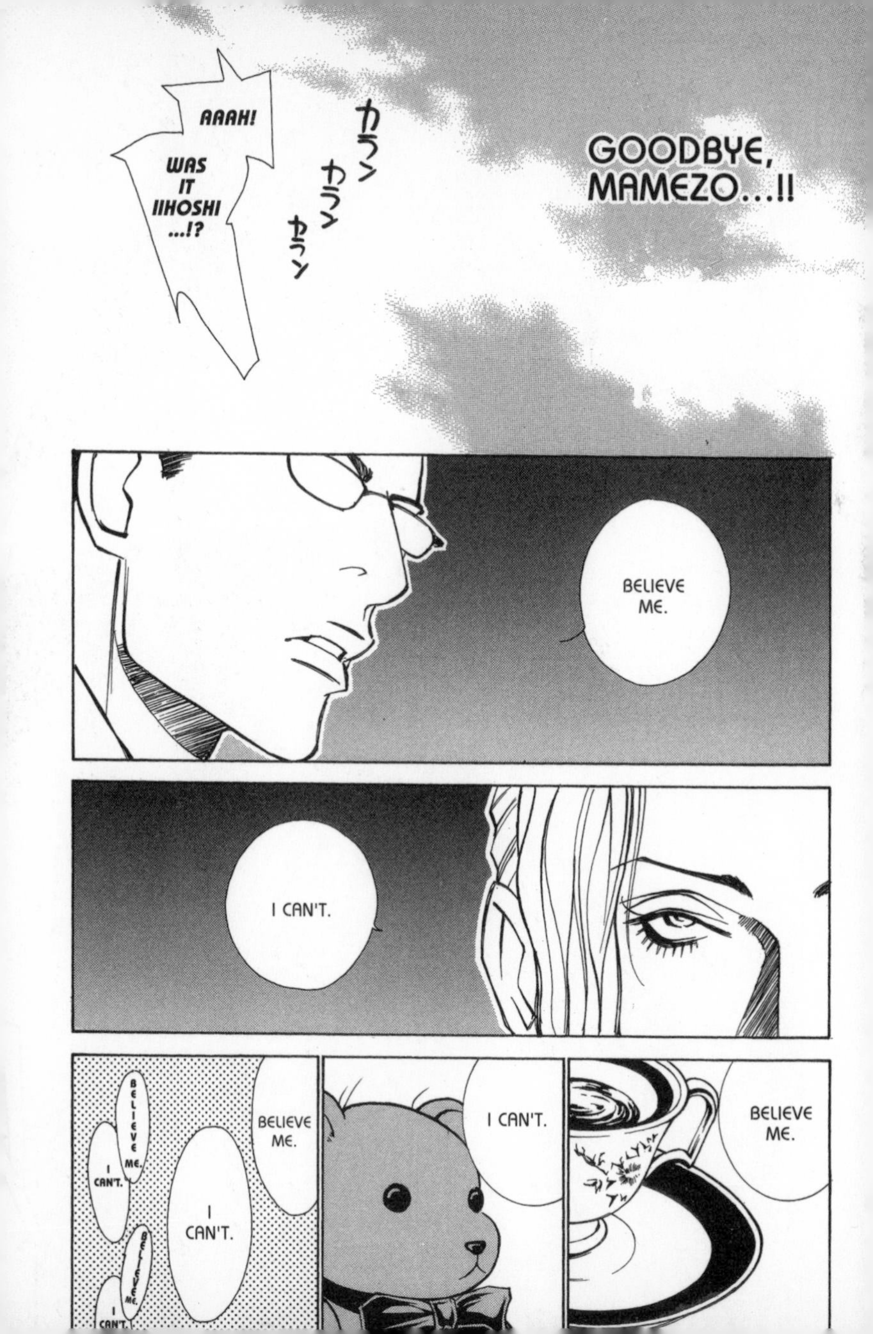
GOODBYE, MAMEZO...!!
カラン
カラン
カラン
AAAH!
WAS IT IIHOSHI ...!?
BELIEVE ME.
I CAN'T.
BELIEVE ME.
I CAN'T.
BELIEVE ME.
I CAN'T.
BELIEVE ME.
I CAN'T.
BELIEVE ME.
I CAN'T.

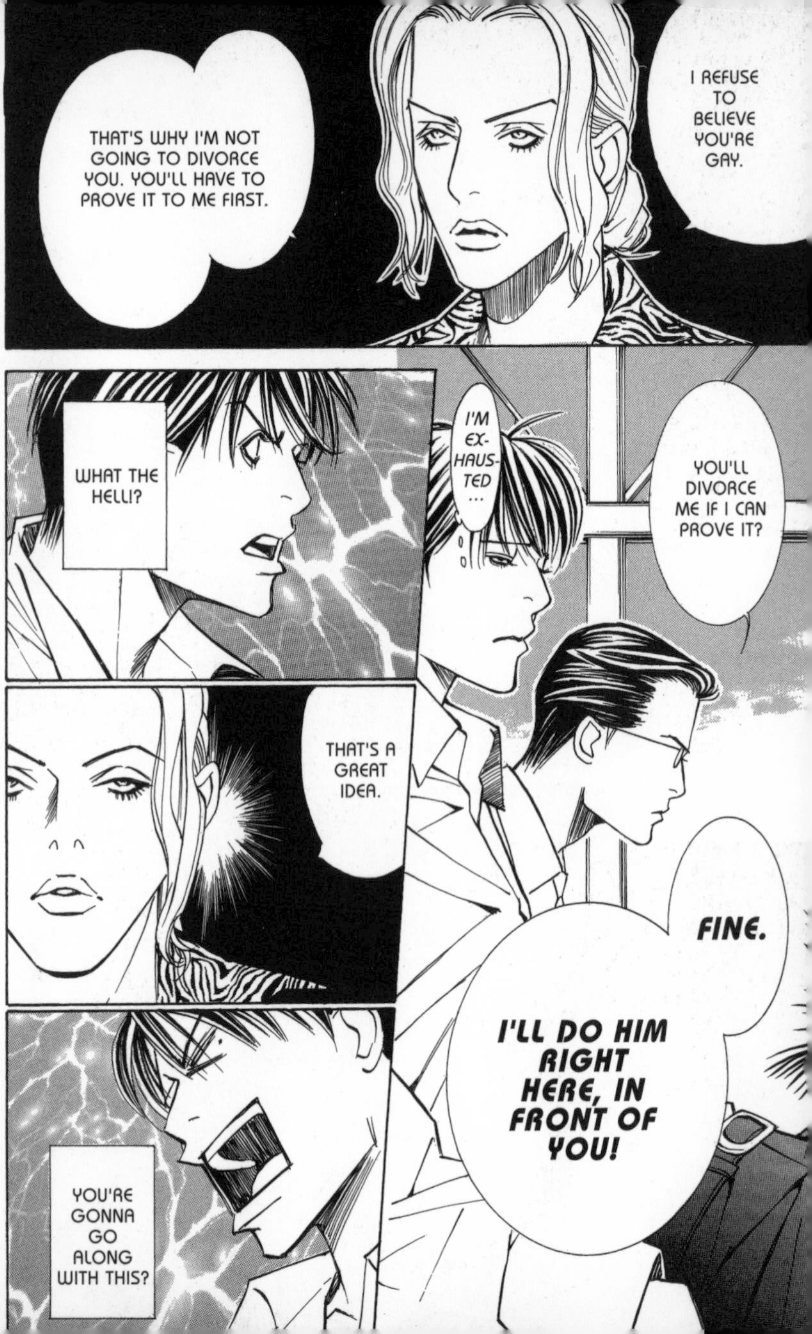
I REFUSE TO BELIEVE YOU'RE GAY.
THAT'S WHY I'M NOT GOING TO DIVORCE YOU. YOU'LL HAVE TO PROVE IT TO ME FIRST.
YOU'LL DIVORCE ME IF I CAN PROVE IT?
I'M EX-HAUS-TED ...
WHAT THE HELL!?
THAT'S A GREAT IDEA.
FINE.
I'LL DO HIM RIGHT HERE, IN FRONT OF YOU!
YOU'RE GONNA GO ALONG WITH THIS?

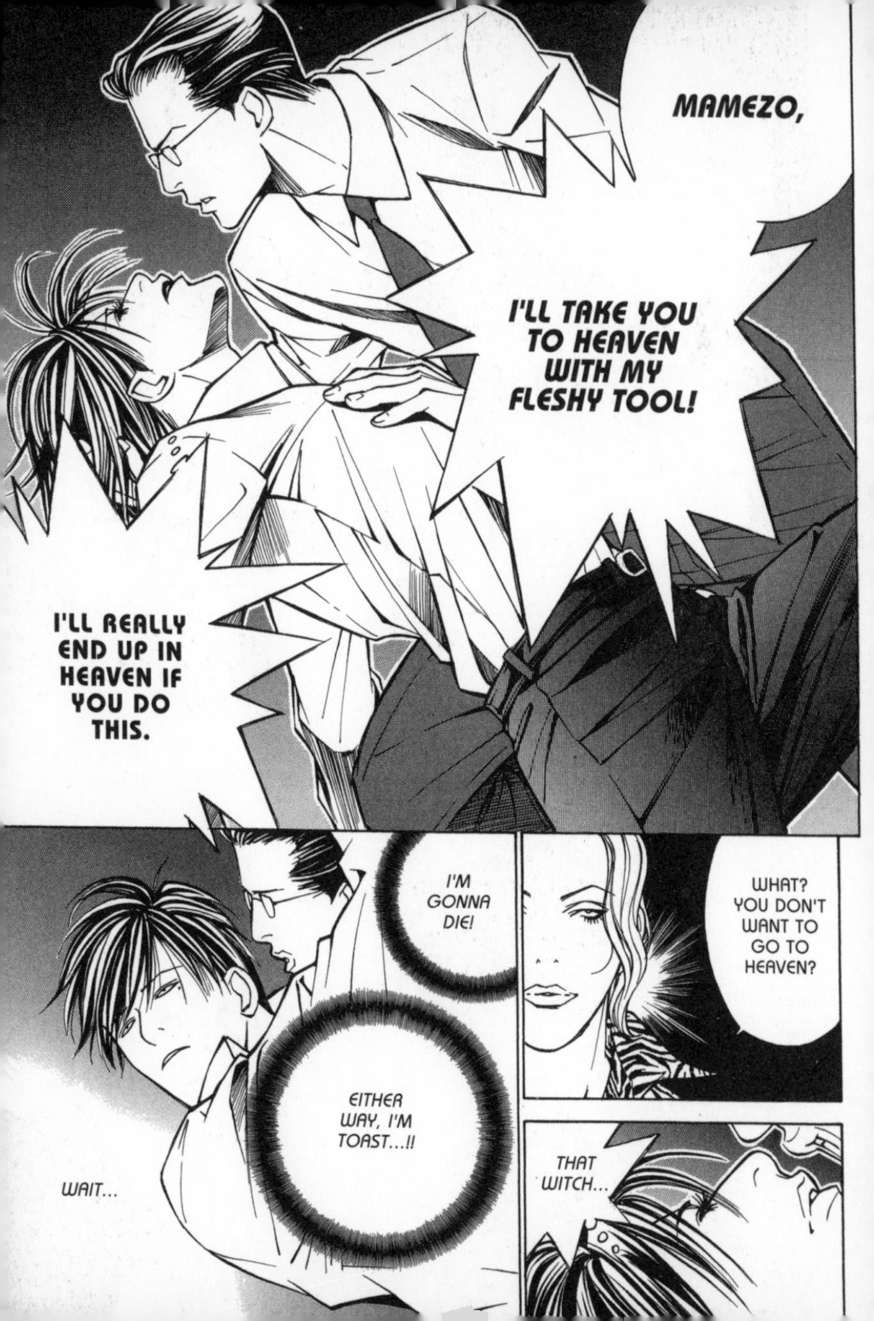
MAMEZO,
I'LL TAKE YOU TO HEAVEN WITH MY FLESHY TOOL!
I'LL REALLY END UP IN HEAVEN IF YOU DO THIS.
WHAT? YOU DON'T WANT TO GO TO HEAVEN?
I'M GONNA DIE!
THAT WITCH...
EITHER WAY, I'M TOAST...!!
WAIT...

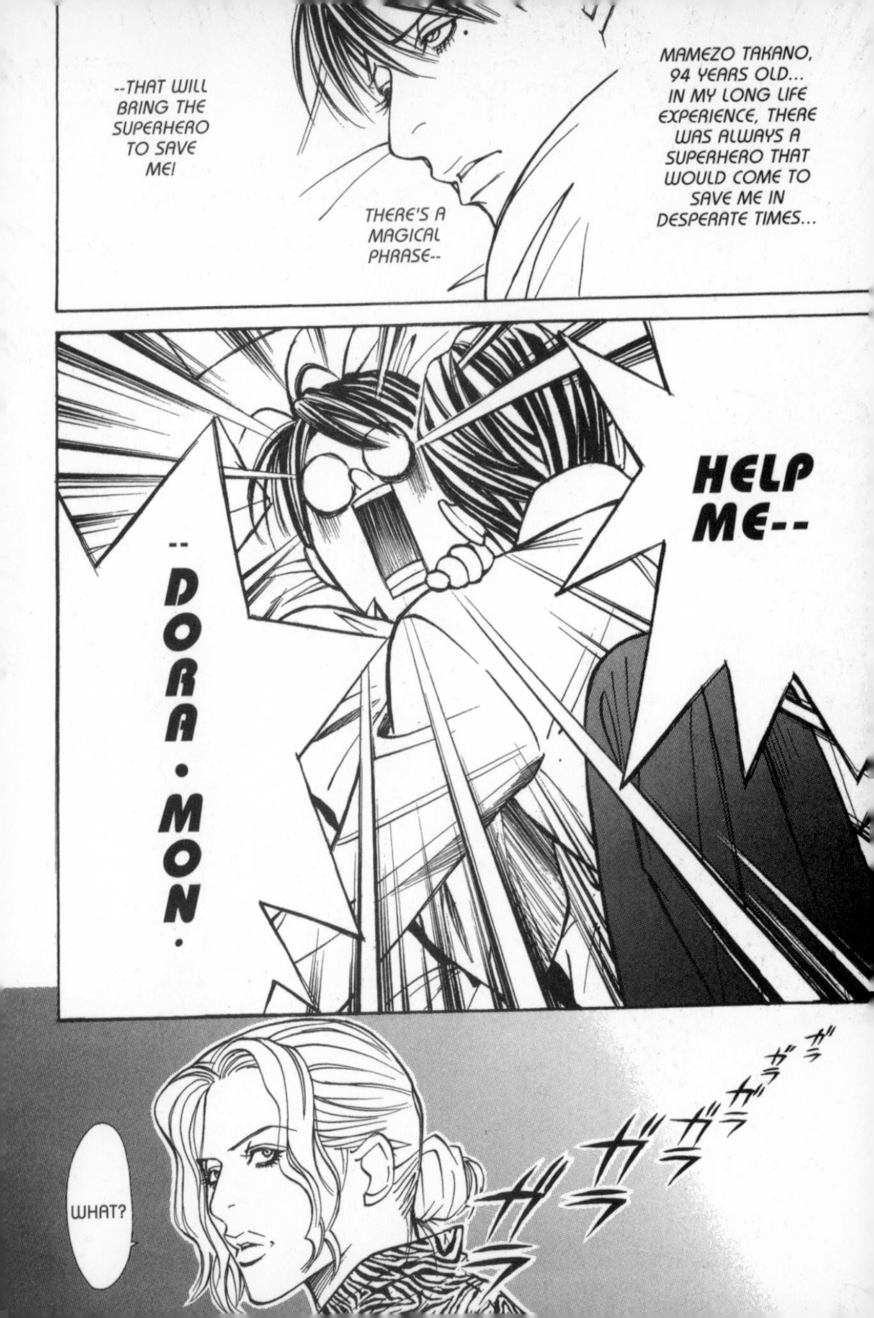
MAMEZO TAKANO, 94 YEARS OLD... IN MY LONG LIFE EXPERIENCE, THERE WAS ALWAYS A SUPERHERO THAT WOULD COME TO SAVE ME IN DESPERATE TIMES...
THERE'S A MAGICAL PHRASE--
--THAT WILL BRING THE SUPERHERO TO SAVE ME!
HELP ME--
--DORA·MON·
ガラ ガラ ガラ ガラ
WHAT?

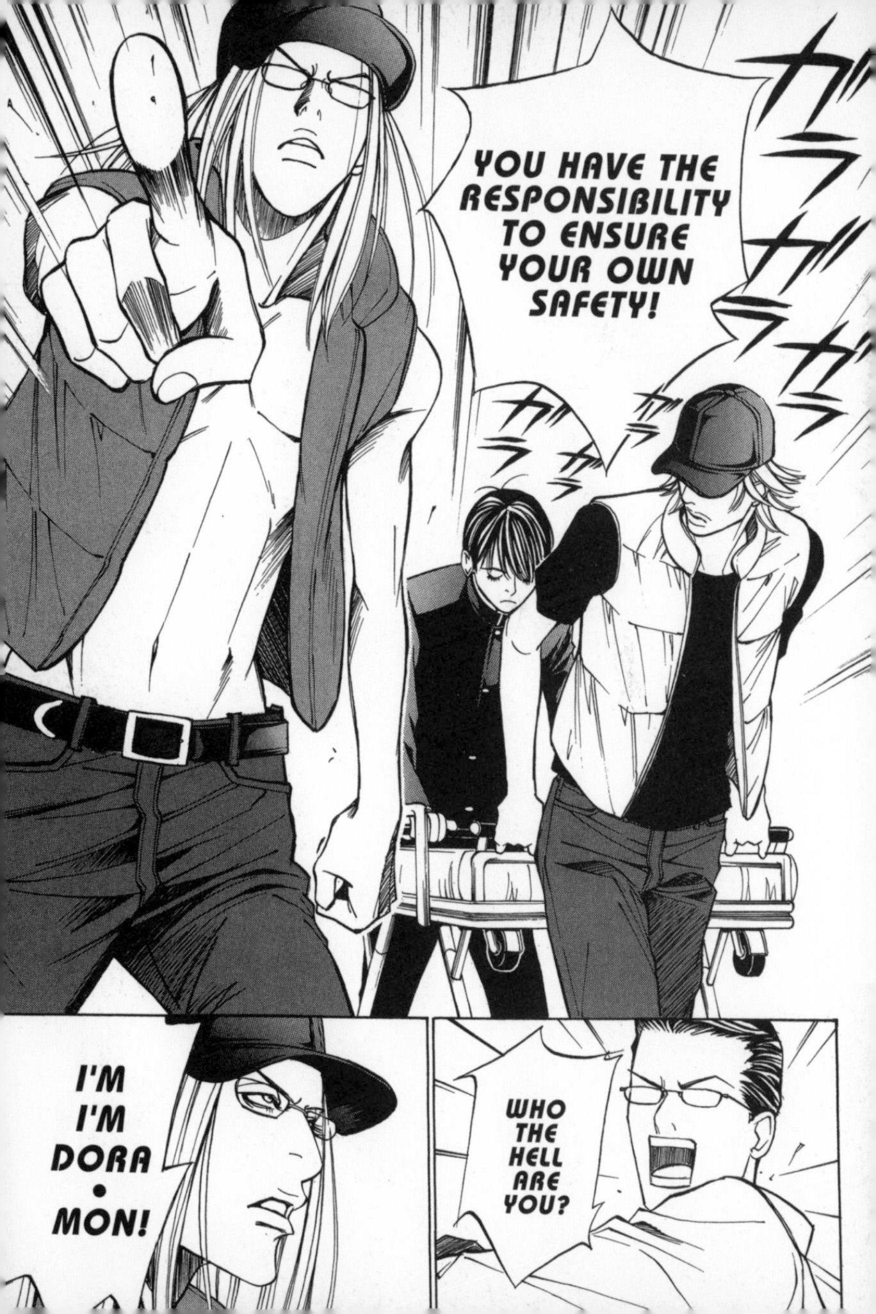
YOU HAVE THE RESPONSIBILITY TO ENSURE YOUR OWN SAFETY!
WHO THE HELL ARE YOU?
I'M I'M DORA • MON!

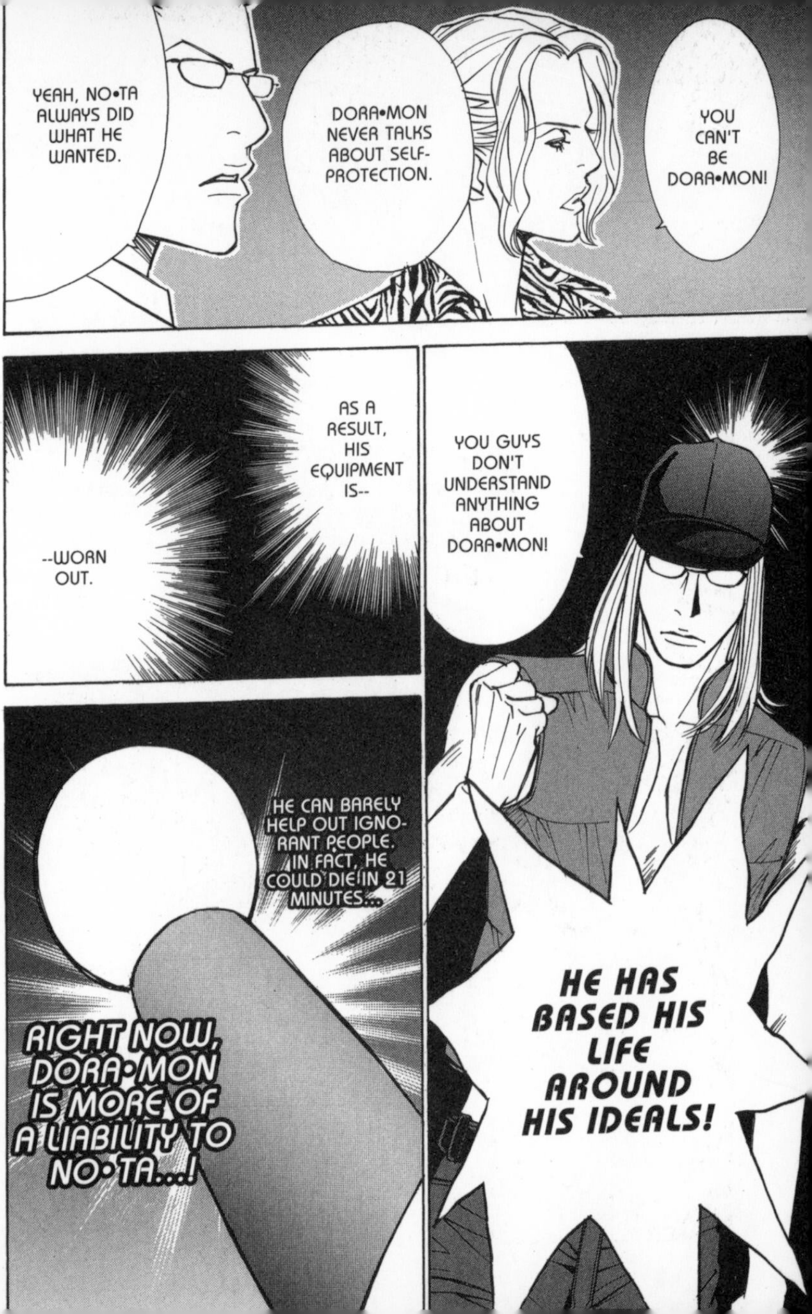
YOU CAN'T BE DORA•MON!
DORA•MON NEVER TALKS ABOUT SELF-PROTECTION.
YEAH, NO•TA ALWAYS DID WHAT HE WANTED.
YOU GUYS DON'T UNDERSTAND ANYTHING ABOUT DORA•MON!
HE HAS BASED HIS LIFE AROUND HIS IDEALS!
AS A RESULT, HIS EQUIPMENT IS--
--WORN OUT.
HE CAN BARELY HELP OUT IGNORANT PEOPLE. IN FACT, HE COULD DIE IN 21 MINUTES...
RIGHT NOW, DORA•MON IS MORE OF A LIABILITY TO NO•TA...!

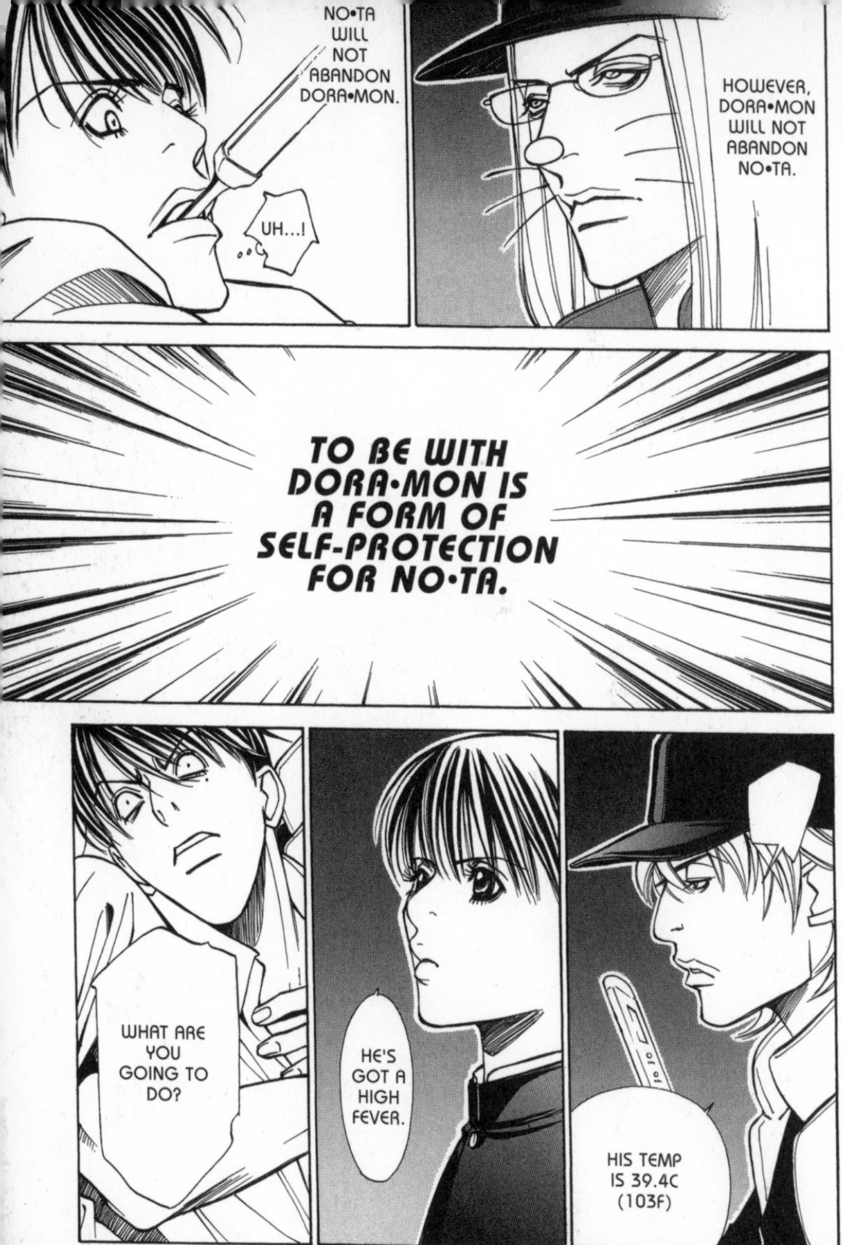

NO•TA WILL NOT ABANDON DORA•MON.
UH...!
HOWEVER, DORA•MON WILL NOT ABANDON NO•TA.
TO BE WITH DORA•MON IS A FORM OF SELF-PROTECTION FOR NO•TA.
WHAT ARE YOU GOING TO DO?
HE'S GOT A HIGH FEVER.
HIS TEMP IS 39.4C (103F)

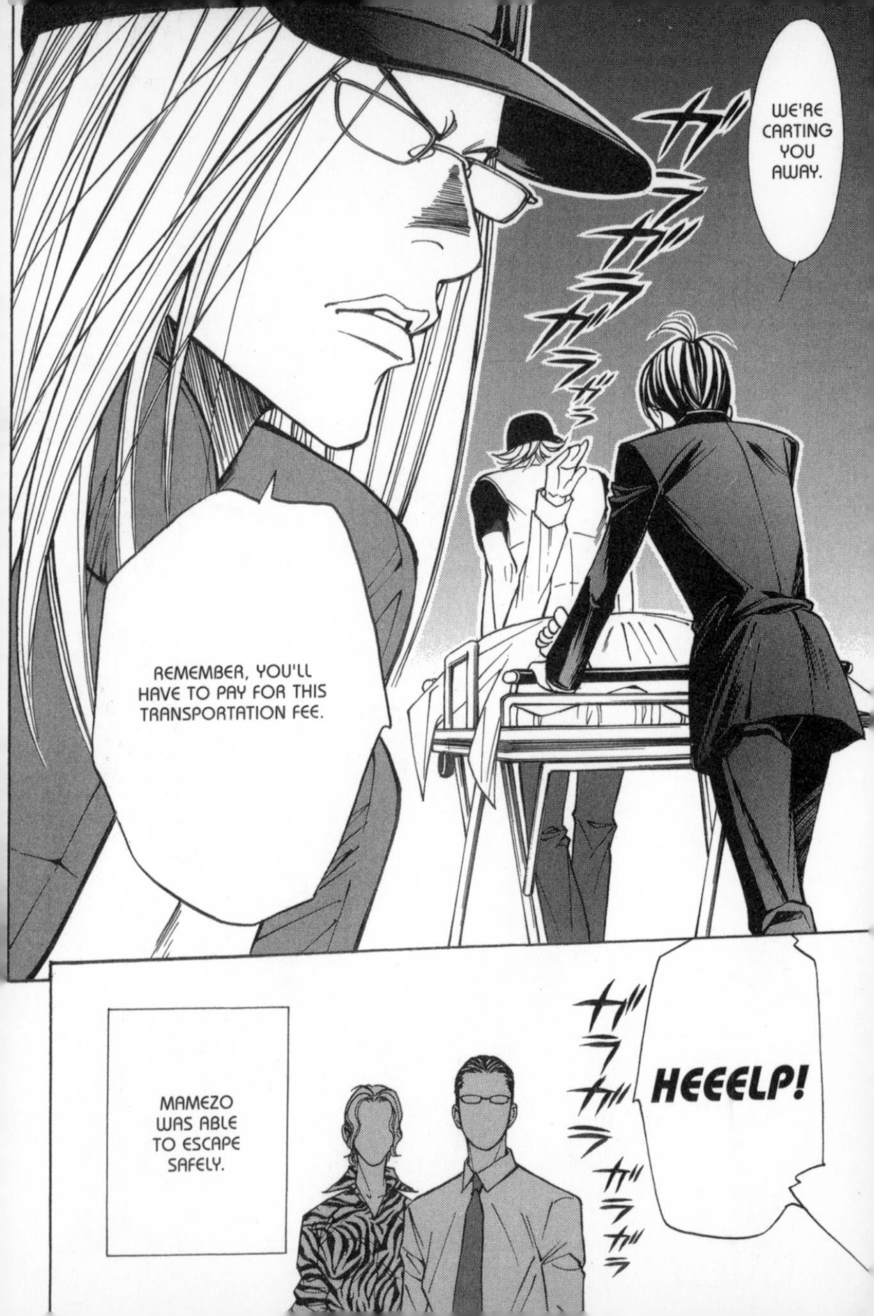
WE'RE CARTING YOU AWAY.
REMEMBER, YOU'LL HAVE TO PAY FOR THIS TRANSPORTATION FEE.
HEEELP!
MAMEZO WAS ABLE TO ESCAPE SAFELY.

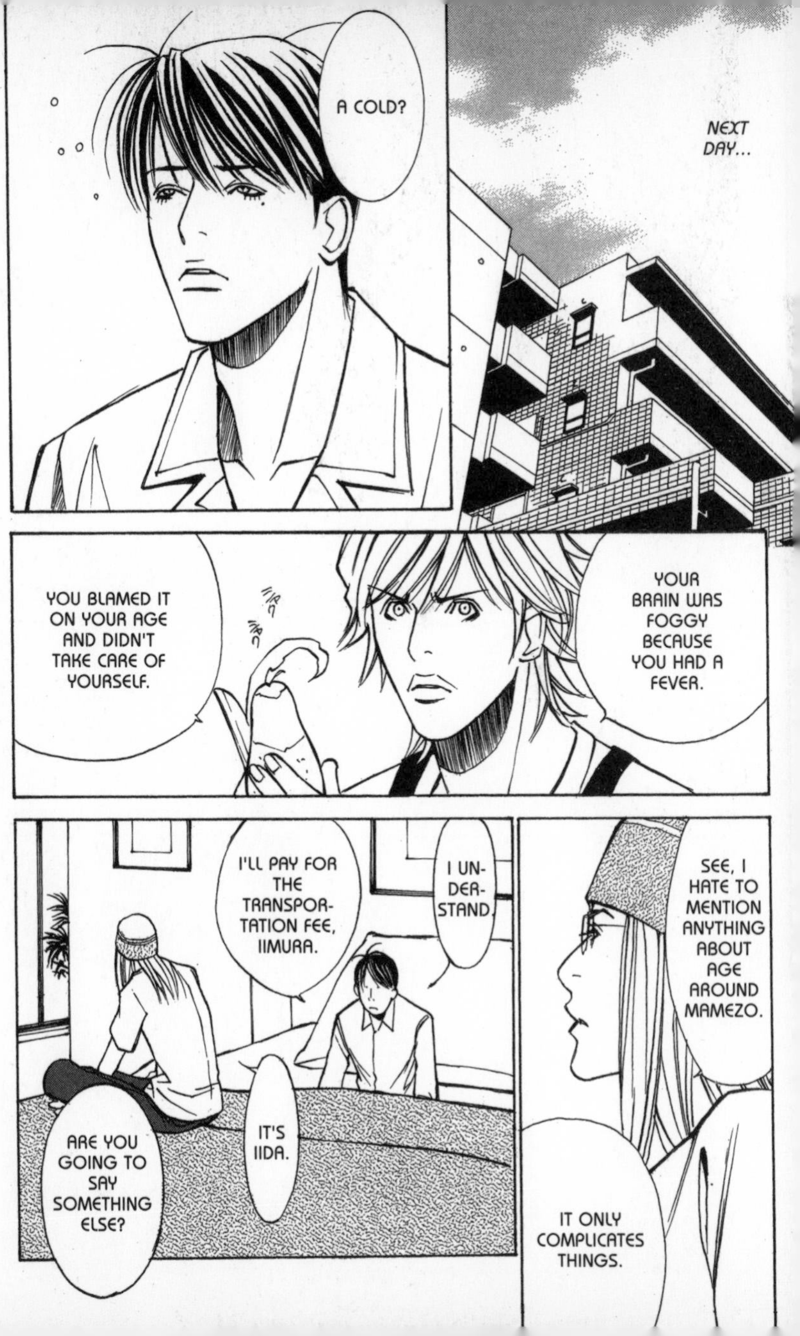
NEXT DAY...
A COLD?
YOUR BRAIN WAS FOGGY BECAUSE YOU HAD A FEVER.
YOU BLAMED IT ON YOUR AGE AND DIDN'T TAKE CARE OF YOURSELF.
SEE, I HATE TO MENTION ANYTHING ABOUT AGE AROUND MAMEZO.
IT ONLY COMPLICATES THINGS.
I UNDER-STAND.
I'LL PAY FOR THE TRANSPOR-TATION FEE, IIMURA.
IT'S IIDA.
ARE YOU GOING TO SAY SOMETHING ELSE?

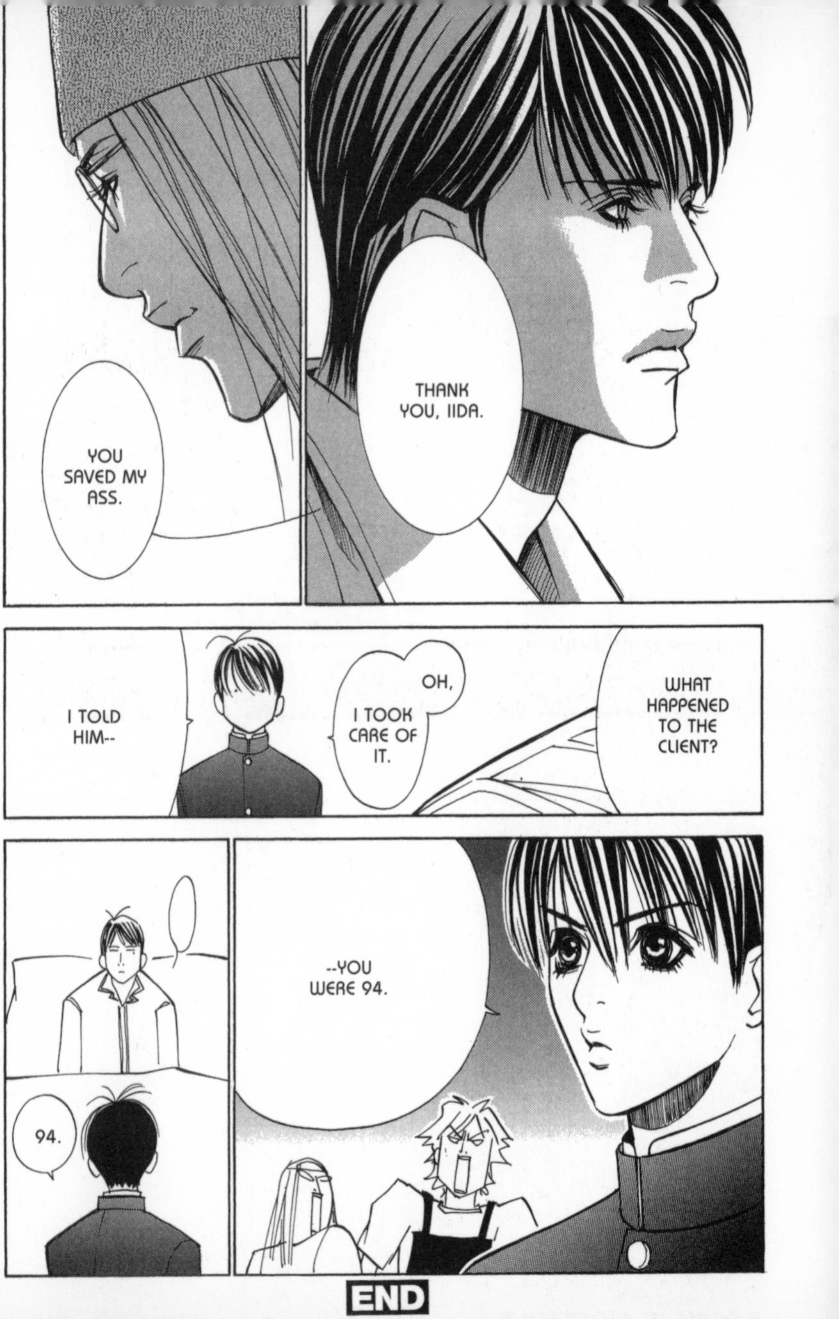
THANK YOU, IIDA.
YOU SAVED MY ASS.
WHAT HAPPENED TO THE CLIENT?
OH, I TOOK CARE OF IT.
I TOLD HIM--
--YOU WERE 94.
94.
END

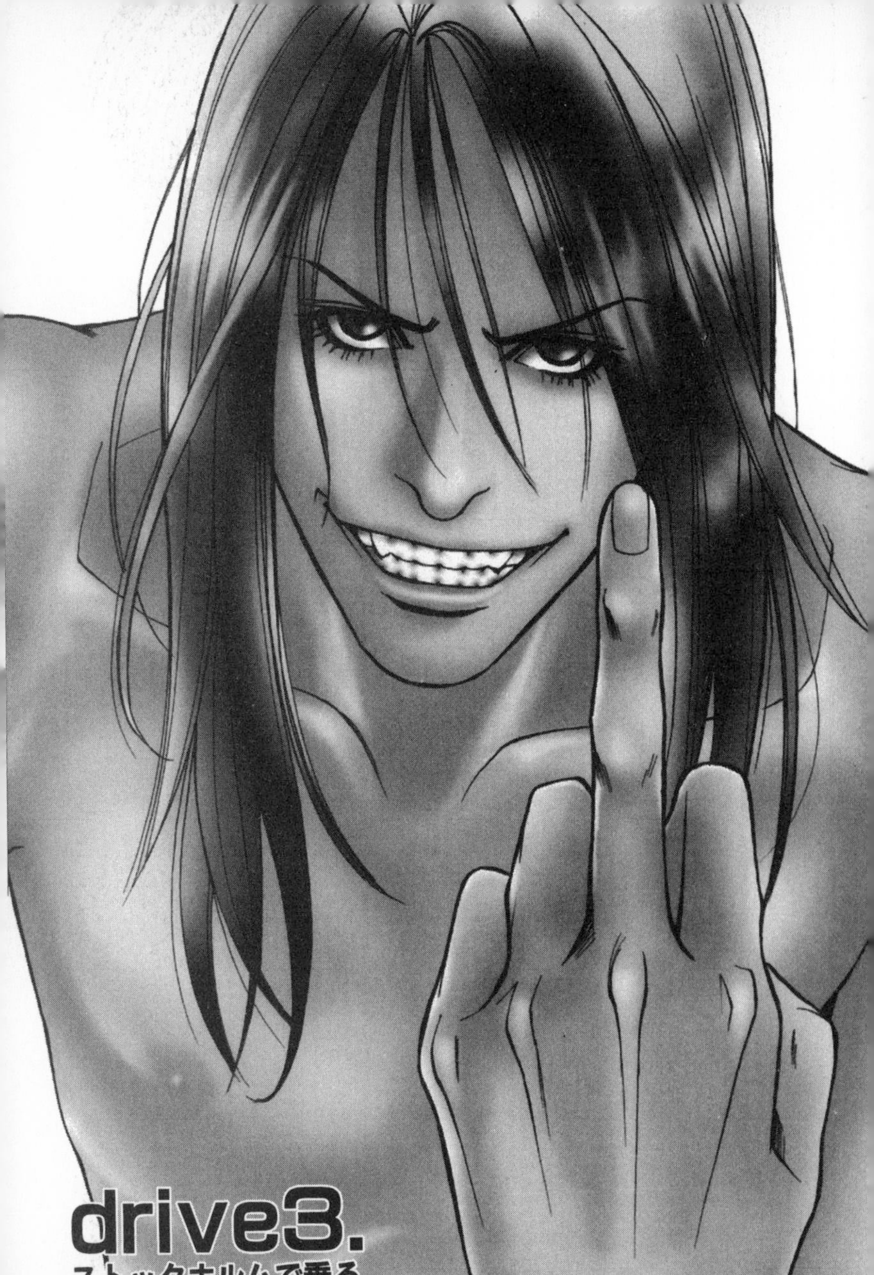

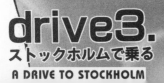

drive3.
ストックホルムで乗る
A DRIVE TO STOCKHOLM

CHERRY DRIVE

A MYSTERIOUS, GAY SITE THAT HELPS PEOPLE GET REVENGE FOR A RAPE, OR RAVISH A WARM BODY FOR THE NIGHT...
THEY ACCEPT ALL KINDS OF OFFERS TO PLEASE THEIR CLIENTS...

THEY'RE OUR FRIENDS.

EVERYONE LOVES THEM.
CHERRY DRIVE

WE ALL WANT TO MEET THEM.
CHERRY DRIVE.

WE'LL FOLLOW YOU TO THE ENDS OF THE EARTH
COME ON, CLAP WITH US (IN PARADISE)
CHERRY DRIVE

I, I, I...
(I'M A MONKEY)
I LOVE YOU, OUR CHERRY DRIVE!

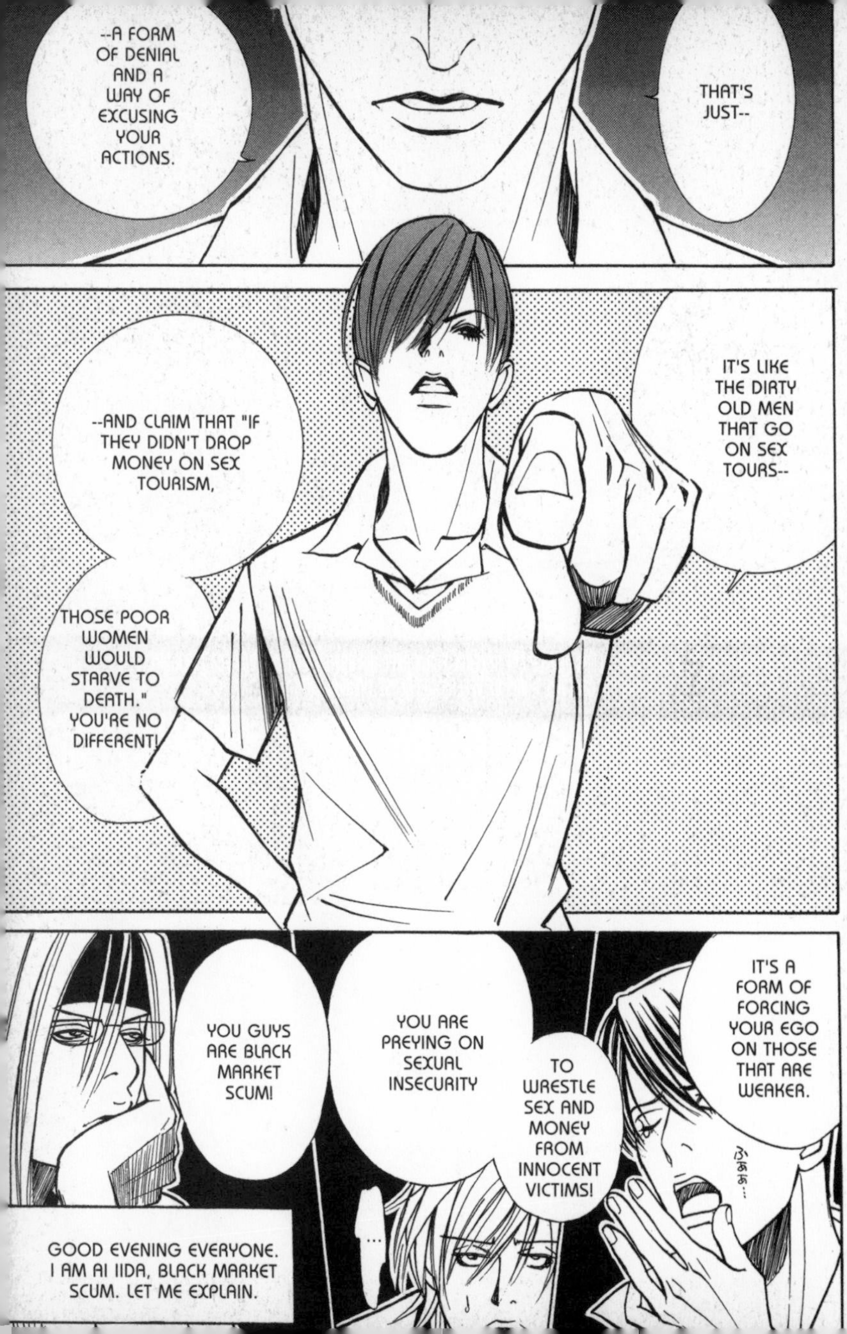
THAT'S JUST--
--A FORM OF DENIAL AND A WAY OF EXCUSING YOUR ACTIONS.
IT'S LIKE THE DIRTY OLD MEN THAT GO ON SEX TOURS--
--AND CLAIM THAT "IF THEY DIDN'T DROP MONEY ON SEX TOURISM,
THOSE POOR WOMEN WOULD STARVE TO DEATH." YOU'RE NO DIFFERENT!
IT'S A FORM OF FORCING YOUR EGO ON THOSE THAT ARE WEAKER.
ふぁあ…
YOU ARE PREYING ON SEXUAL INSECURITY
TO WRESTLE SEX AND MONEY FROM INNOCENT VICTIMS!
...
YOU GUYS ARE BLACK MARKET SCUM!
GOOD EVENING EVERYONE. I AM AI IIDA, BLACK MARKET SCUM. LET ME EXPLAIN.

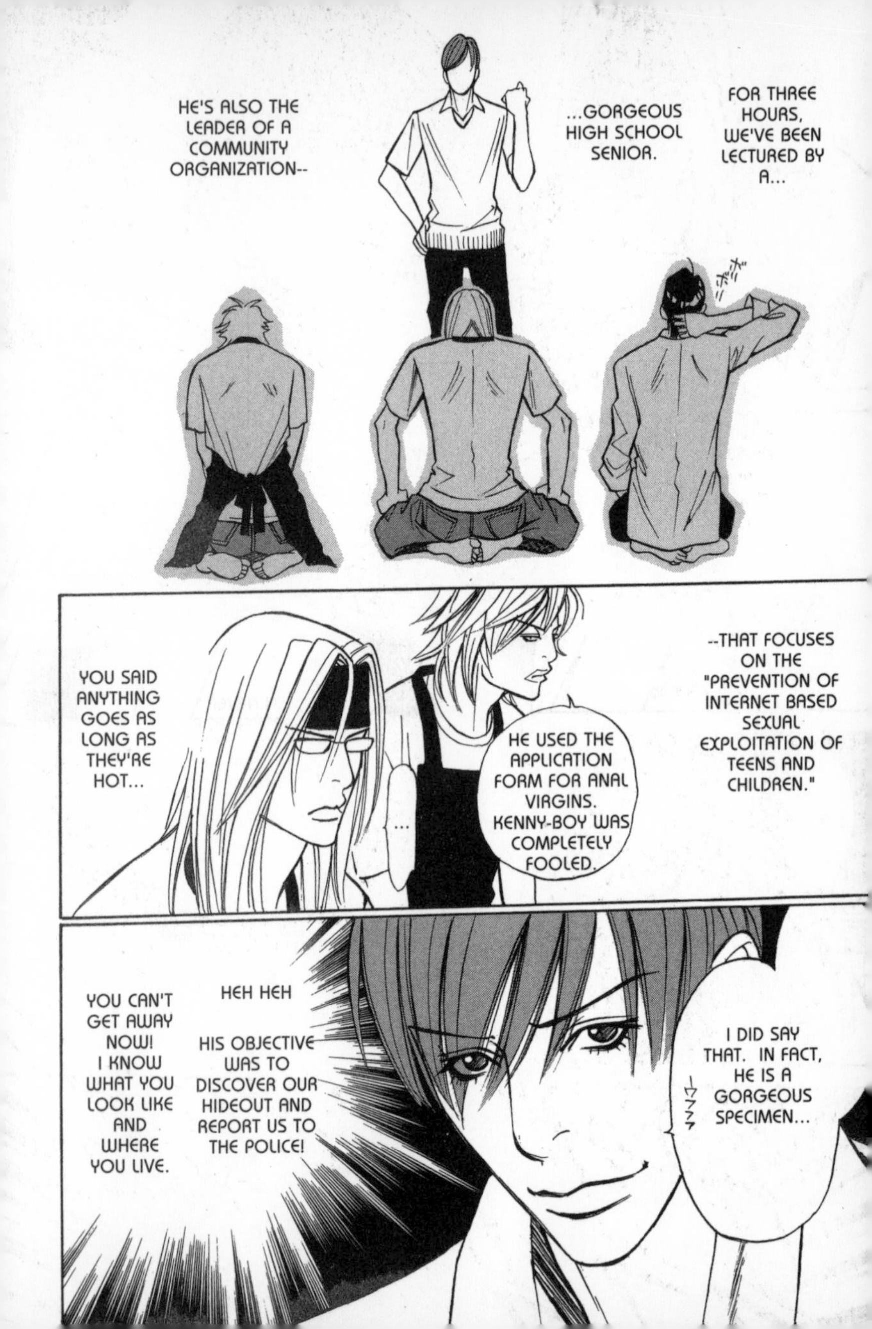
FOR THREE HOURS, WE'VE BEEN LECTURED BY A...
...GORGEOUS HIGH SCHOOL SENIOR.
HE'S ALSO THE LEADER OF A COMMUNITY ORGANIZATION--
--THAT FOCUSES ON THE "PREVENTION OF INTERNET BASED SEXUAL EXPLOITATION OF TEENS AND CHILDREN."
HE USED THE APPLICATION FORM FOR ANAL VIRGINS. KENNY-BOY WAS COMPLETELY FOOLED.
...
YOU SAID ANYTHING GOES AS LONG AS THEY'RE HOT...
I DID SAY THAT. IN FACT, HE IS A GORGEOUS SPECIMEN...
HEH HEH
HIS OBJECTIVE WAS TO DISCOVER OUR HIDEOUT AND REPORT US TO THE POLICE!
YOU CAN'T GET AWAY NOW! I KNOW WHAT YOU LOOK LIKE AND WHERE YOU LIVE.

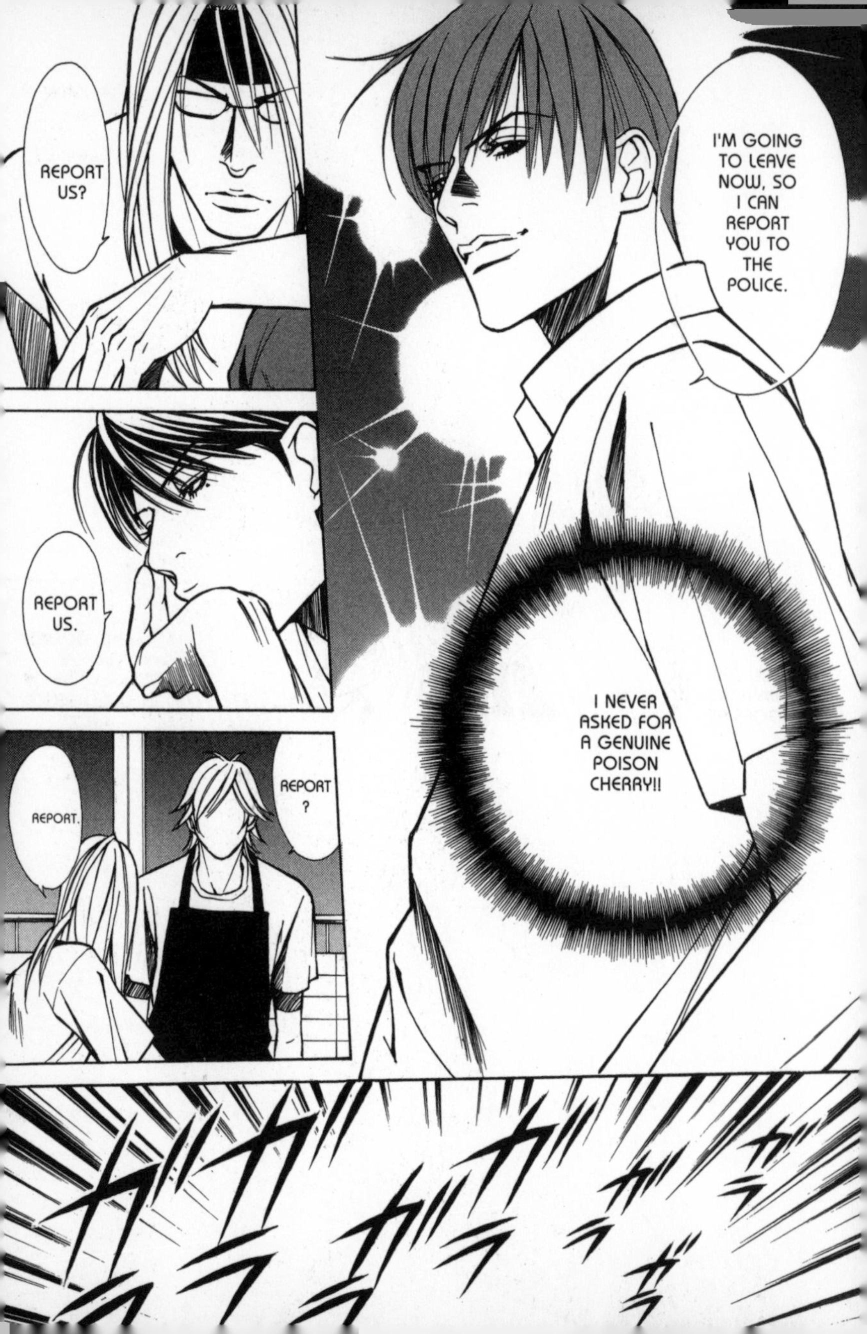
I'M GOING TO LEAVE NOW, SO I CAN REPORT YOU TO THE POLICE.
REPORT US?
REPORT US.
REPORT ?
REPORT.
I NEVER ASKED FOR A GENUINE POISON CHERRY!!

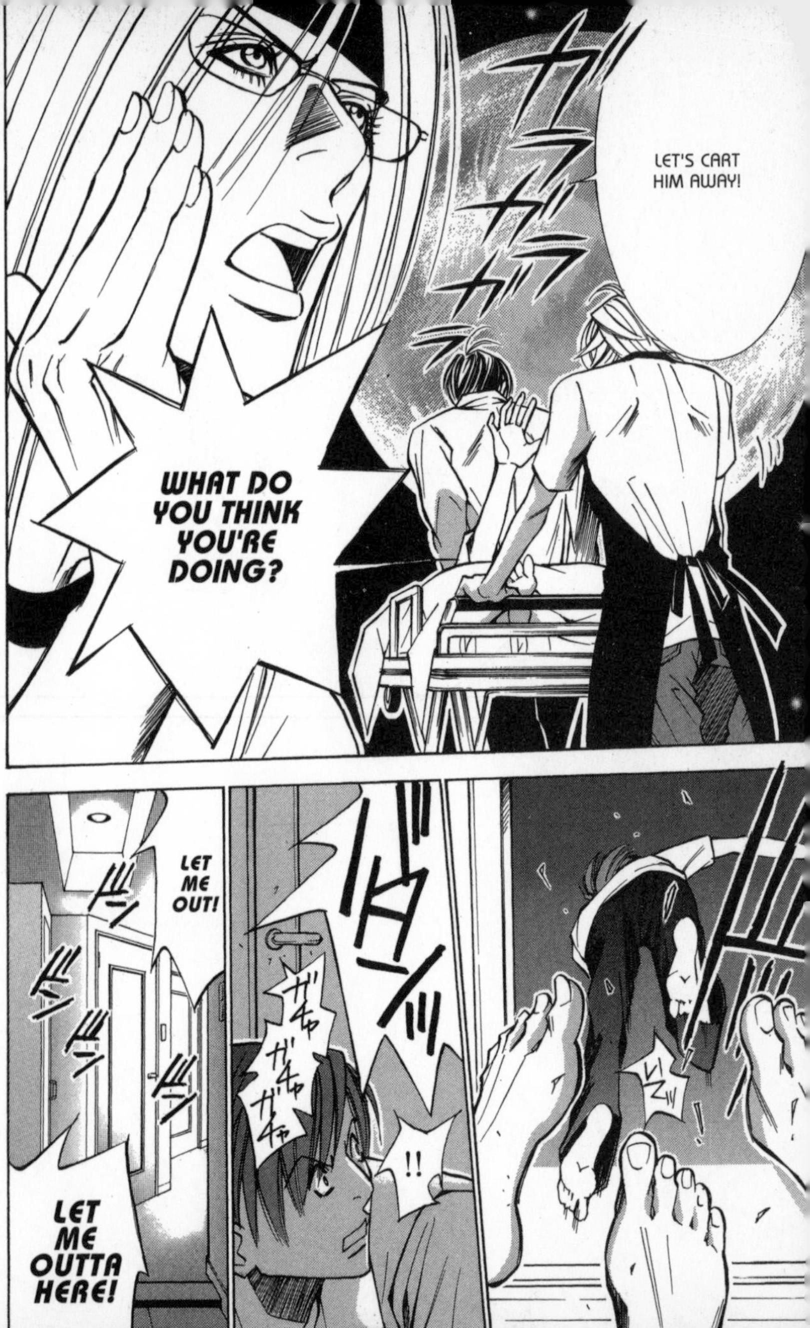
LET'S CART HIM AWAY!
WHAT DO YOU THINK YOU'RE DOING?
!!
LET ME OUT!
LET ME OUTTA HERE!

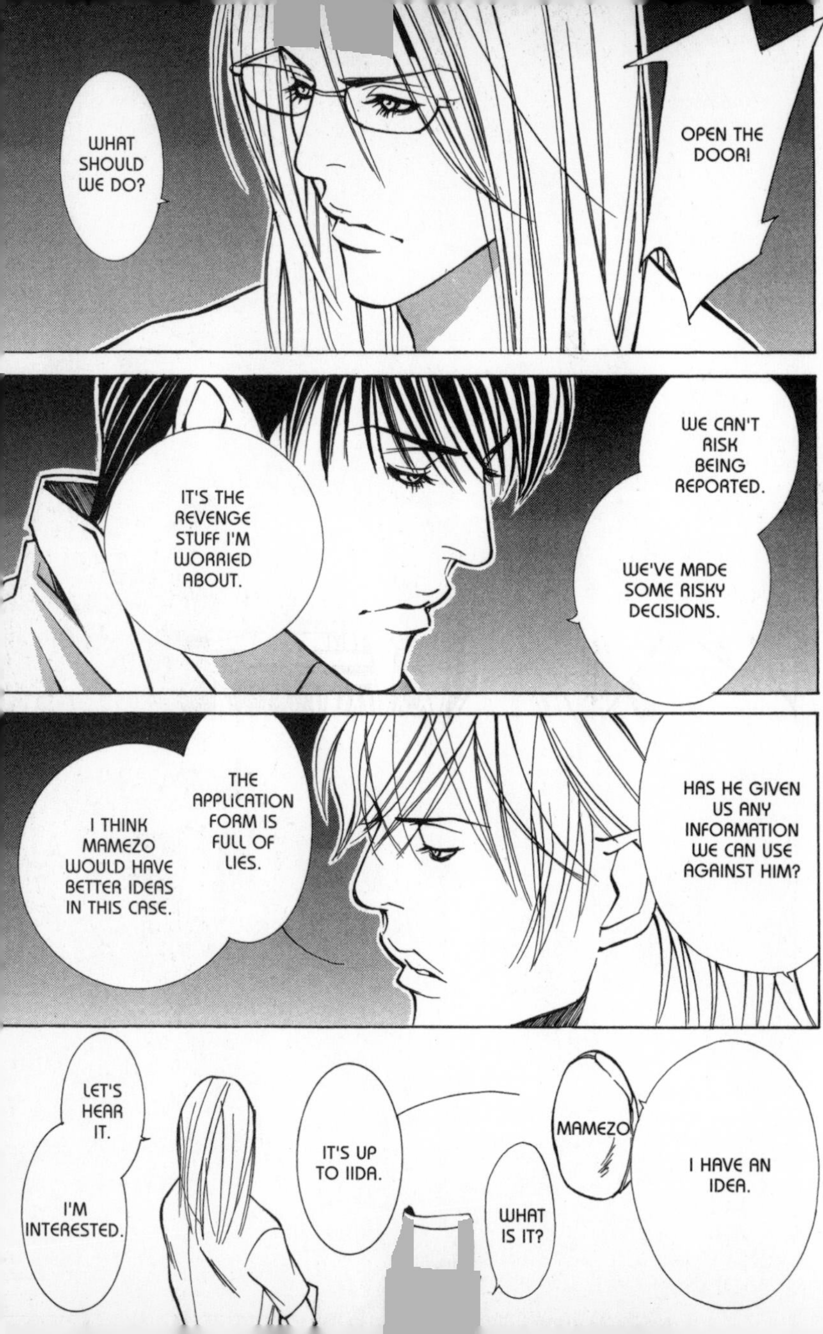
OPEN THE DOOR!
WHAT SHOULD WE DO?
WE CAN'T RISK BEING REPORTED.
WE'VE MADE SOME RISKY DECISIONS.
IT'S THE REVENGE STUFF I'M WORRIED ABOUT.
HAS HE GIVEN US ANY INFORMATION WE CAN USE AGAINST HIM?
THE APPLICATION FORM IS FULL OF LIES.
I THINK MAMEZO WOULD HAVE BETTER IDEAS IN THIS CASE.
I HAVE AN IDEA.
MAMEZO
WHAT IS IT?
IT'S UP TO IIDA.
LET'S HEAR IT.
I'M INTERESTED.

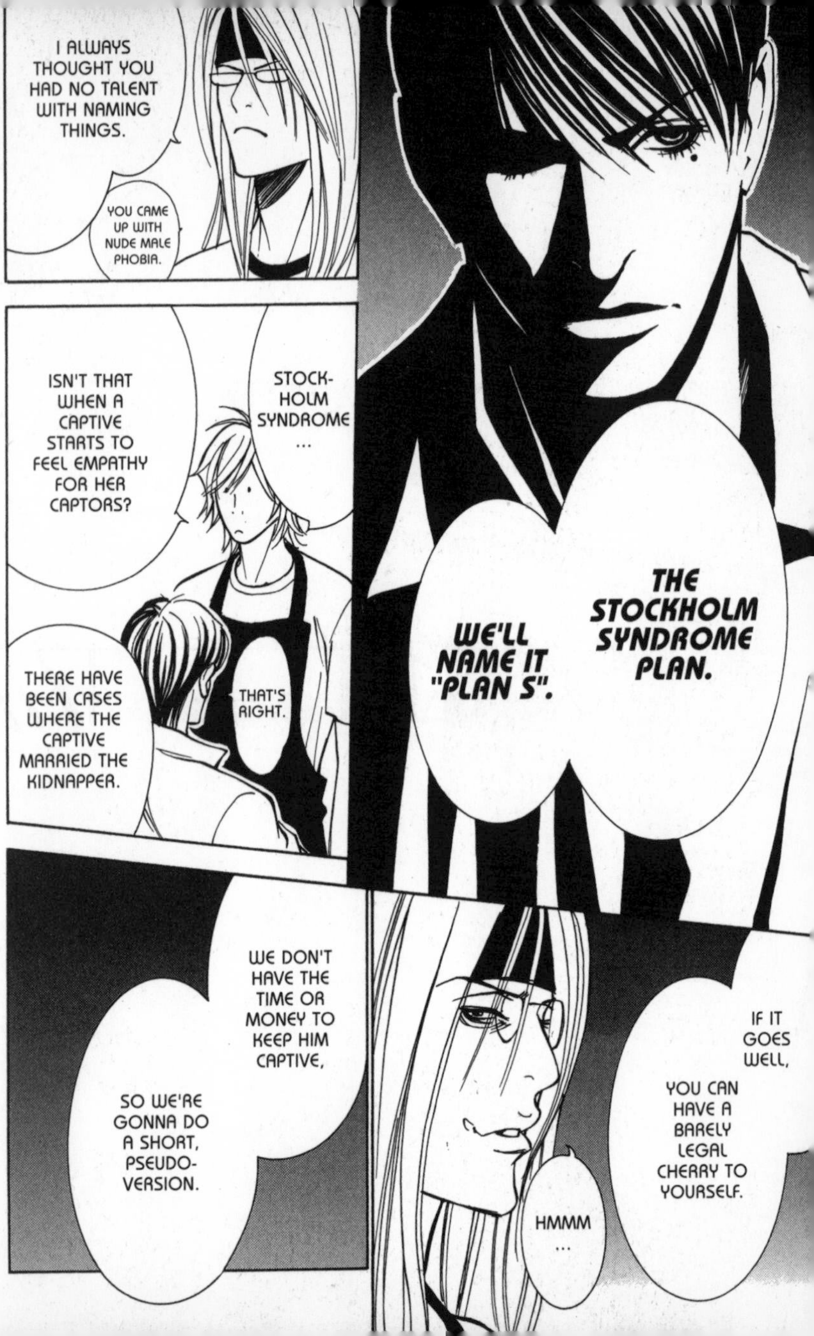
THE STOCKHOLM SYNDROME PLAN.
WE'LL NAME IT "PLAN S".
I ALWAYS THOUGHT YOU HAD NO TALENT WITH NAMING THINGS.
YOU CAME UP WITH NUDE MALE PHOBIA.
STOCK-HOLM SYNDROME ...
ISN'T THAT WHEN A CAPTIVE STARTS TO FEEL EMPATHY FOR HER CAPTORS?
THAT'S RIGHT.
THERE HAVE BEEN CASES WHERE THE CAPTIVE MARRIED THE KIDNAPPER.
IF IT GOES WELL,
YOU CAN HAVE A BARELY LEGAL CHERRY TO YOURSELF.
HMMM ...
WE DON'T HAVE THE TIME OR MONEY TO KEEP HIM CAPTIVE,
SO WE'RE GONNA DO A SHORT, PSEUDO-VERSION.

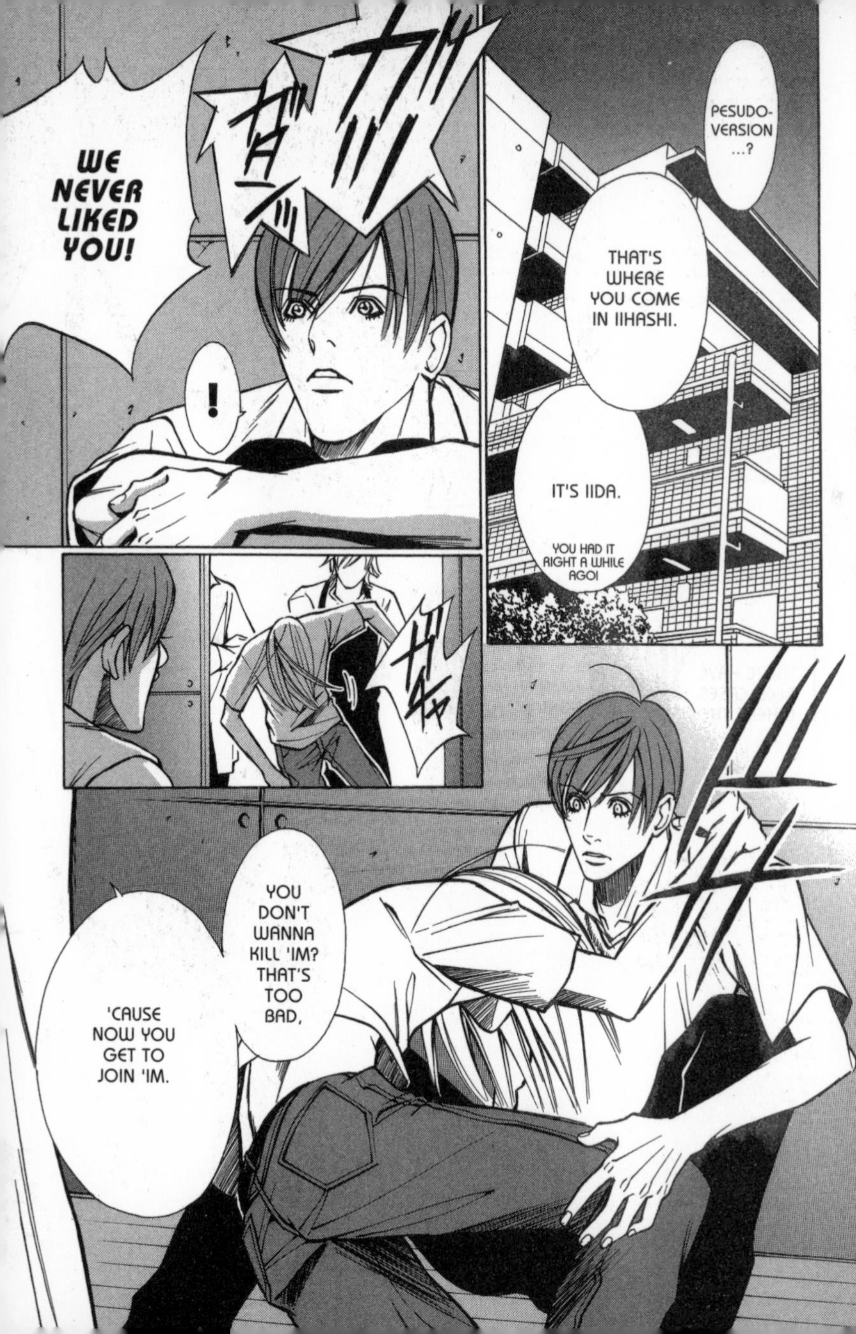
PESUDO-VERSION ...?
THAT'S WHERE YOU COME IN IIHASHI.
IT'S IIDA.
YOU HAD IT RIGHT A WHILE AGO!
WE NEVER LIKED YOU!
!
YOU DON'T WANNA KILL 'IM? THAT'S TOO BAD,
'CAUSE NOW YOU GET TO JOIN 'IM.

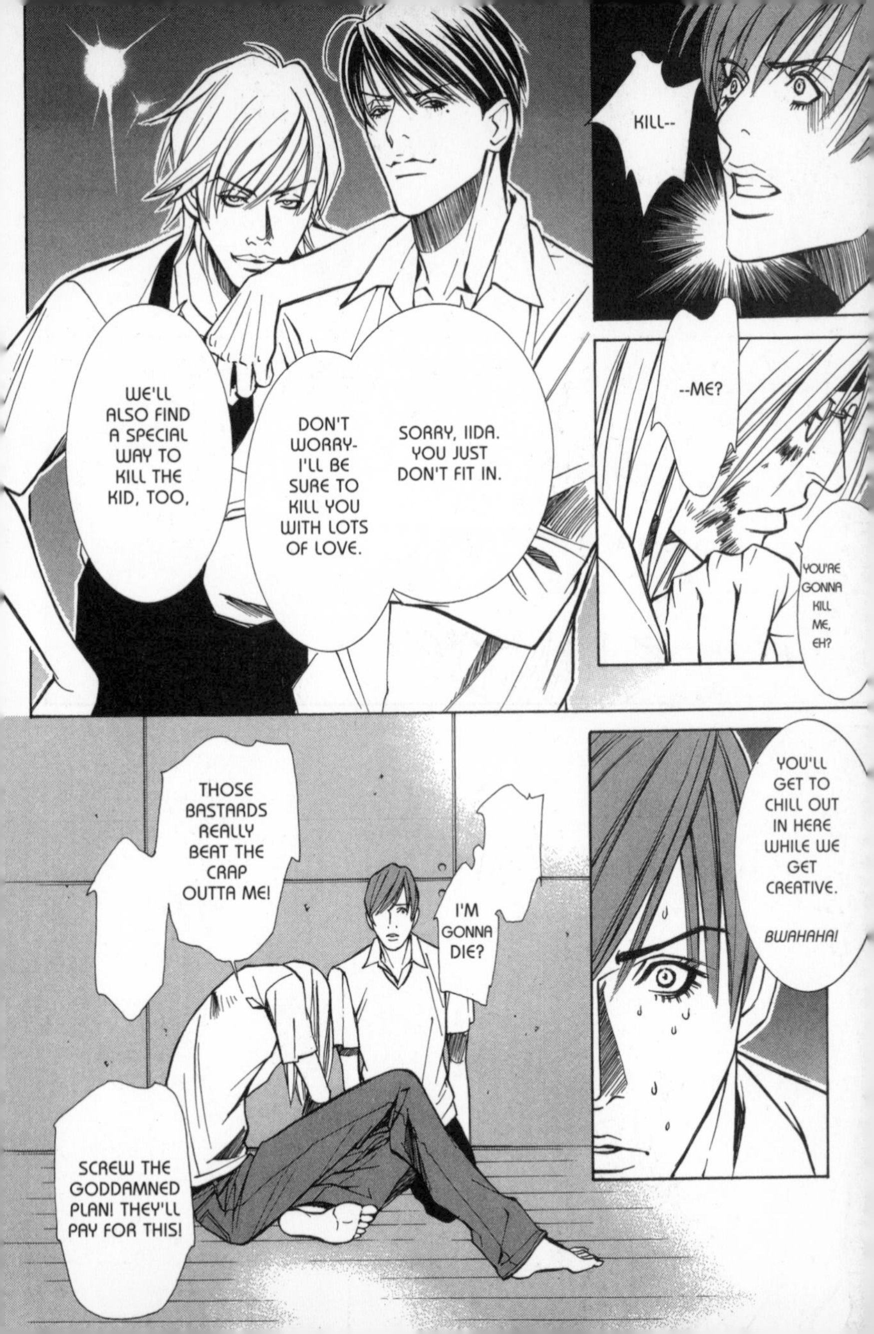
KILL--
--ME?
YOU'RE GONNA KILL ME, EH?
SORRY, IIDA. YOU JUST DON'T FIT IN.
DON'T WORRY- I'LL BE SURE TO KILL YOU WITH LOTS OF LOVE.
WE'LL ALSO FIND A SPECIAL WAY TO KILL THE KID, TOO,
YOU'LL GET TO CHILL OUT IN HERE WHILE WE GET CREATIVE.
BWAHAHA!
I'M GONNA DIE?
THOSE BASTARDS REALLY BEAT THE CRAP OUTTA ME!
SCREW THE GODDAMNED PLAN! THEY'LL PAY FOR THIS!

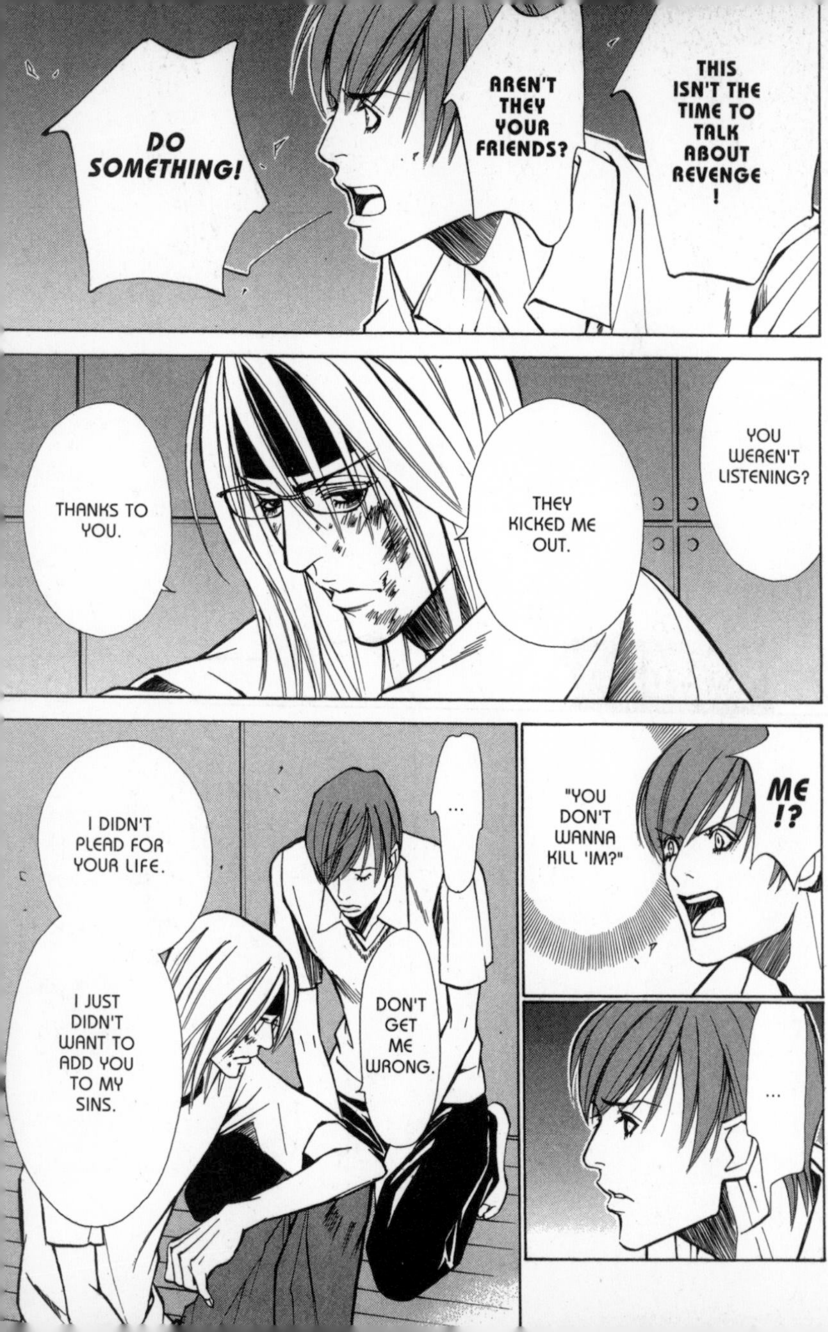
THIS ISN'T THE TIME TO TALK ABOUT REVENGE !
AREN'T THEY YOUR FRIENDS?
DO SOMETHING!
YOU WEREN'T LISTENING?
THEY KICKED ME OUT.
THANKS TO YOU.
ME !?
"YOU DON'T WANNA KILL 'IM?"
...
...
DON'T GET ME WRONG.
I DIDN'T PLEAD FOR YOUR LIFE.
I JUST DIDN'T WANT TO ADD YOU TO MY SINS.

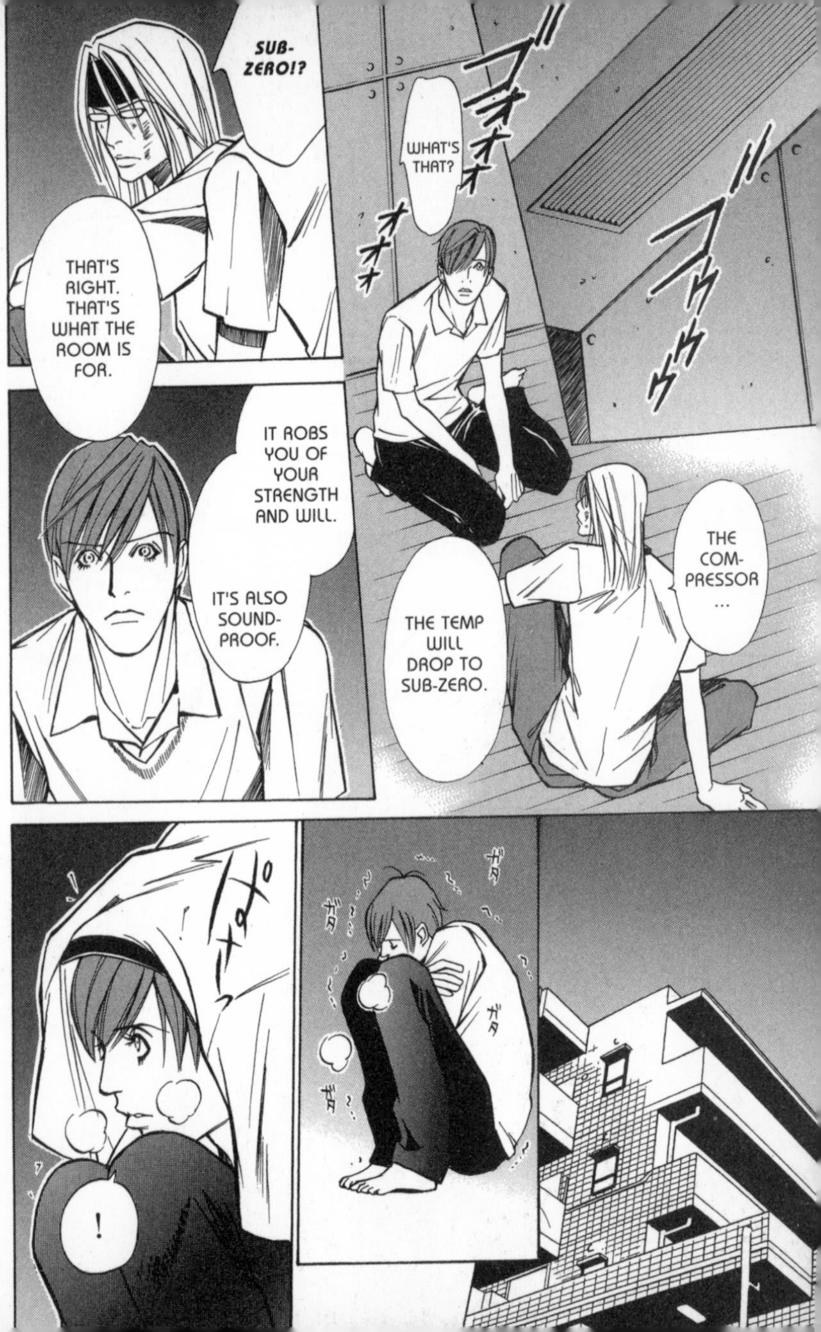
WHAT'S THAT?
THE COMPRESSOR...
THE TEMP WILL DROP TO SUB-ZERO.
SUB-ZERO!?
THAT'S RIGHT. THAT'S WHAT THE ROOM IS FOR.
IT ROBS YOU OF YOUR STRENGTH AND WILL.
IT'S ALSO SOUND-PROOF.
!

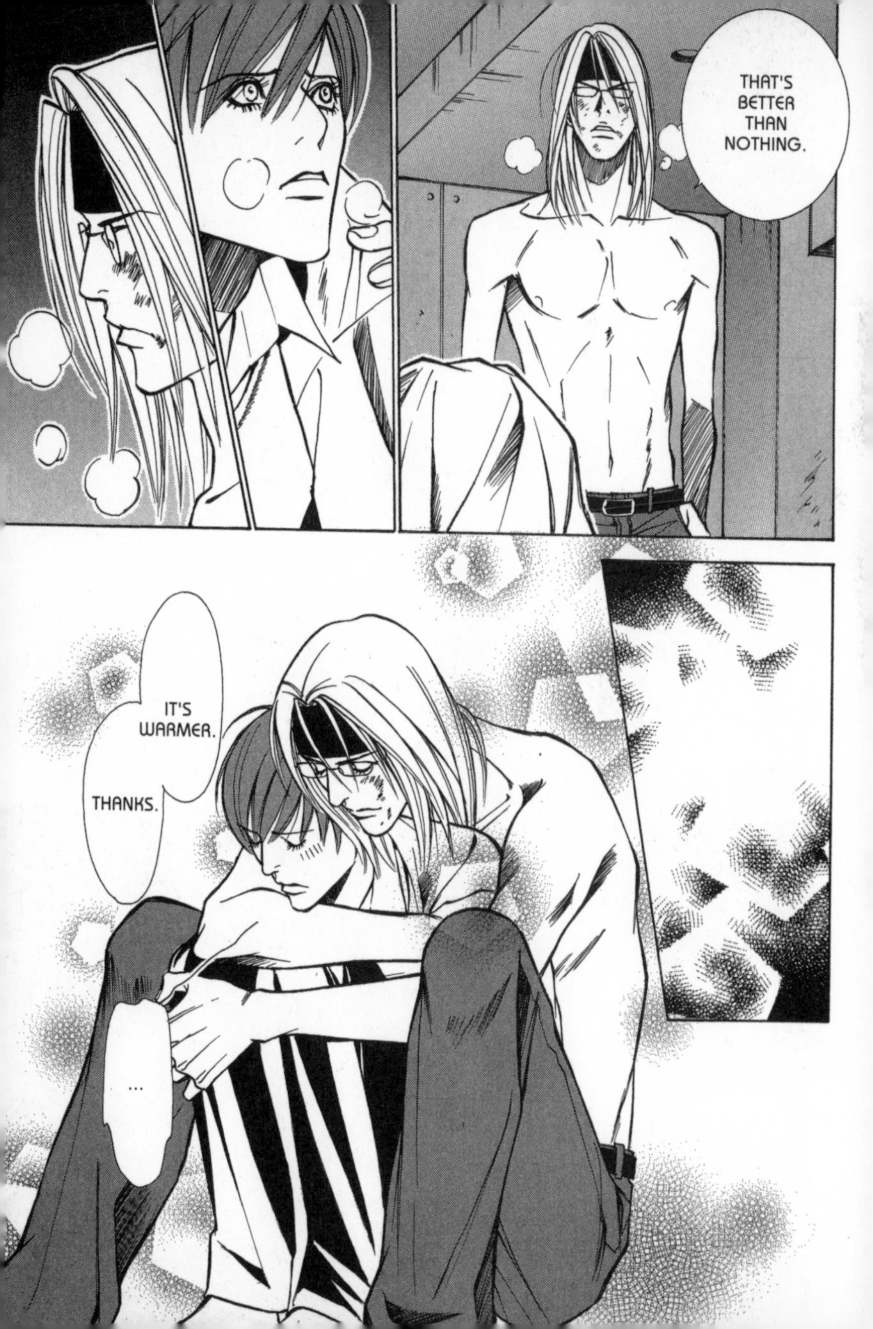
THAT'S BETTER THAN NOTHING.
IT'S WARMER.
THANKS.
...

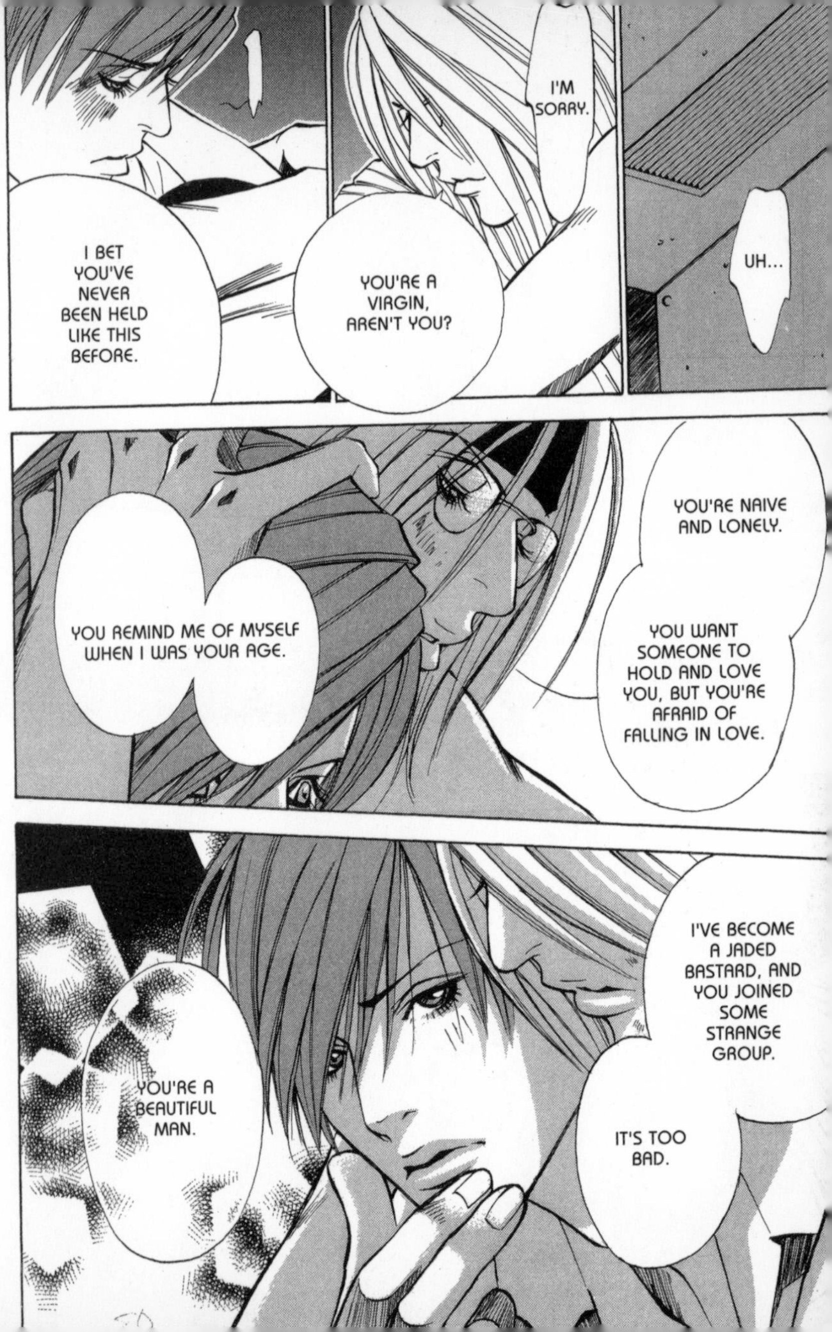
UH...
I'M SORRY.
YOU'RE A VIRGIN, AREN'T YOU?
I BET YOU'VE NEVER BEEN HELD LIKE THIS BEFORE.
YOU'RE NAIVE AND LONELY.
YOU WANT SOMEONE TO HOLD AND LOVE YOU, BUT YOU'RE AFRAID OF FALLING IN LOVE.
YOU REMIND ME OF MYSELF WHEN I WAS YOUR AGE.
I'VE BECOME A JADED BASTARD, AND YOU JOINED SOME STRANGE GROUP.
IT'S TOO BAD.
YOU'RE A BEAUTIFUL MAN.

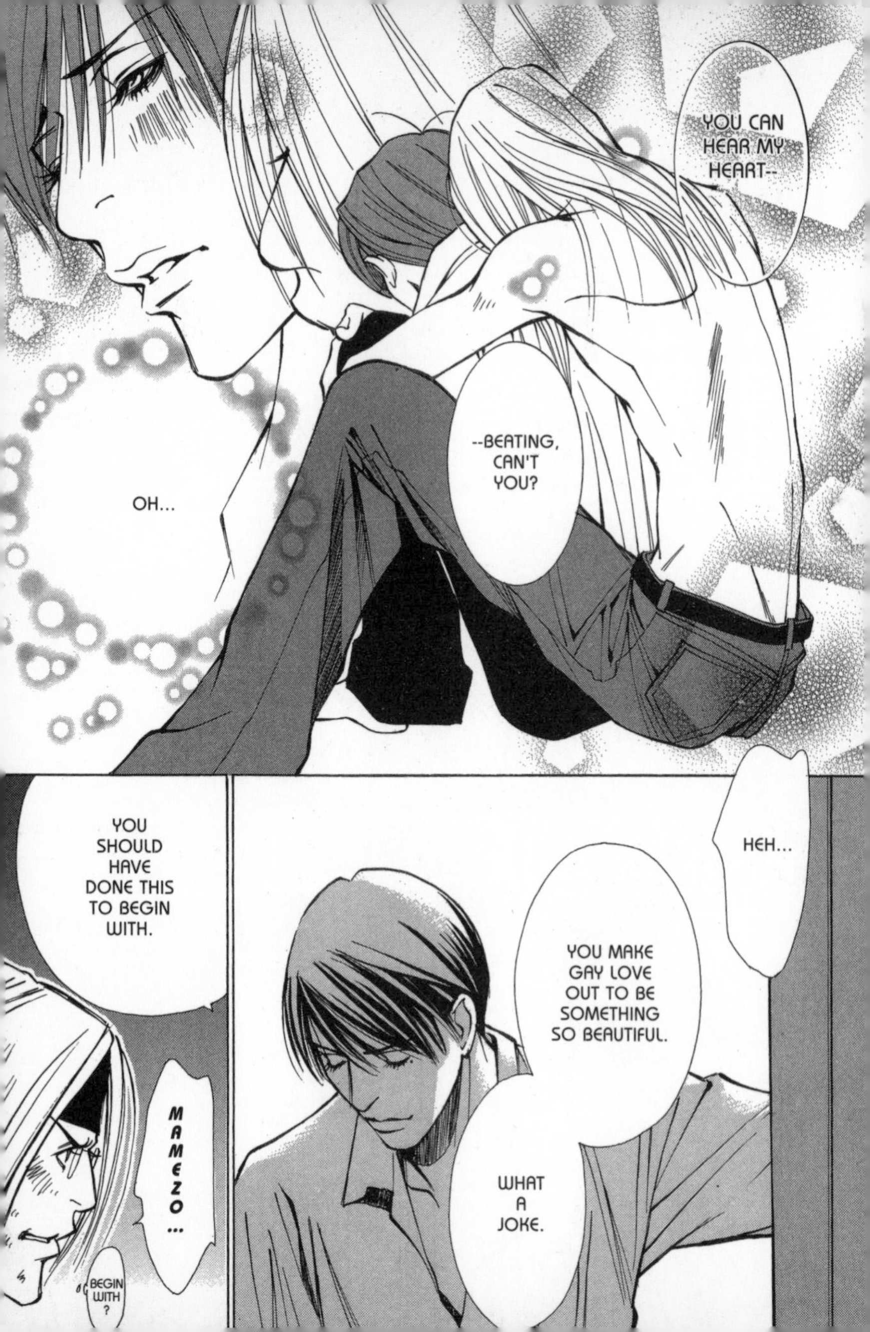
YOU CAN HEAR MY HEART--
--BEATING, CAN'T YOU?
OH...
HEH...
YOU MAKE GAY LOVE OUT TO BE SOMETHING SO BEAUTIFUL.
WHAT A JOKE.
YOU SHOULD HAVE DONE THIS TO BEGIN WITH.
MAMEZO...
BEGIN WITH?

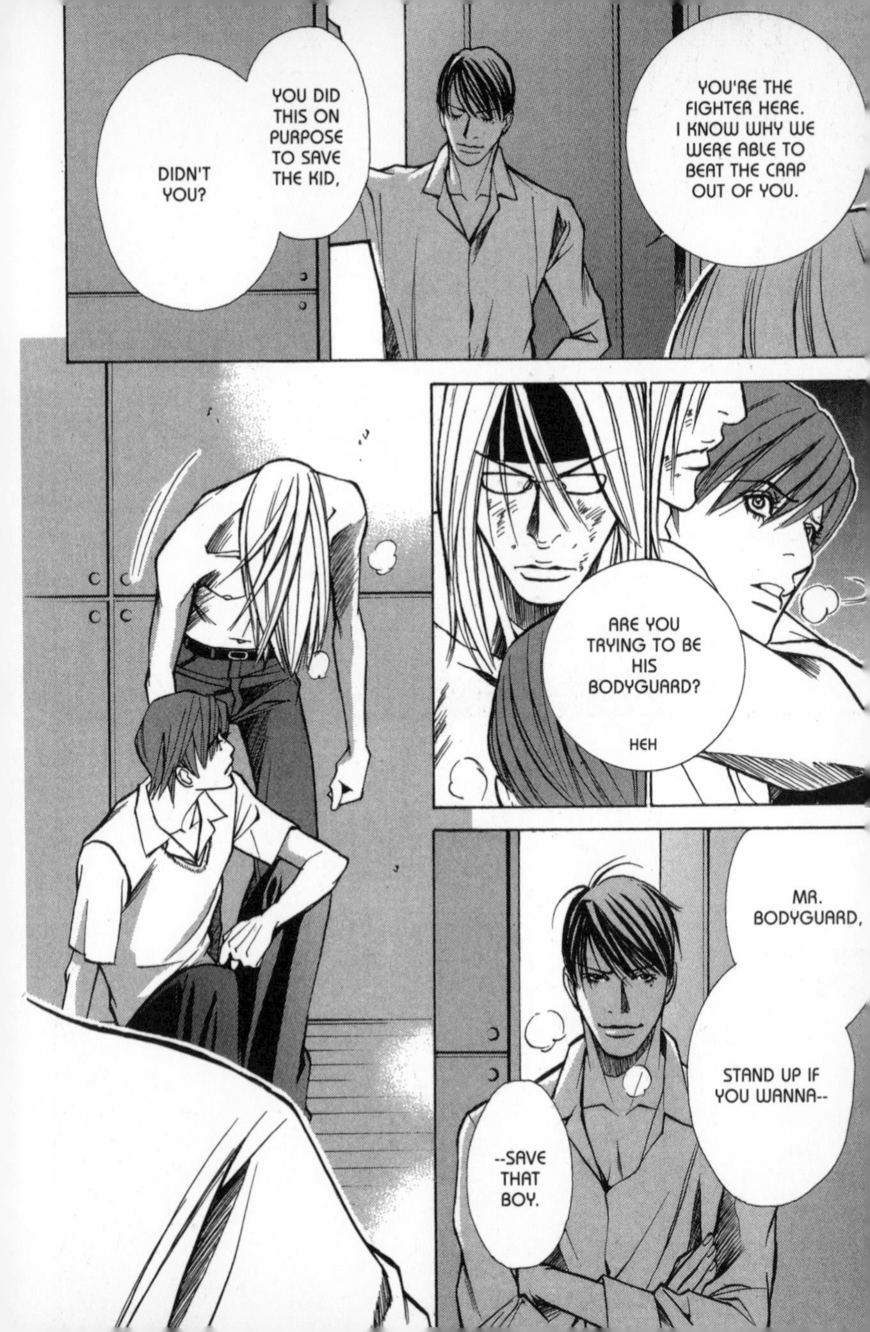
YOU'RE THE FIGHTER HERE. I KNOW WHY WE WERE ABLE TO BEAT THE CRAP OUT OF YOU.
YOU DID THIS ON PURPOSE TO SAVE THE KID,
DIDN'T YOU?
ARE YOU TRYING TO BE HIS BODYGUARD?
HEH
MR. BODYGUARD,
STAND UP IF YOU WANNA--
--SAVE THAT BOY.

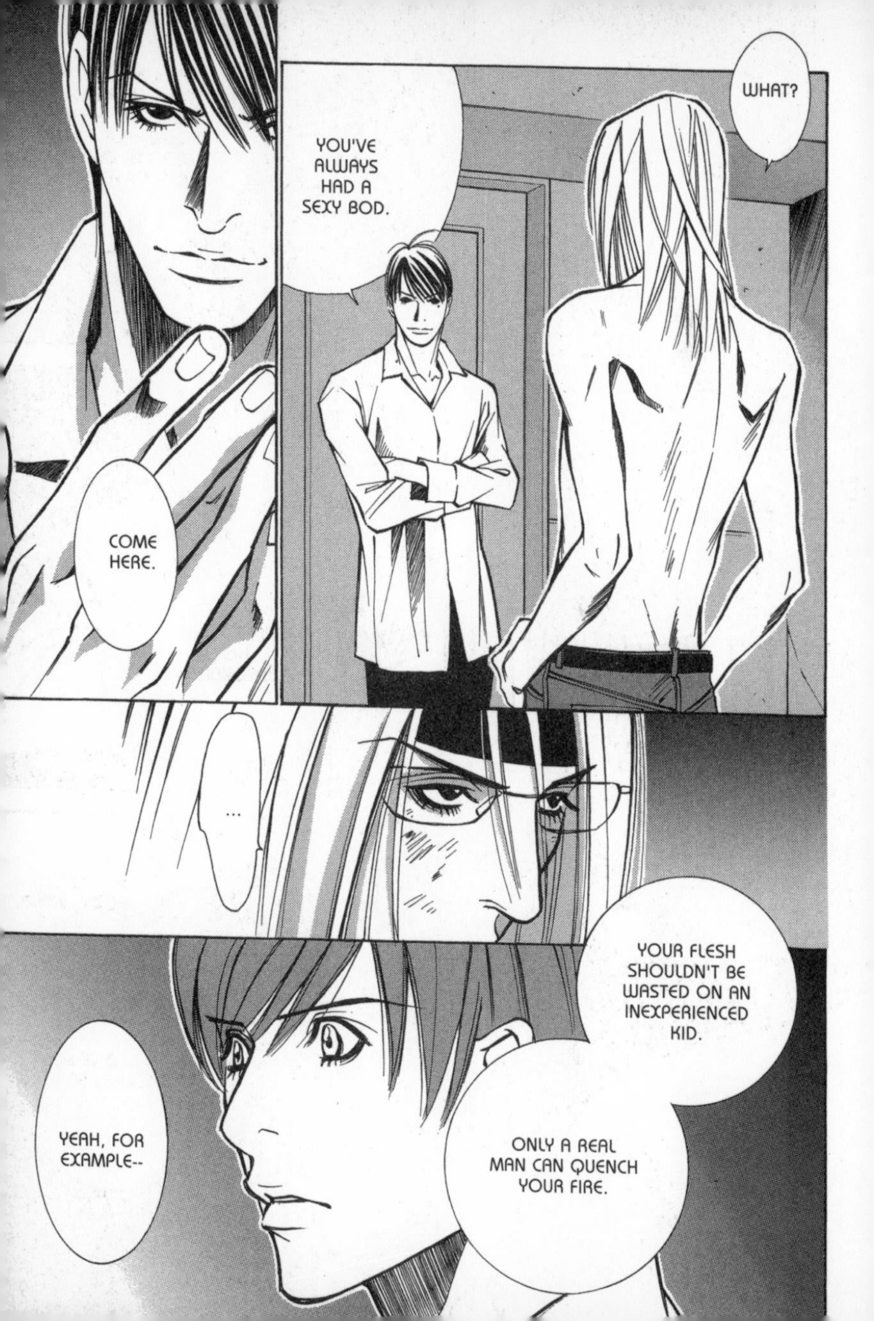
WHAT?
YOU'VE ALWAYS HAD A SEXY BOD.
COME HERE.
...
YOUR FLESH SHOULDN'T BE WASTED ON AN INEXPERIENCED KID.
ONLY A REAL MAN CAN QUENCH YOUR FIRE.
YEAH, FOR EXAMPLE--

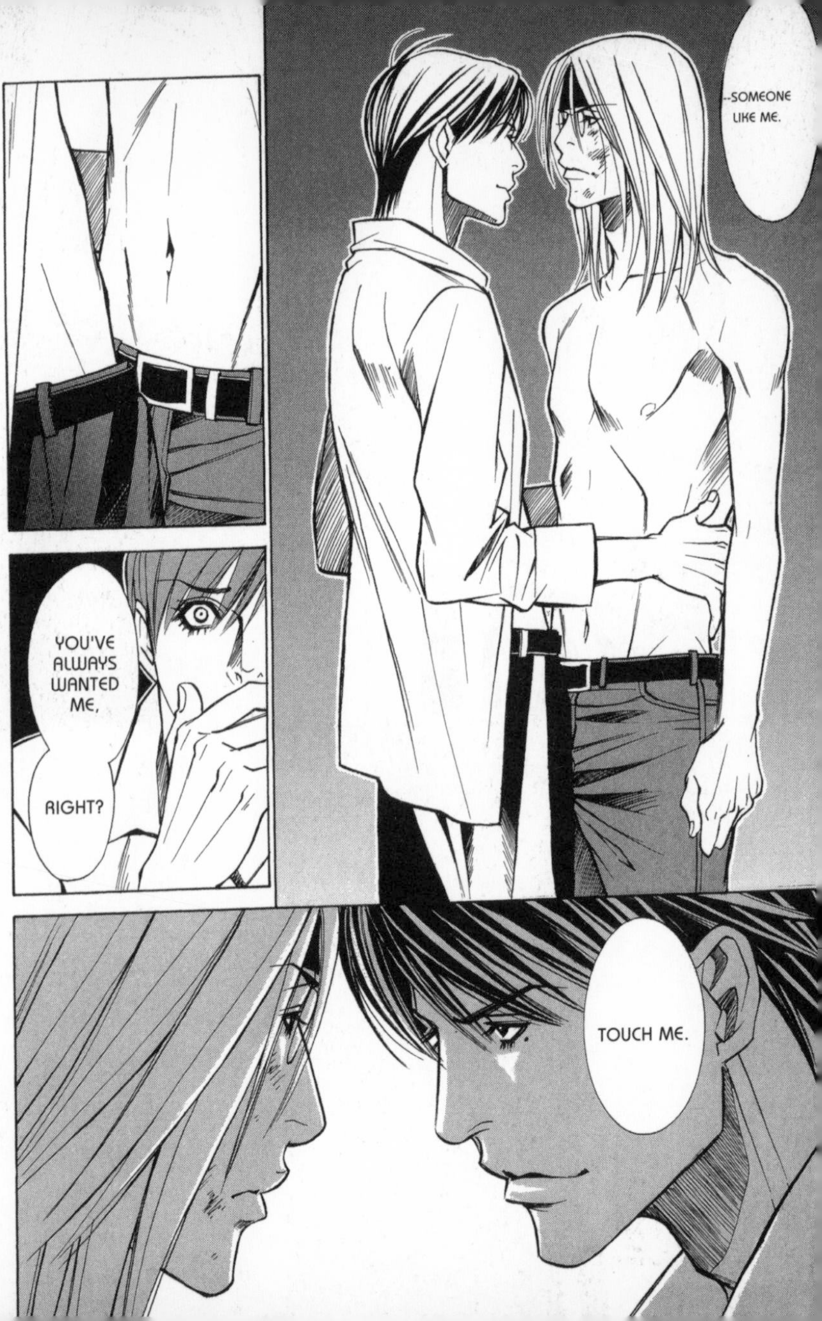
--SOMEONE LIKE ME.
YOU'VE ALWAYS WANTED ME,
RIGHT?
TOUCH ME.

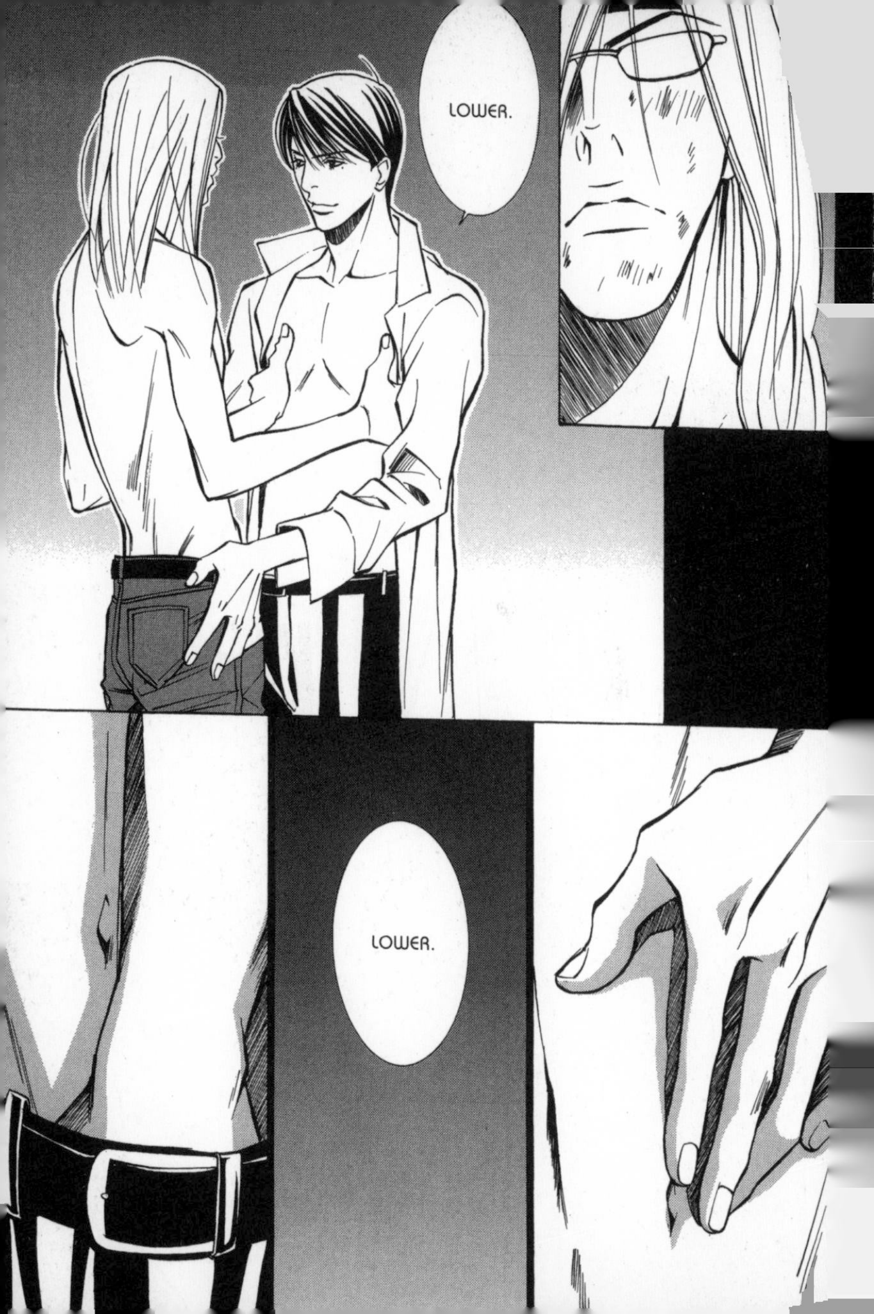
LOWER.
LOWER.

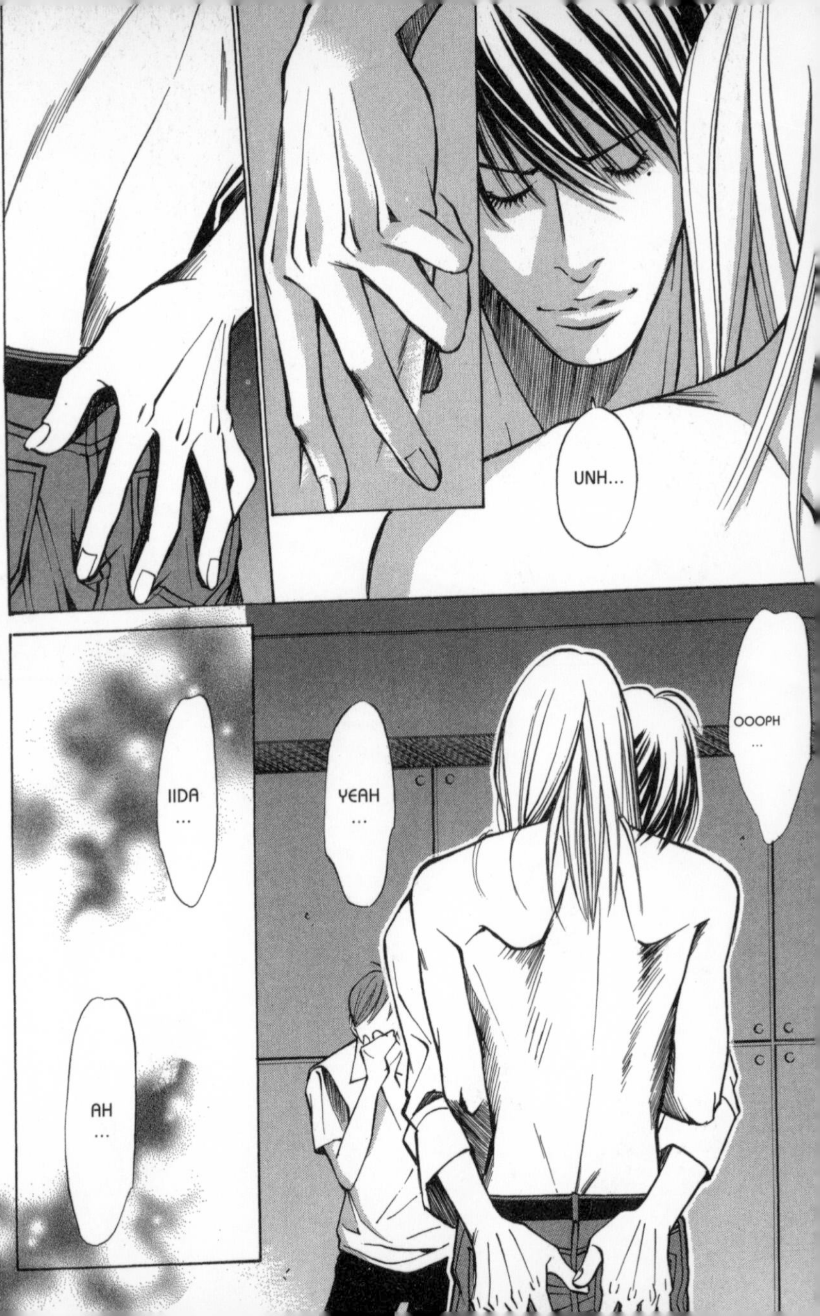
UNH...
OOOPH ...
YEAH ...
IIDA ...
AH ...

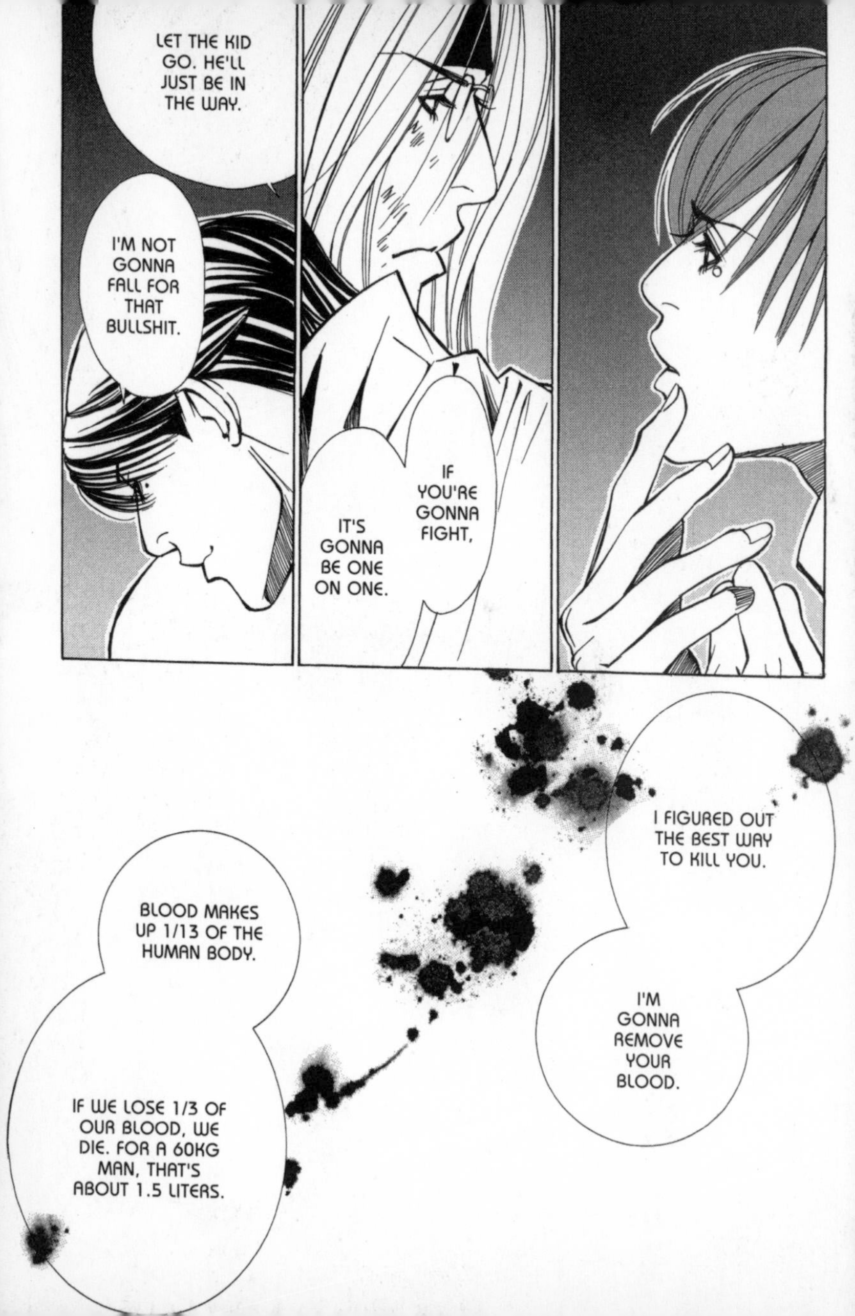
LET THE KID GO. HE'LL JUST BE IN THE WAY.
I'M NOT GONNA FALL FOR THAT BULLSHIT.
IF YOU'RE GONNA FIGHT,
IT'S GONNA BE ONE ON ONE.
I FIGURED OUT THE BEST WAY TO KILL YOU.
I'M GONNA REMOVE YOUR BLOOD.
BLOOD MAKES UP 1/13 OF THE HUMAN BODY.
IF WE LOSE 1/3 OF OUR BLOOD, WE DIE. FOR A 60KG MAN, THAT'S ABOUT 1.5 LITERS.

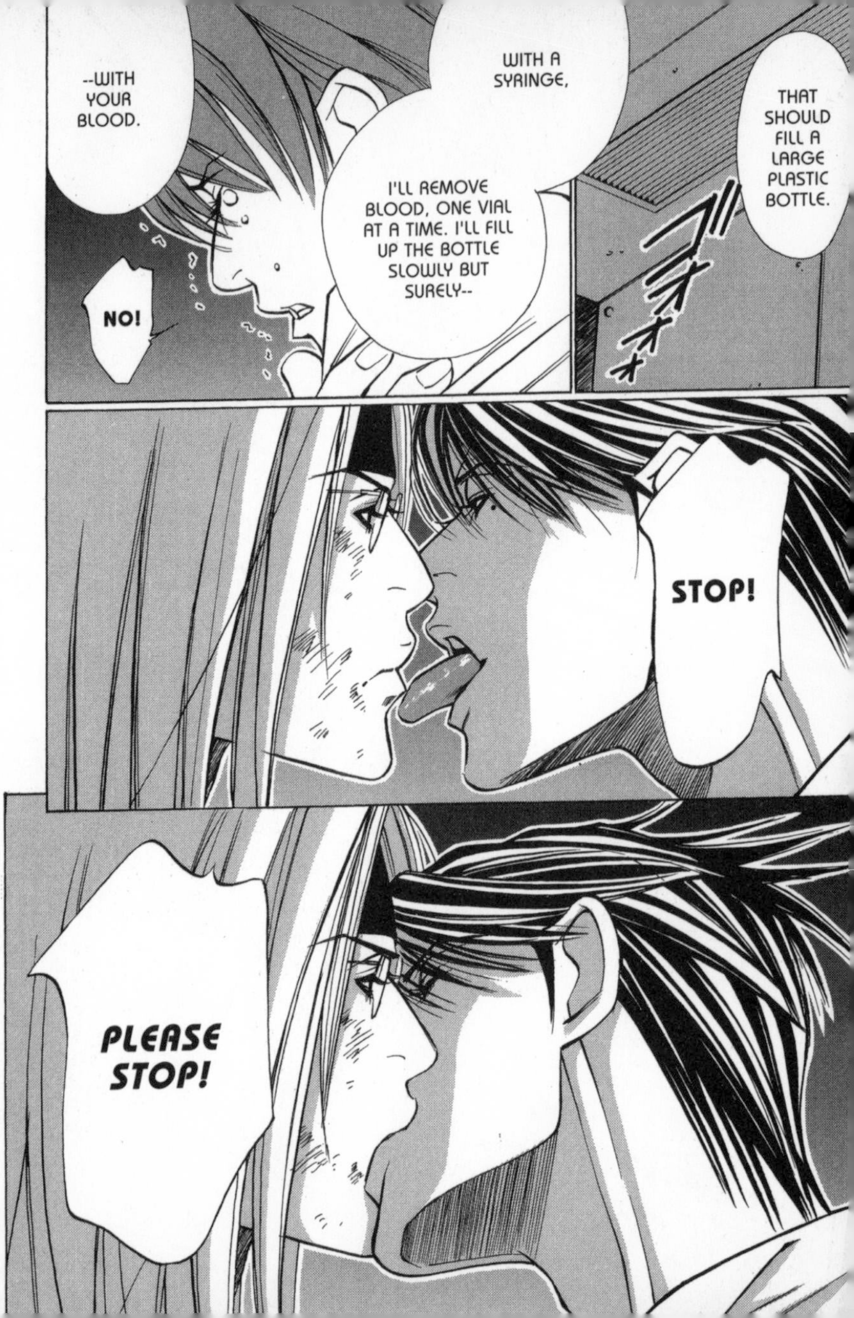
THAT SHOULD FILL A LARGE PLASTIC BOTTLE.
WITH A SYRINGE,
I'LL REMOVE BLOOD, ONE VIAL AT A TIME. I'LL FILL UP THE BOTTLE SLOWLY BUT SURELY--
--WITH YOUR BLOOD.
NO!
STOP!
PLEASE STOP!

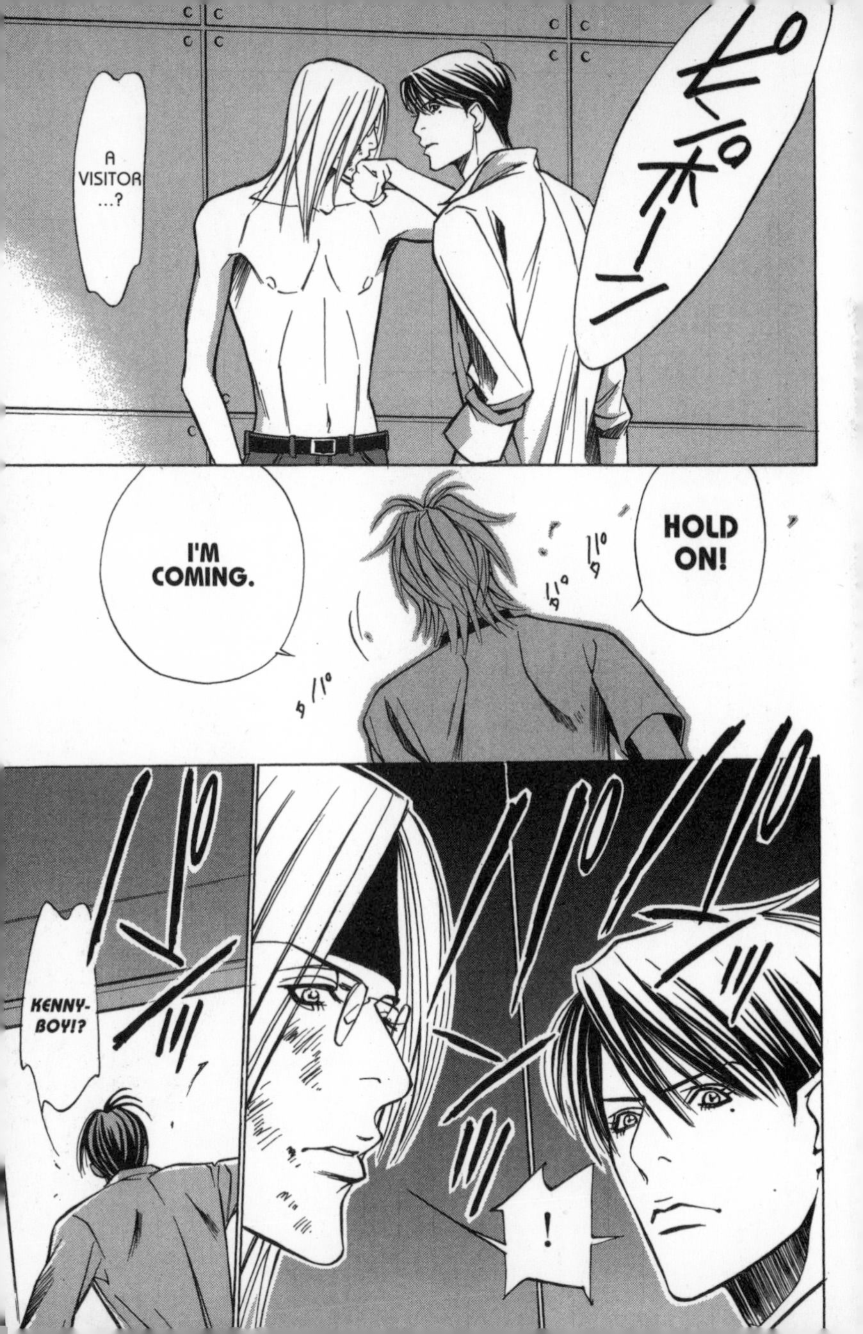
A VISITOR ...?
HOLD ON!
I'M COMING.
KENNY-BOY!?
!

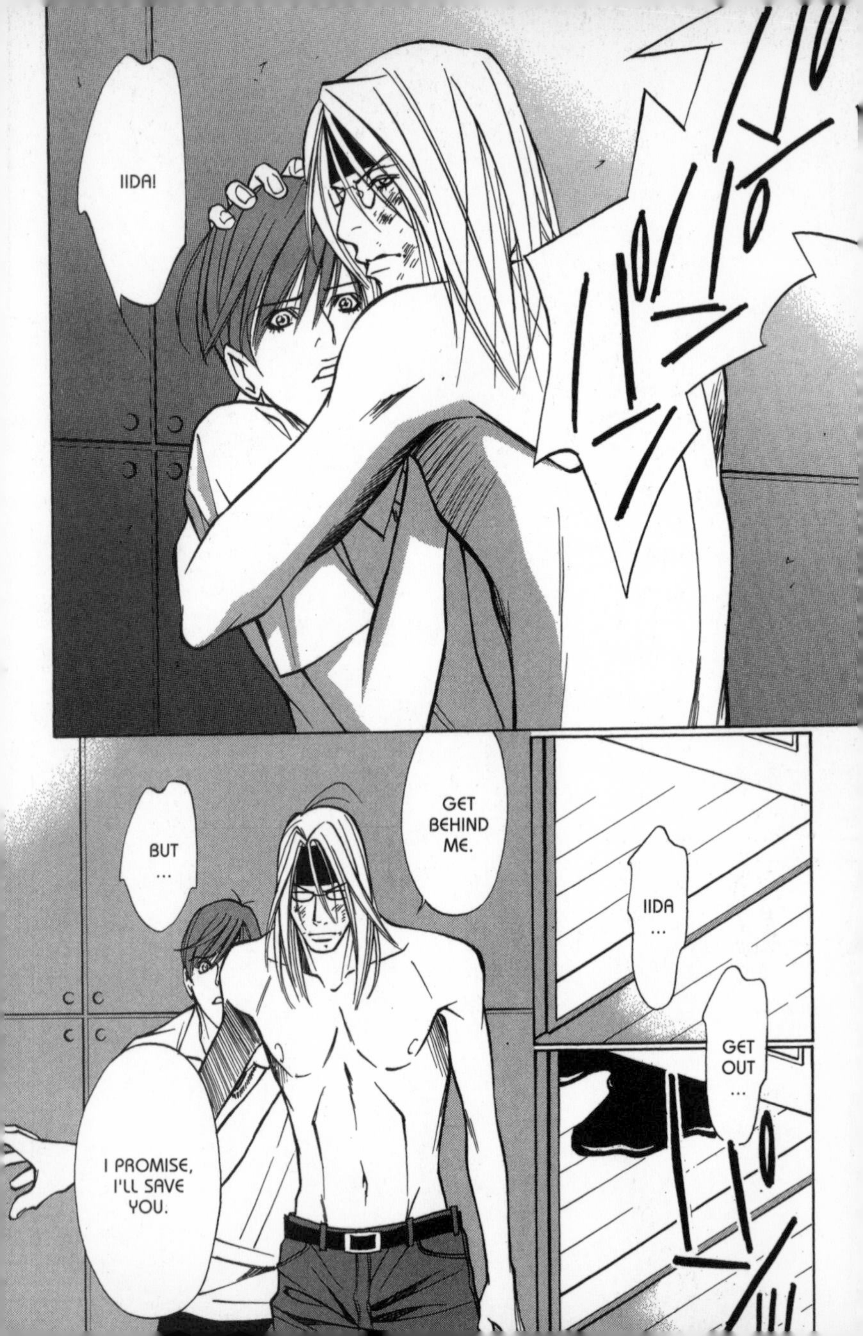
IIDA!
GET BEHIND ME.
BUT ...
I PROMISE, I'LL SAVE YOU.
IIDA ...
GET OUT ...

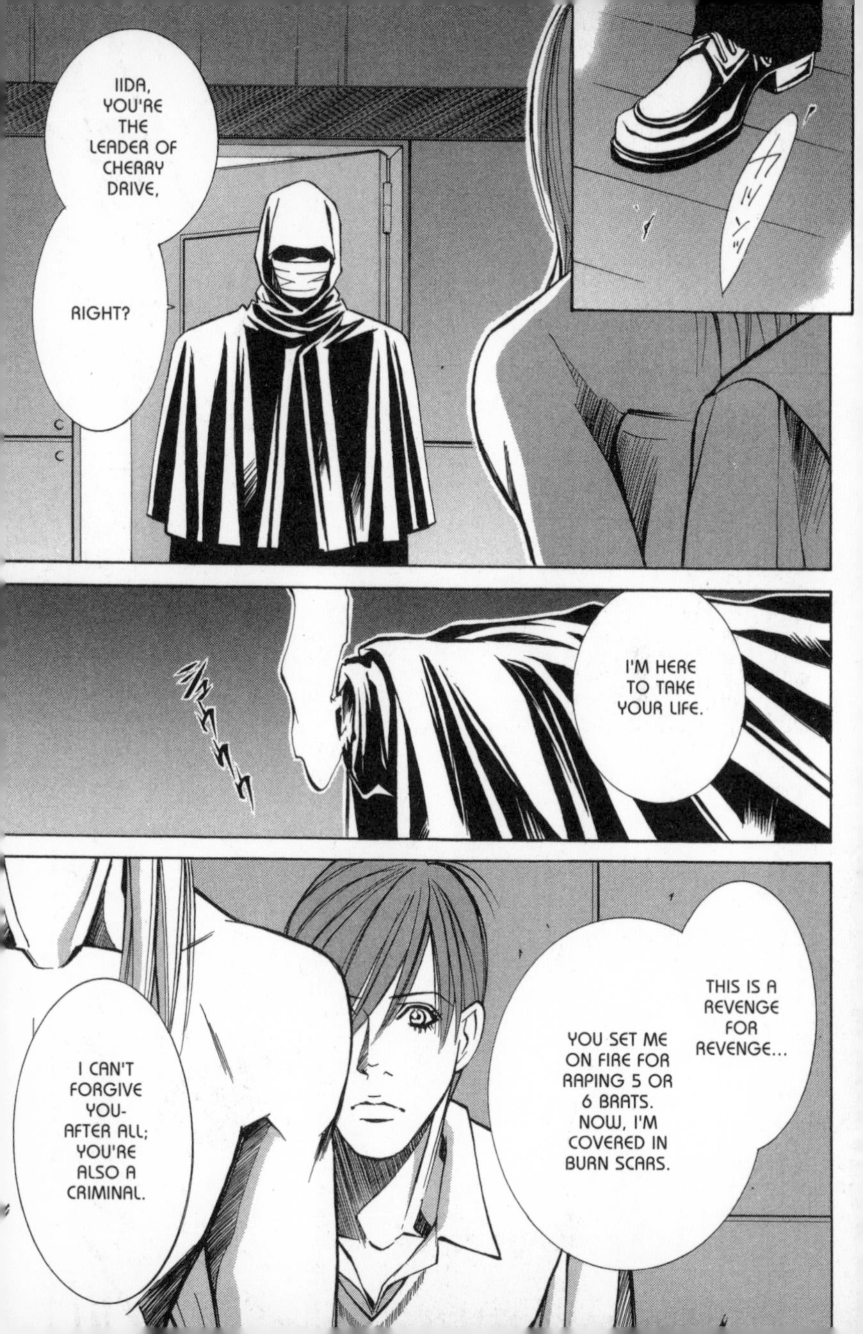
IIDA, YOU'RE THE LEADER OF CHERRY DRIVE,
RIGHT?
I'M HERE TO TAKE YOUR LIFE.
THIS IS A REVENGE FOR REVENGE...
YOU SET ME ON FIRE FOR RAPING 5 OR 6 BRATS. NOW, I'M COVERED IN BURN SCARS.
I CAN'T FORGIVE YOU- AFTER ALL; YOU'RE ALSO A CRIMINAL.

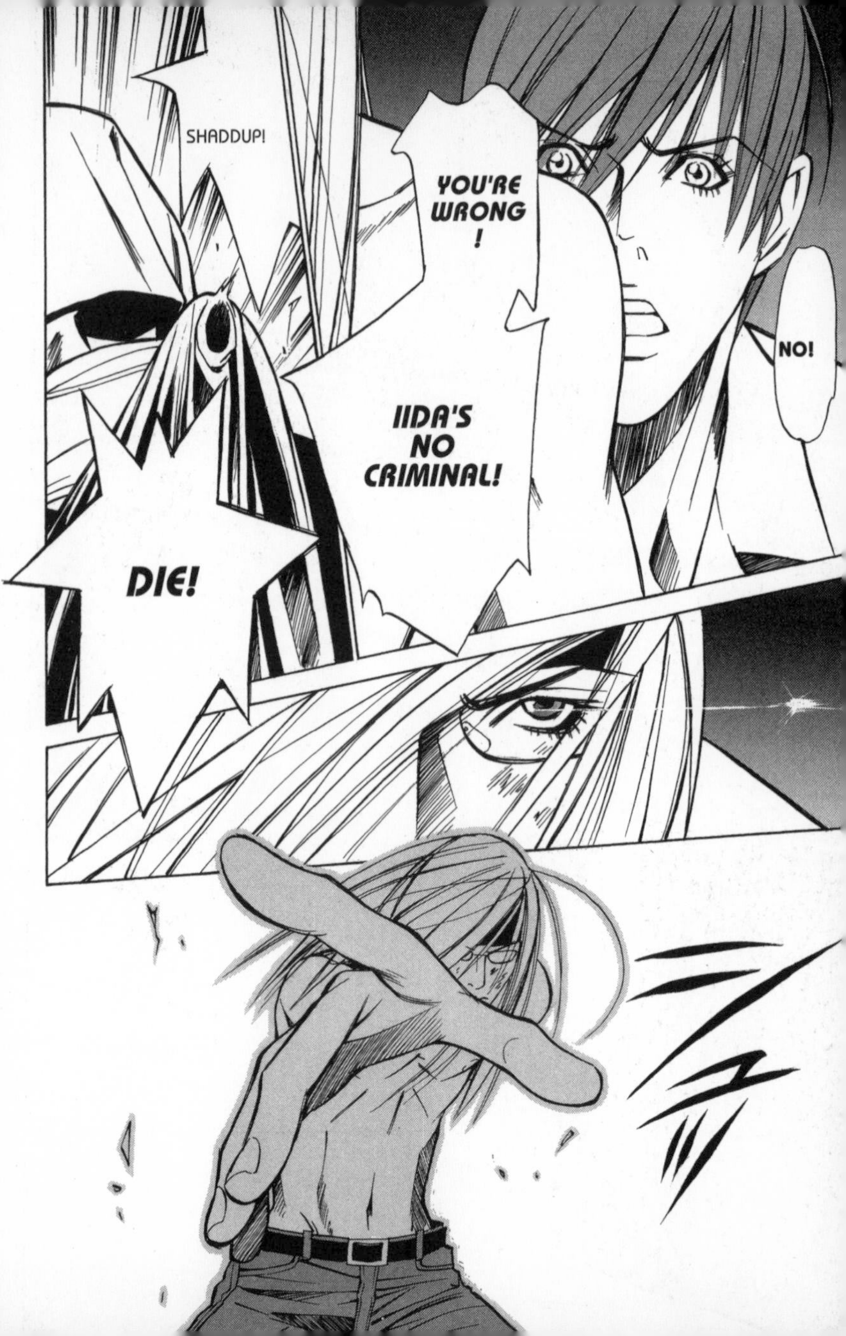
NO!
YOU'RE WRONG!
IIDA'S NO CRIMINAL!
SHADDUP!
DIE!

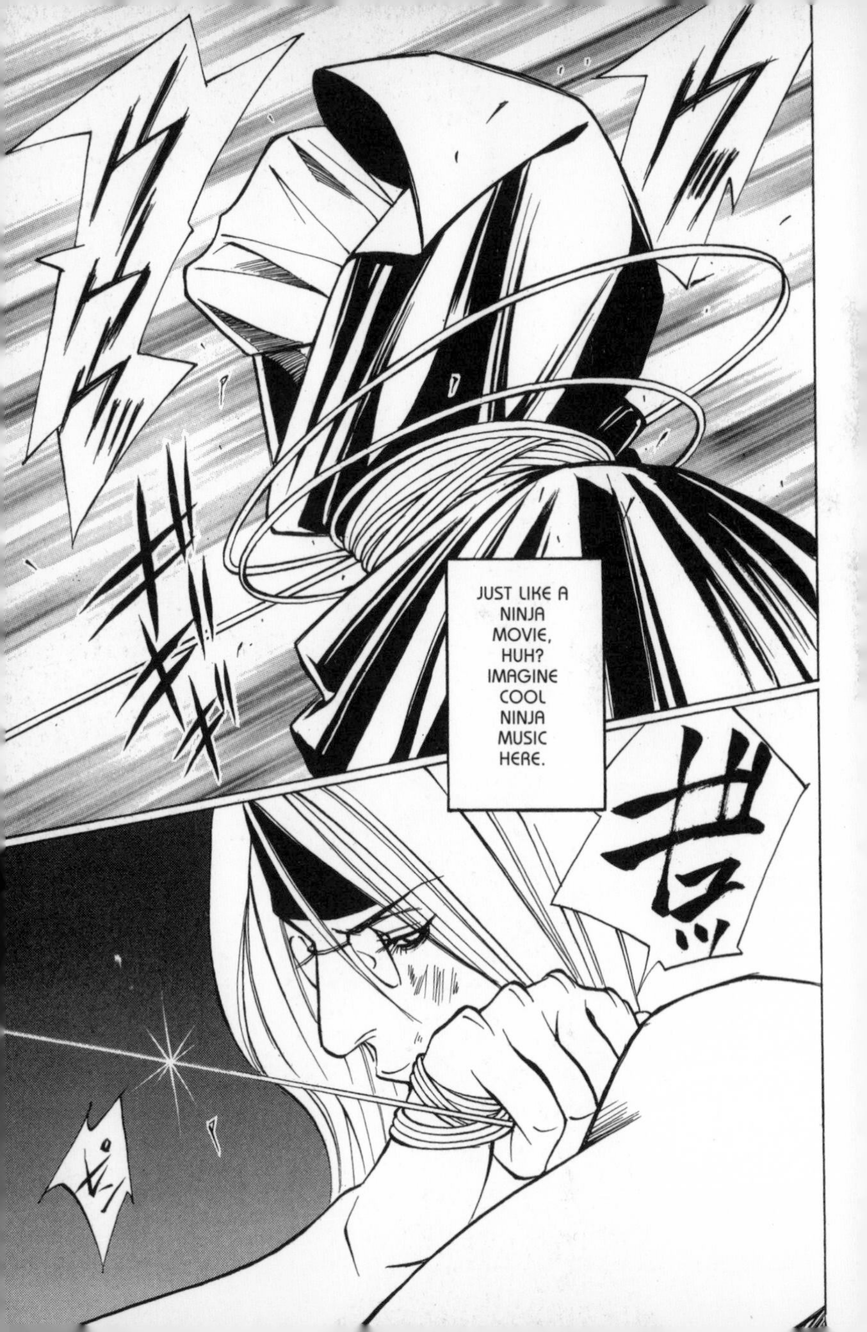
JUST LIKE A NINJA MOVIE, HUH? IMAGINE COOL NINJA MUSIC HERE.

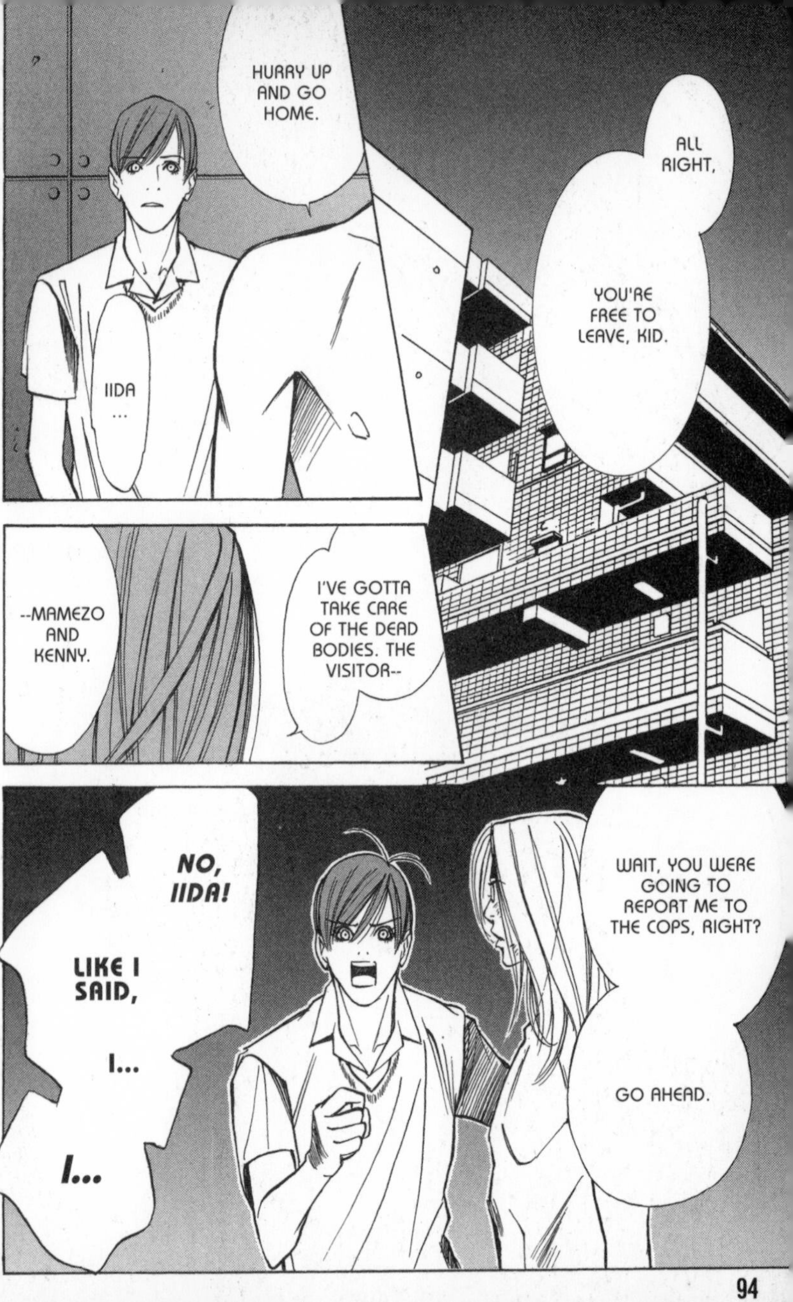
HURRY UP AND GO HOME.
ALL RIGHT,
YOU'RE FREE TO LEAVE, KID.
IIDA ...
I'VE GOTTA TAKE CARE OF THE DEAD BODIES. THE VISITOR--
--MAMEZO AND KENNY.
NO, IIDA!
LIKE I SAID,
I...
I...
WAIT, YOU WERE GOING TO REPORT ME TO THE COPS, RIGHT?
GO AHEAD.

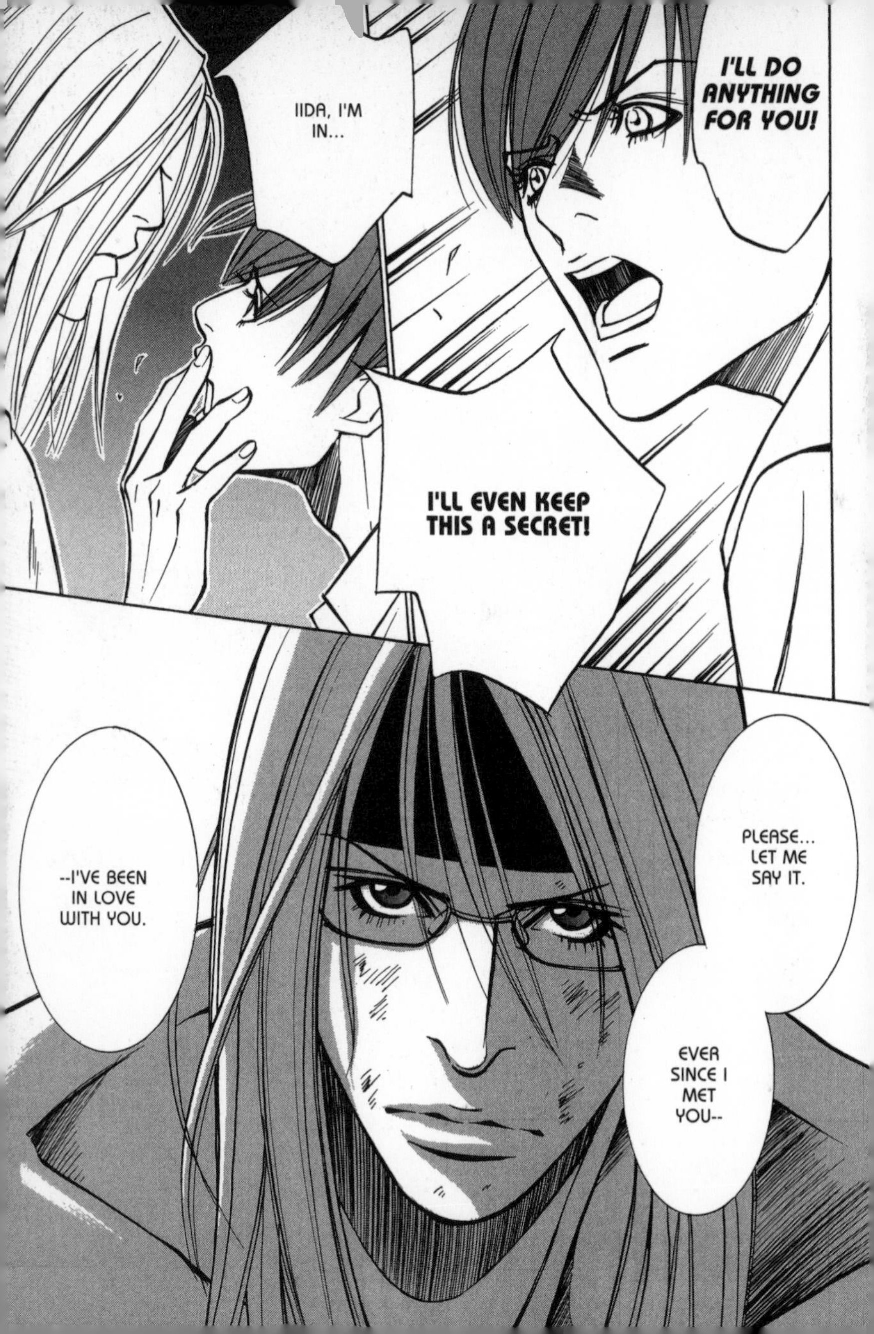
I'LL DO ANYTHING FOR YOU!
IIDA, I'M IN...
I'LL EVEN KEEP THIS A SECRET!
PLEASE... LET ME SAY IT.
EVER SINCE I MET YOU--
--I'VE BEEN IN LOVE WITH YOU.

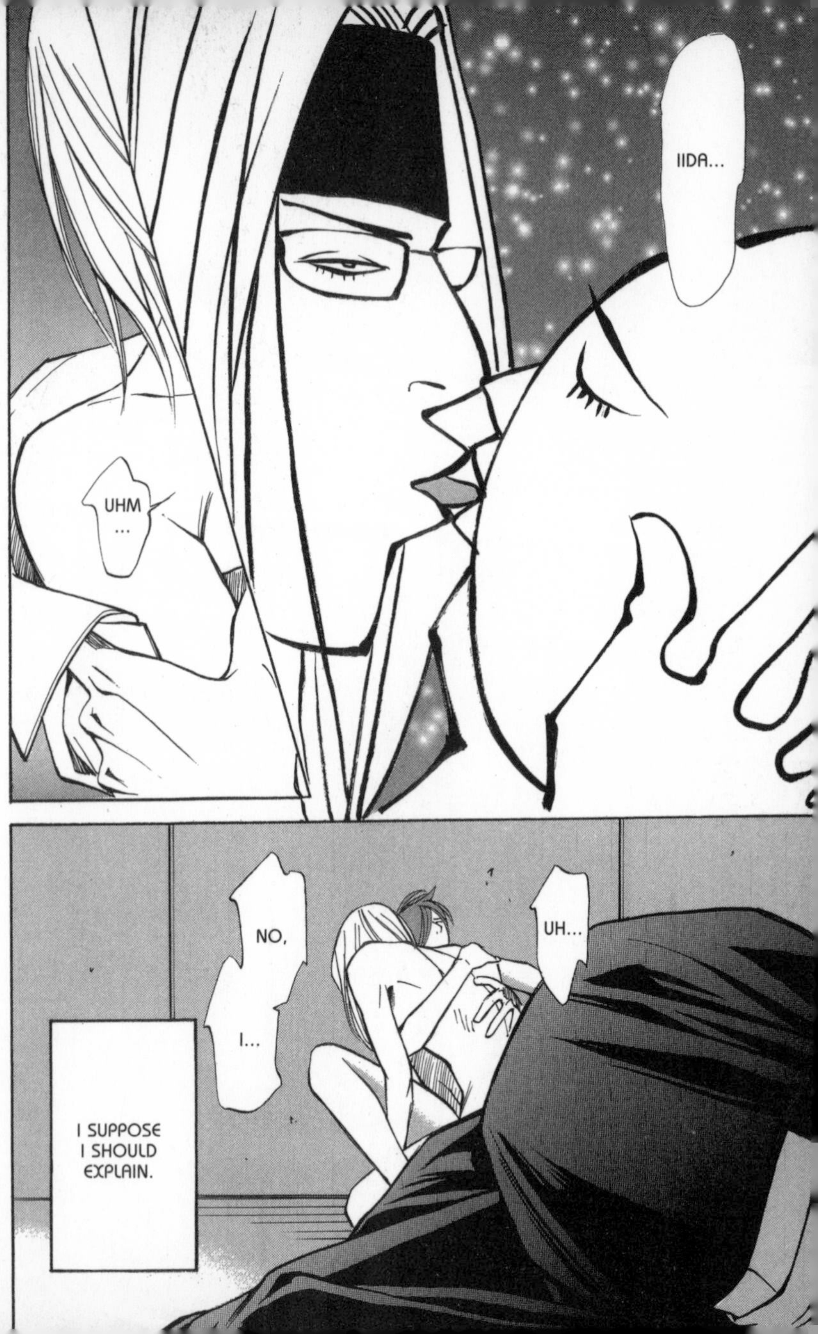
IIDA...
UHM ...
UH...
NO,
I...
I SUPPOSE I SHOULD EXPLAIN.

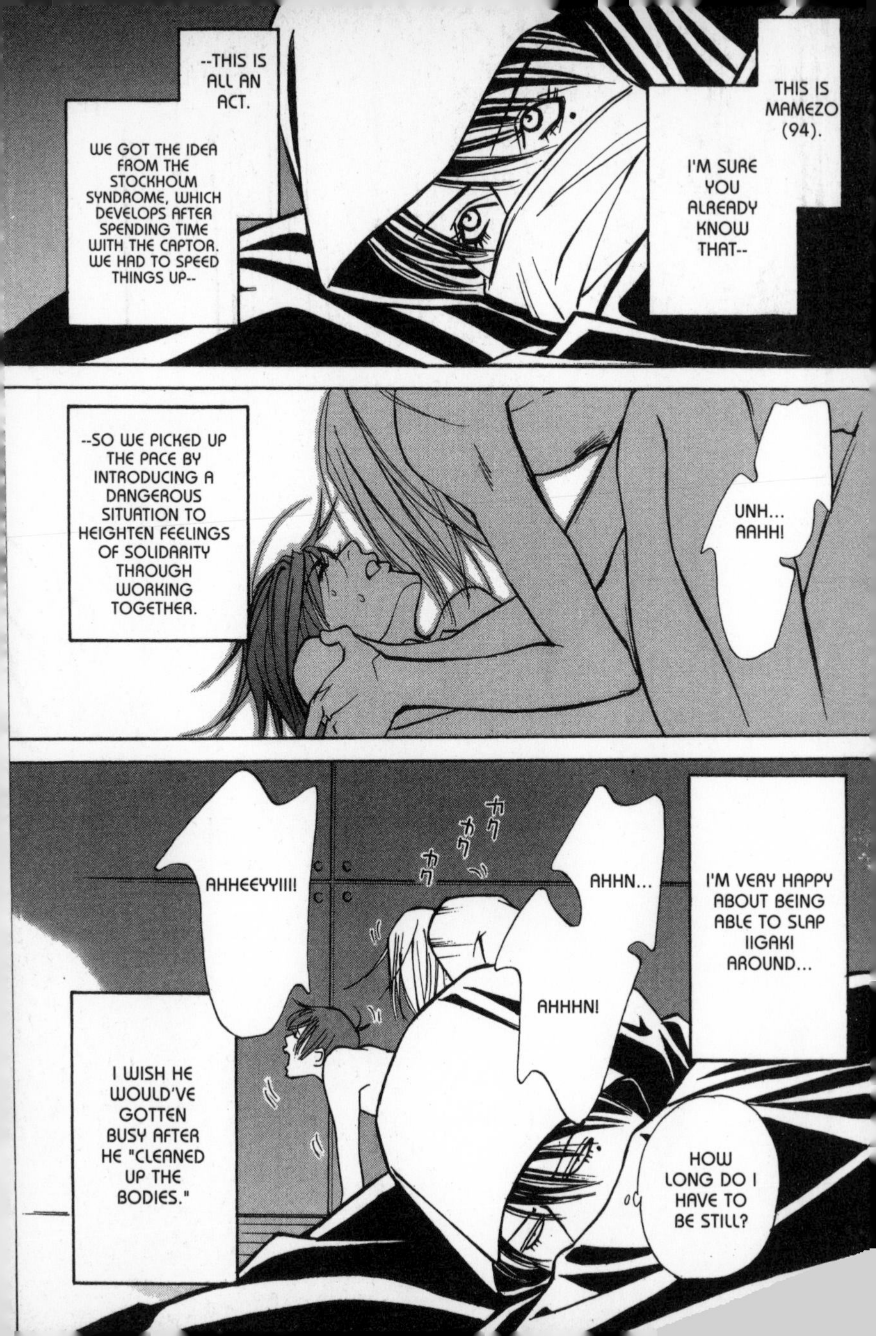
THIS IS MAMEZO (94).
I'M SURE YOU ALREADY KNOW THAT--
--THIS IS ALL AN ACT.
WE GOT THE IDEA FROM THE STOCKHOLM SYNDROME, WHICH DEVELOPS AFTER SPENDING TIME WITH THE CAPTOR. WE HAD TO SPEED THINGS UP--
UNH... AAHH!
--SO WE PICKED UP THE PACE BY INTRODUCING A DANGEROUS SITUATION TO HEIGHTEN FEELINGS OF SOLIDARITY THROUGH WORKING TOGETHER.
I'M VERY HAPPY ABOUT BEING ABLE TO SLAP IIGAKI AROUND...
AHHN...
AHHHN!
カク カク カク
AHHEEYYIIII!
HOW LONG DO I HAVE TO BE STILL?
I WISH HE WOULD'VE GOTTEN BUSY AFTER HE "CLEANED UP THE BODIES."

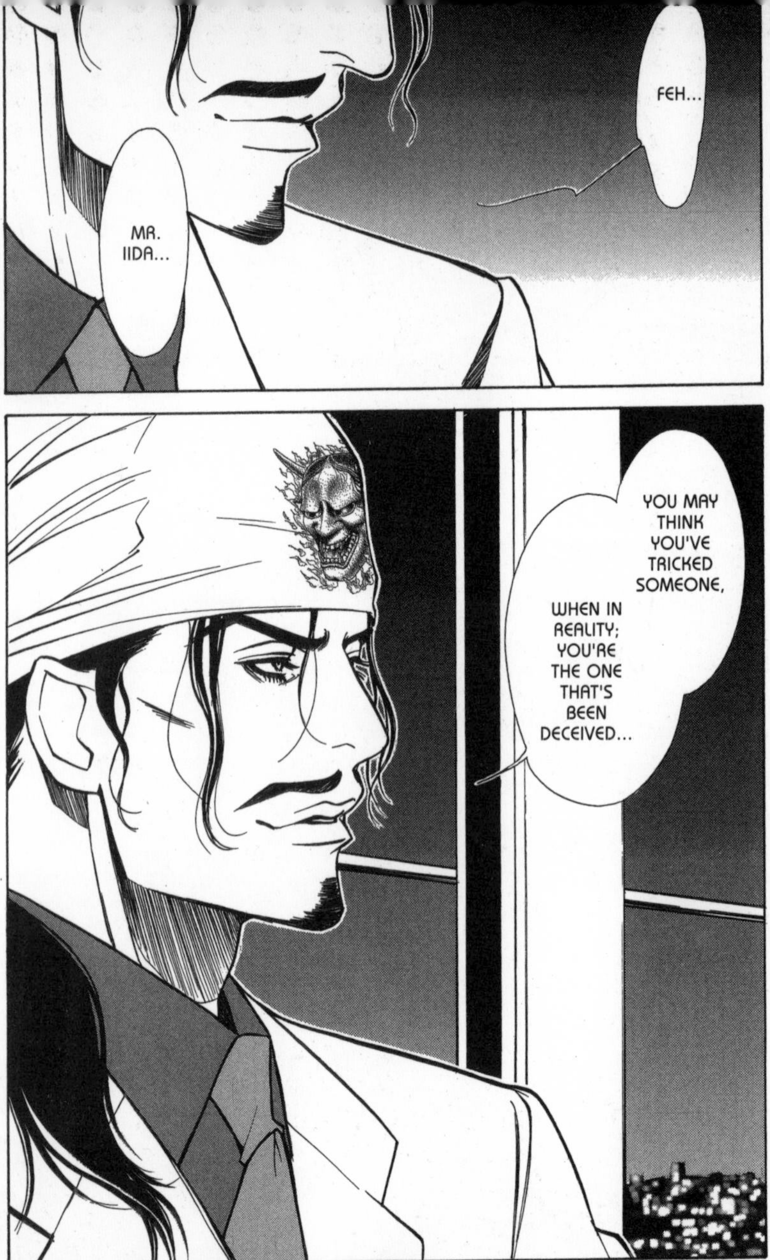
FEH...
MR. IIDA...
YOU MAY THINK YOU'VE TRICKED SOMEONE,
WHEN IN REALITY; YOU'RE THE ONE THAT'S BEEN DECEIVED...

END

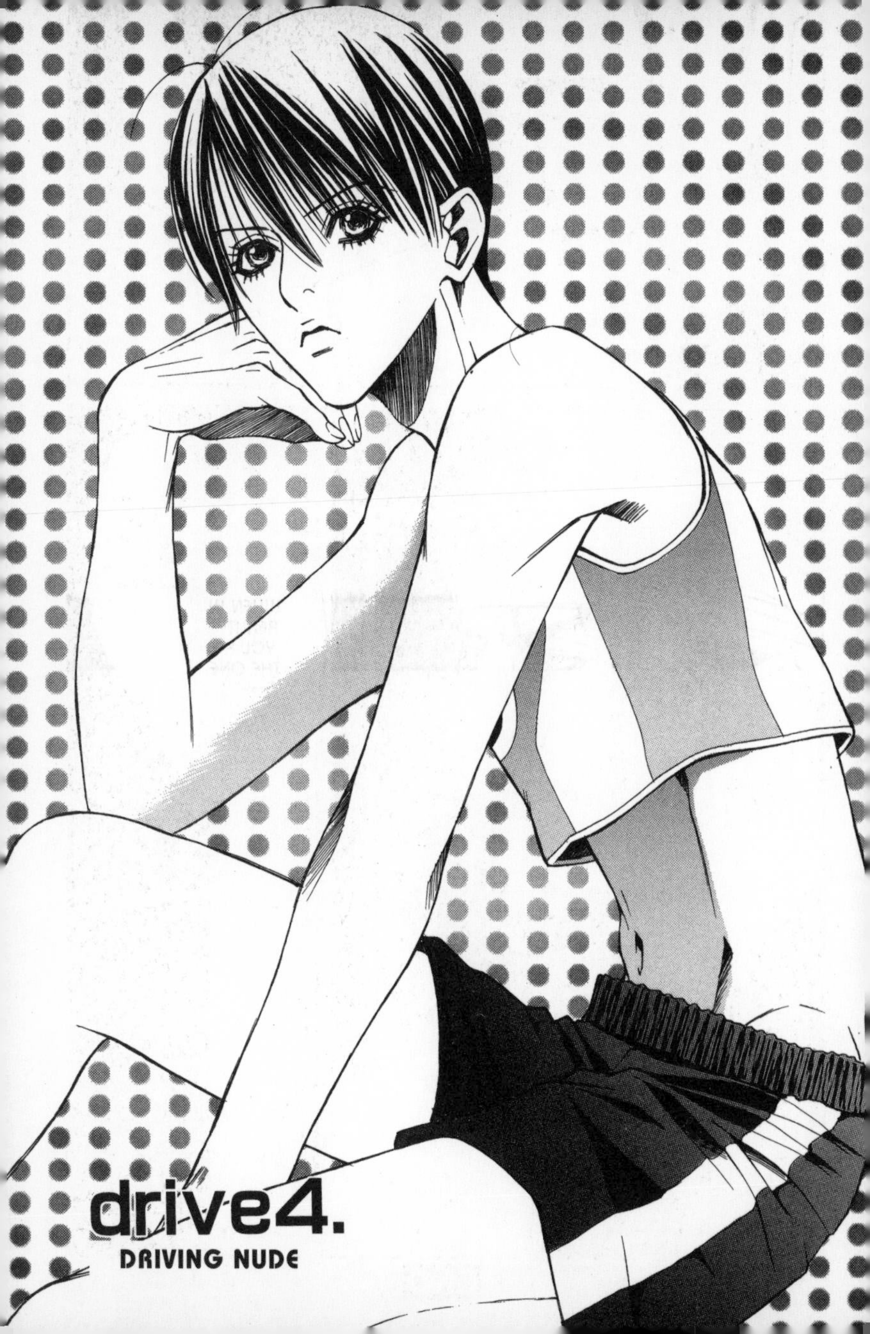
drive4.
DRIVING NUDE

CD Cherry Drive

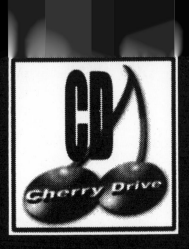

A MYSTERIOUS, GAY SITE THAT HELPS PEOPLE GET REVENGE FOR A RAPE, OR RAVISH A WARM BODY FOR THE NIGHT...
THEY ACCEPT ALL KINDS OF OFFERS TO PLEASE THEIR CLIENTS...

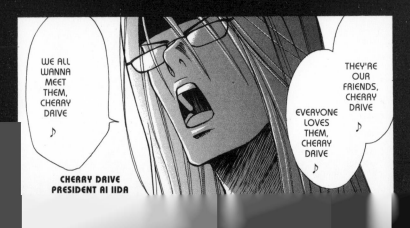

THEY'RE OUR FRIENDS, CHERRY DRIVE ♪
EVERYONE LOVES THEM, CHERRY DRIVE ♪
WE ALL WANNA MEET THEM, CHERRY DRIVE ♪
CHERRY DRIVE PRESIDENT AI IIDA

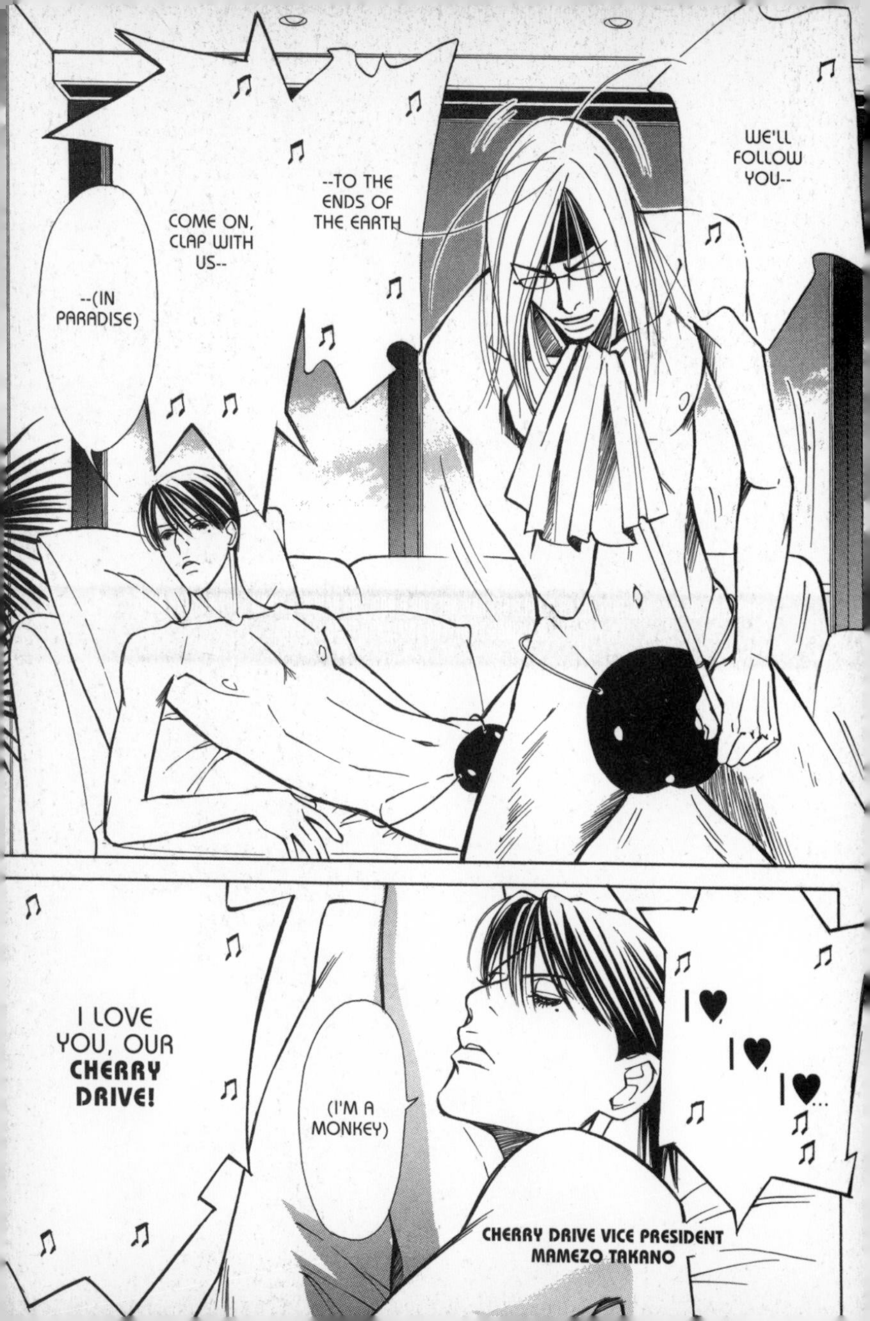
WE'LL FOLLOW YOU--
--TO THE ENDS OF THE EARTH
COME ON, CLAP WITH US--
--(IN PARADISE)
I♥, I♥, I♥...
CHERRY DRIVE VICE PRESIDENT MAMEZO TAKANO
(I'M A MONKEY)
I LOVE YOU, OUR CHERRY DRIVE!

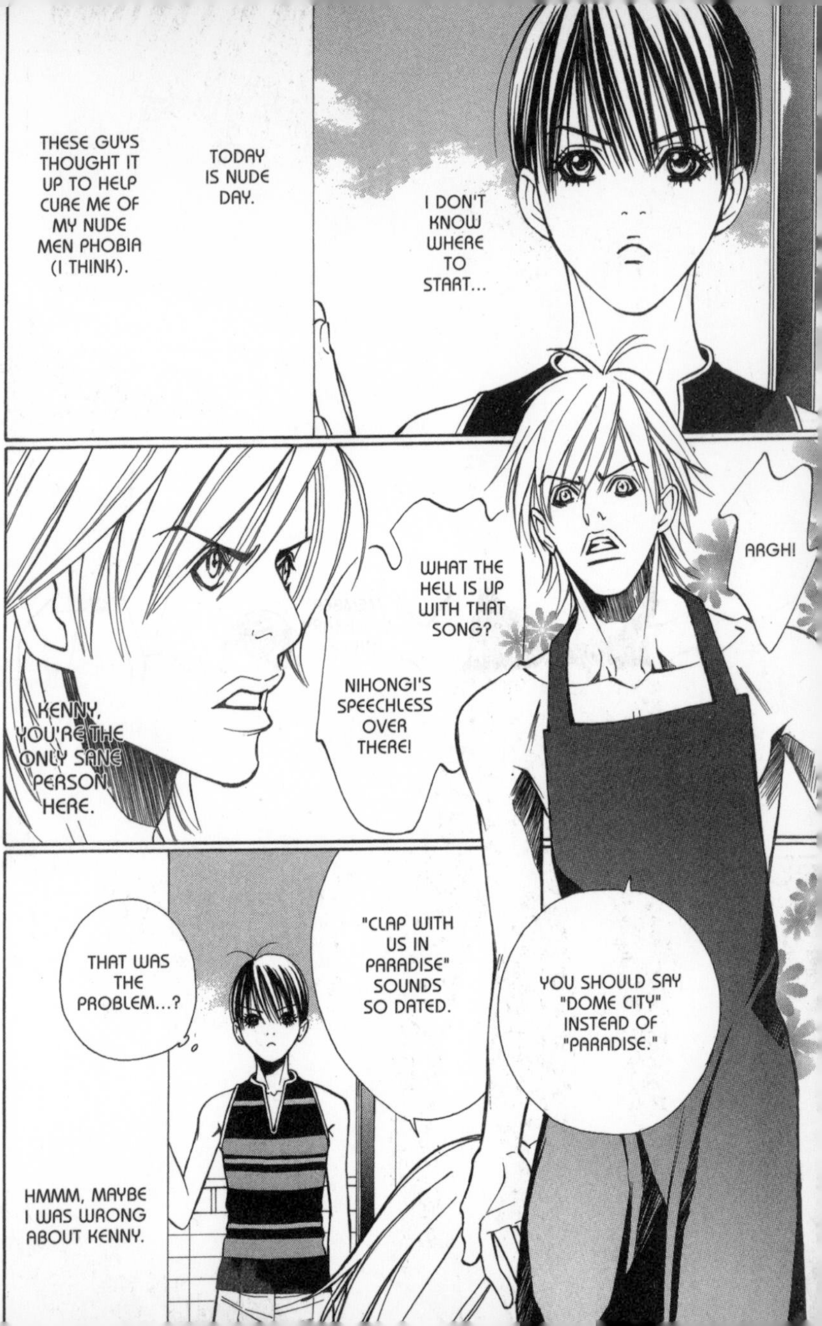
I DON'T KNOW WHERE TO START...
TODAY IS NUDE DAY.
THESE GUYS THOUGHT IT UP TO HELP CURE ME OF MY NUDE MEN PHOBIA (I THINK).
ARGH!
WHAT THE HELL IS UP WITH THAT SONG?
NIHONGI'S SPEECHLESS OVER THERE!
KENNY, YOU'RE THE ONLY SANE PERSON HERE.
YOU SHOULD SAY "DOME CITY" INSTEAD OF "PARADISE."
"CLAP WITH US IN PARADISE" SOUNDS SO DATED.
THAT WAS THE PROBLEM...?
HMMM, MAYBE I WAS WRONG ABOUT KENNY.

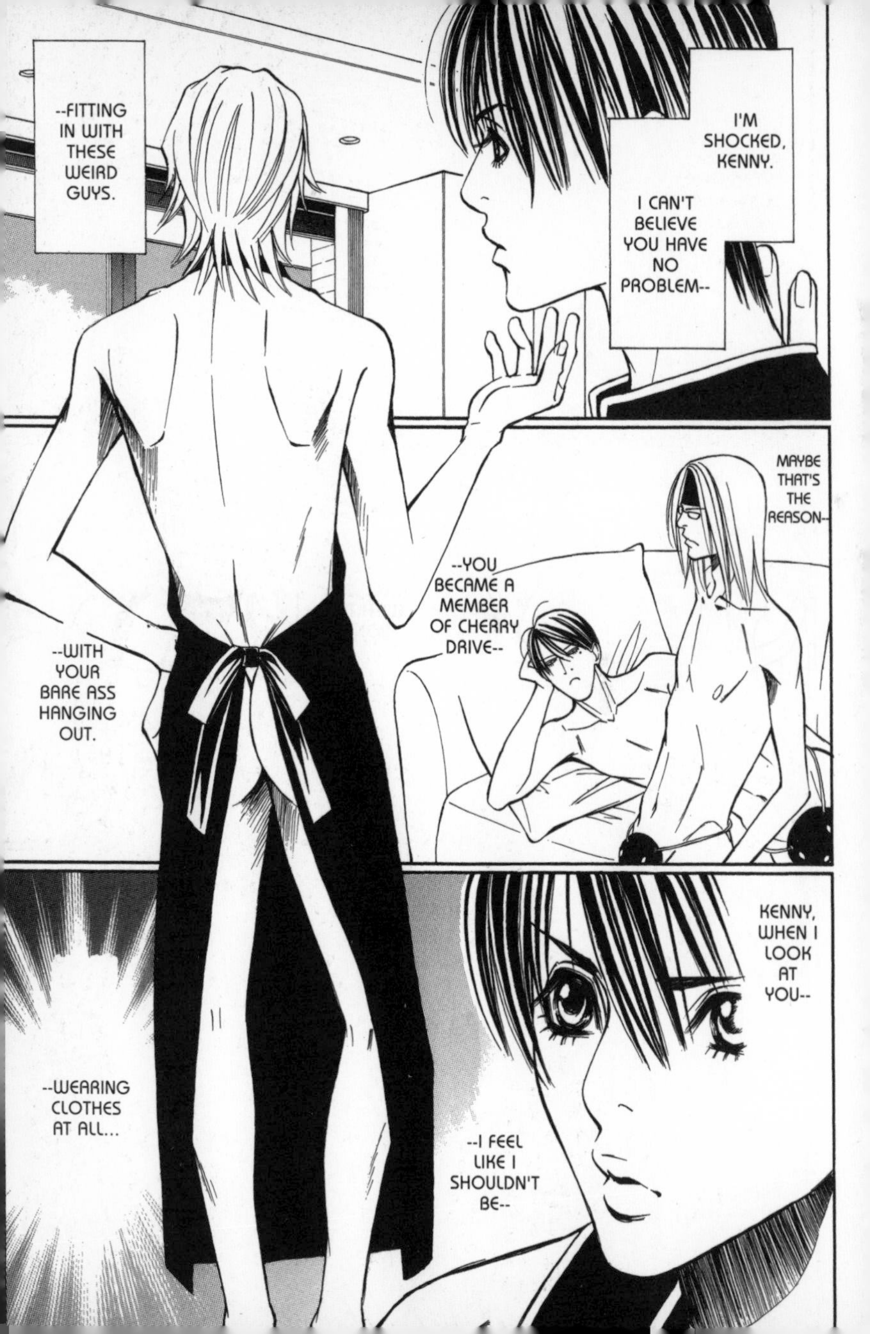
I'M SHOCKED, KENNY.
I CAN'T BELIEVE YOU HAVE NO PROBLEM--
--FITTING IN WITH THESE WEIRD GUYS.
MAYBE THAT'S THE REASON--
--YOU BECAME A MEMBER OF CHERRY DRIVE--
--WITH YOUR BARE ASS HANGING OUT.
KENNY, WHEN I LOOK AT YOU--
--I FEEL LIKE I SHOULDN'T BE--
--WEARING CLOTHES AT ALL...

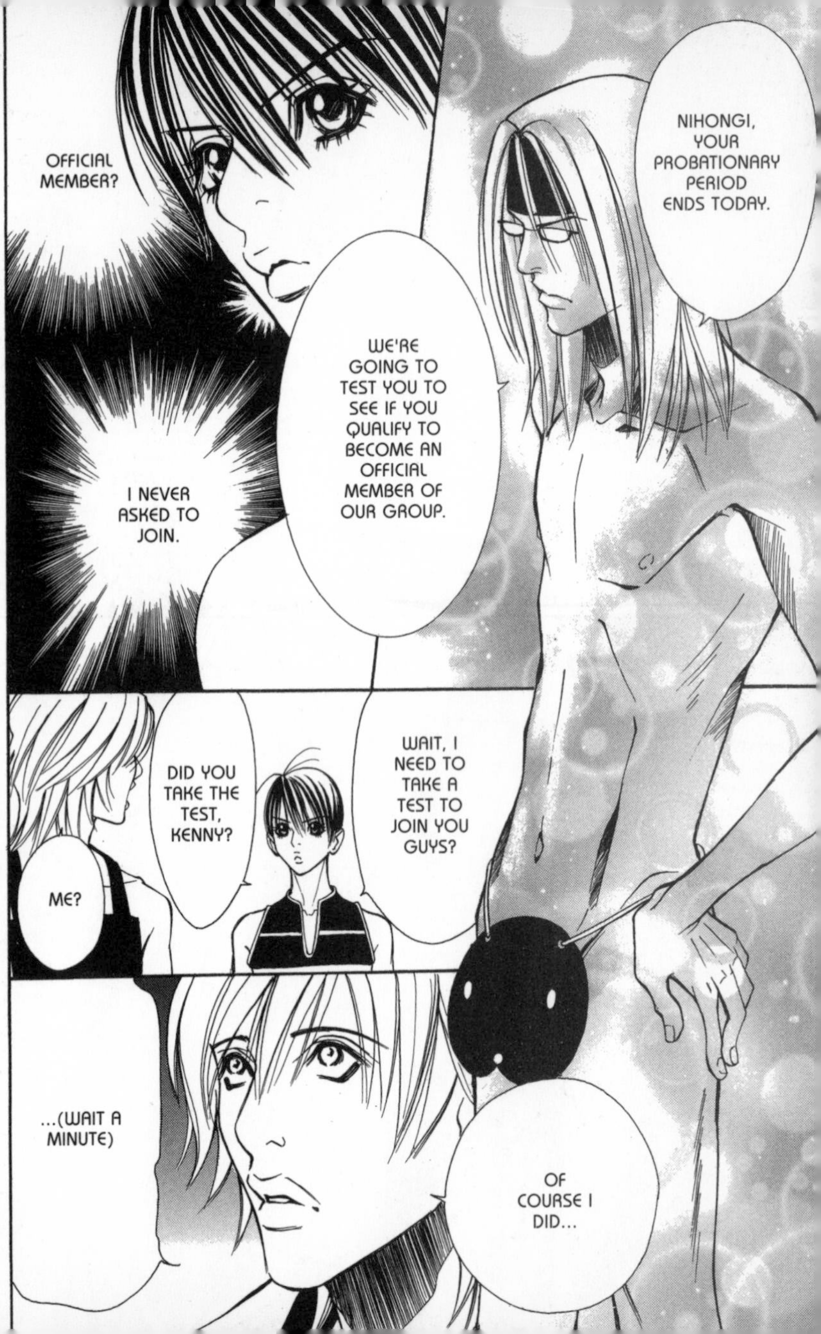
NIHONGI, YOUR PROBATIONARY PERIOD ENDS TODAY.
WE'RE GOING TO TEST YOU TO SEE IF YOU QUALIFY TO BECOME AN OFFICIAL MEMBER OF OUR GROUP.
OFFICIAL MEMBER?
I NEVER ASKED TO JOIN.
WAIT, I NEED TO TAKE A TEST TO JOIN YOU GUYS?
DID YOU TAKE THE TEST, KENNY?
ME?
OF COURSE I DID...
...(WAIT A MINUTE)

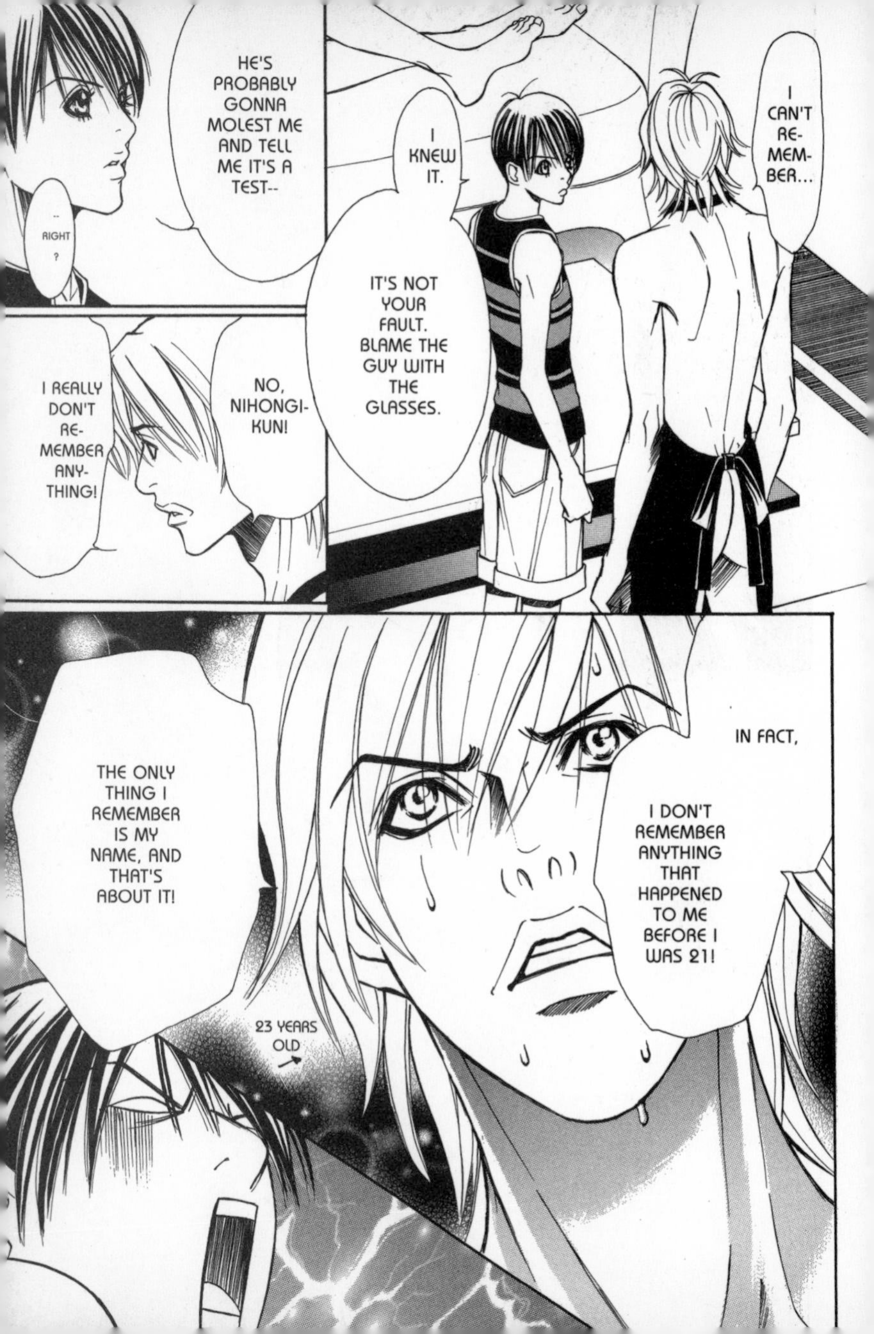
I CAN'T RE-MEM-BER...
I KNEW IT.
IT'S NOT YOUR FAULT. BLAME THE GUY WITH THE GLASSES.
HE'S PROBABLY GONNA MOLEST ME AND TELL ME IT'S A TEST--
--RIGHT?
NO, NIHONGI-KUN!
I REALLY DON'T RE-MEMBER ANY-THING!
IN FACT,
I DON'T REMEMBER ANYTHING THAT HAPPENED TO ME BEFORE I WAS 21!
THE ONLY THING I REMEMBER IS MY NAME, AND THAT'S ABOUT IT!
23 YEARS OLD

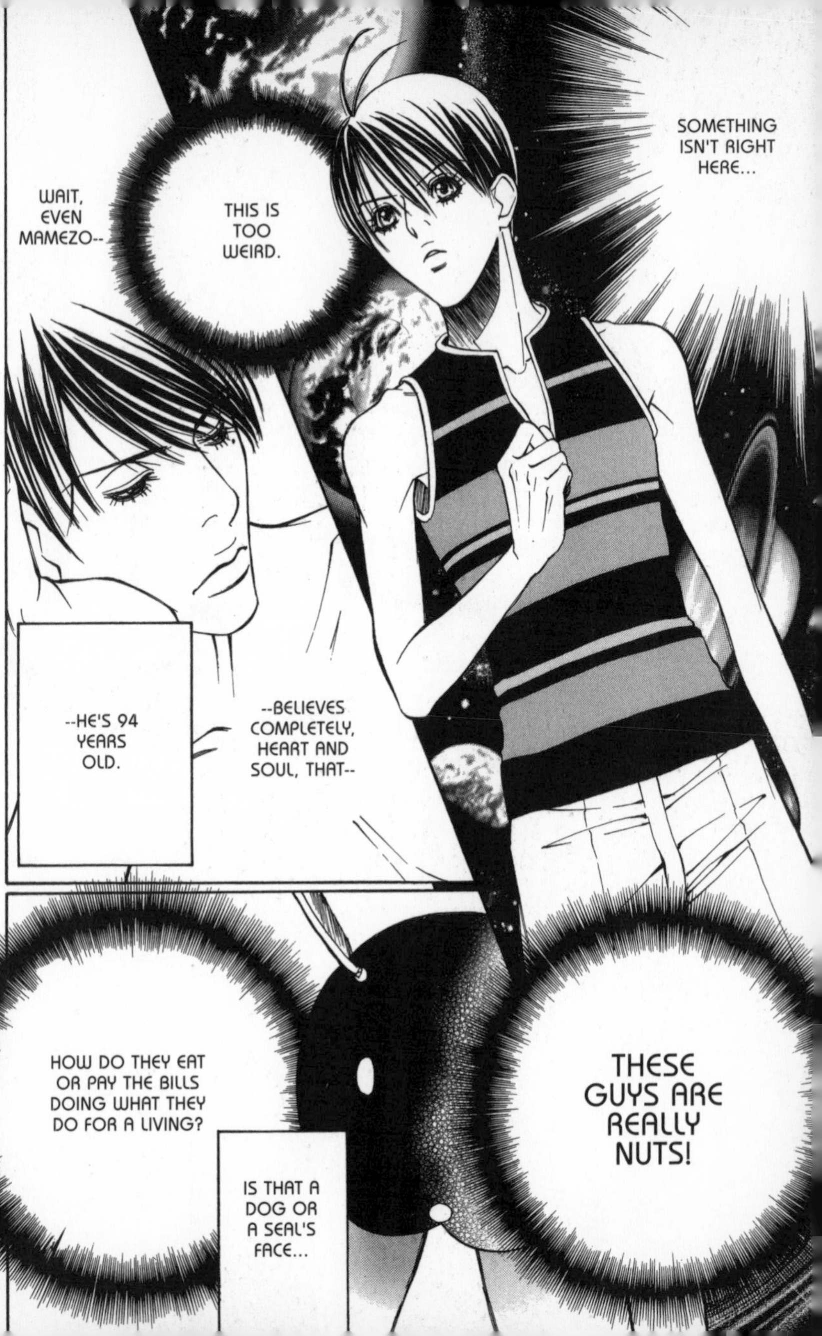
SOMETHING ISN'T RIGHT HERE...
THIS IS TOO WEIRD.
WAIT, EVEN MAMEZO--
--BELIEVES COMPLETELY, HEART AND SOUL, THAT--
--HE'S 94 YEARS OLD.
THESE GUYS ARE REALLY NUTS!
IS THAT A DOG OR A SEAL'S FACE...
HOW DO THEY EAT OR PAY THE BILLS DOING WHAT THEY DO FOR A LIVING?

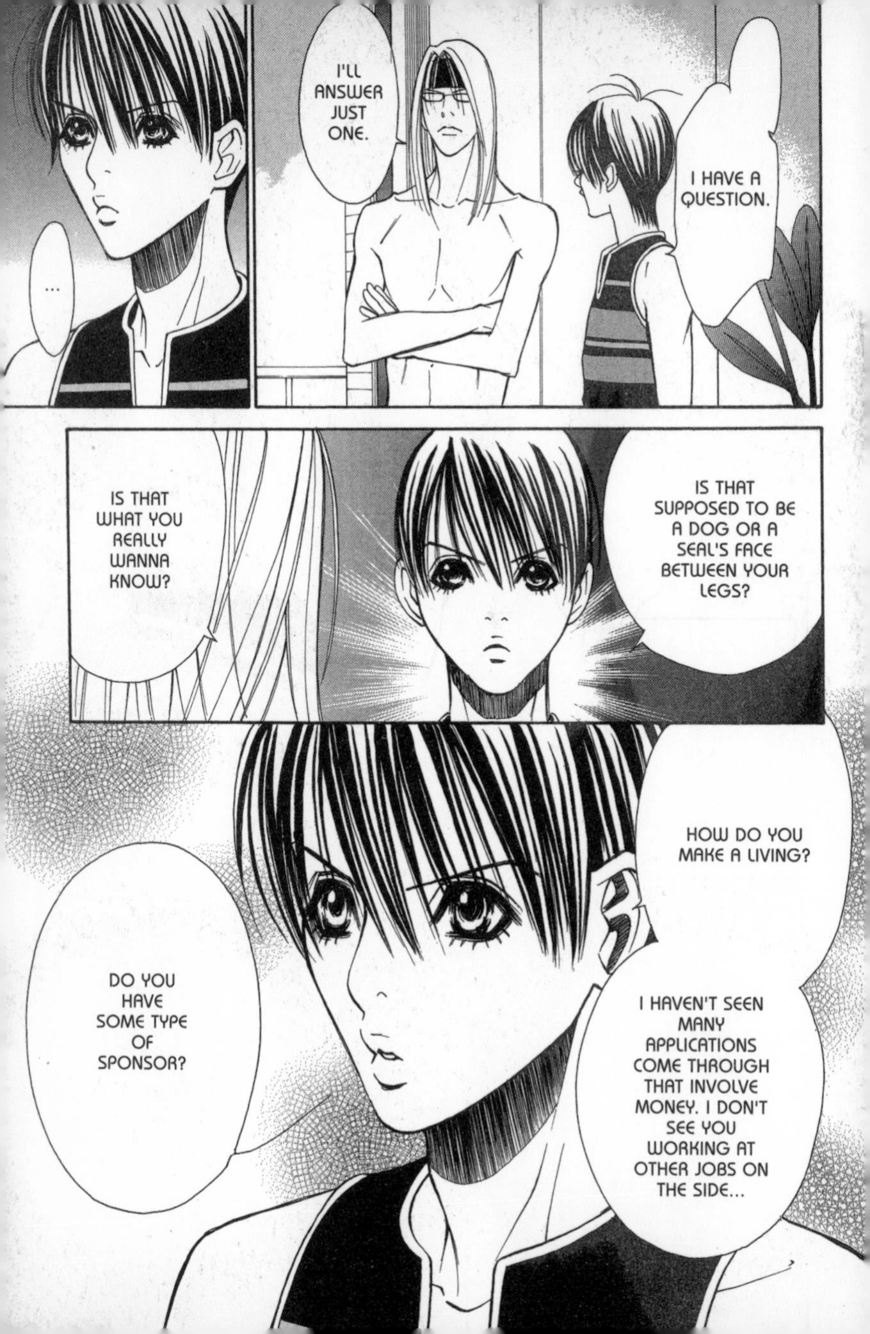
I HAVE A QUESTION.
I'LL ANSWER JUST ONE.
...
IS THAT SUPPOSED TO BE A DOG OR A SEAL'S FACE BETWEEN YOUR LEGS?
IS THAT WHAT YOU REALLY WANNA KNOW?
HOW DO YOU MAKE A LIVING?
I HAVEN'T SEEN MANY APPLICATIONS COME THROUGH THAT INVOLVE MONEY. I DON'T SEE YOU WORKING AT OTHER JOBS ON THE SIDE...
DO YOU HAVE SOME TYPE OF SPONSOR?

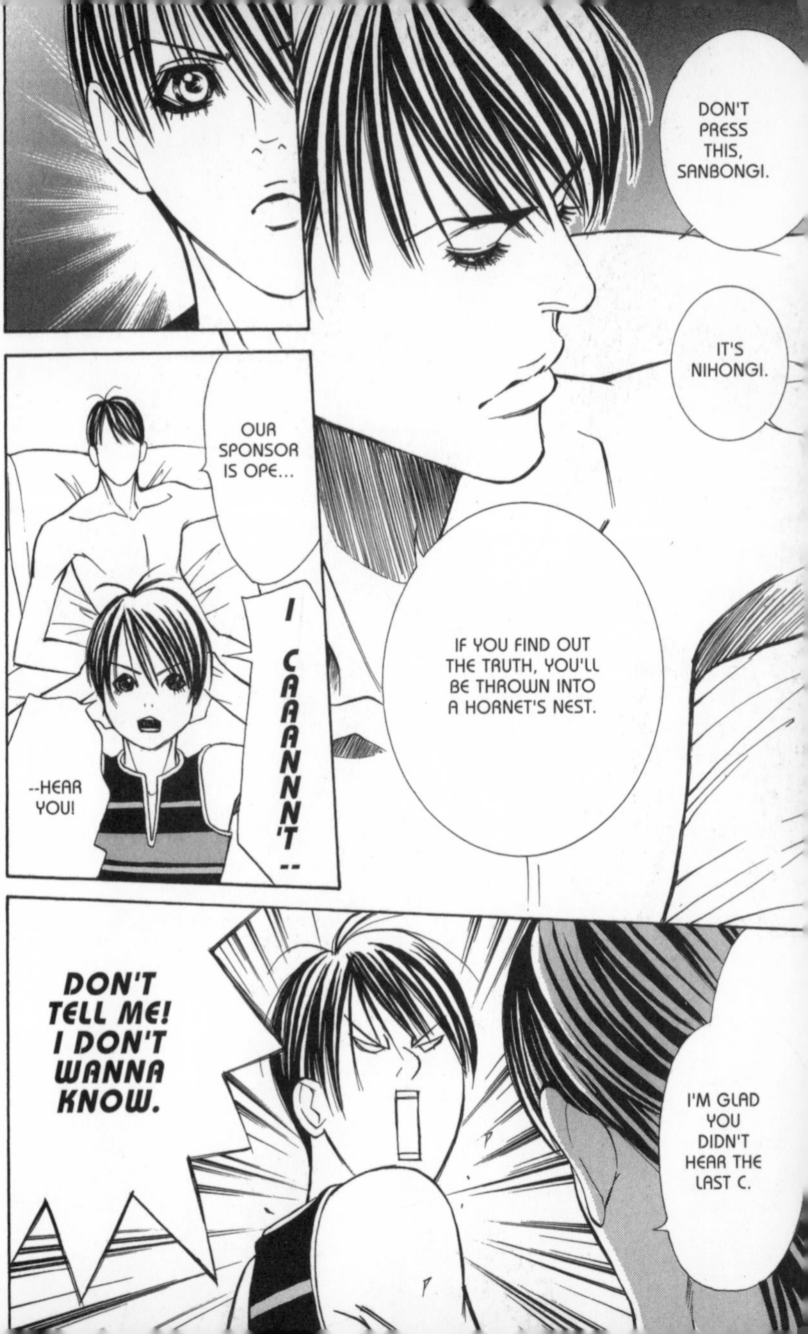
DON'T PRESS THIS, SANBONGI.
IT'S NIHONGI.
OUR SPONSOR IS OPE...
IF YOU FIND OUT THE TRUTH, YOU'LL BE THROWN INTO A HORNET'S NEST.
I CAAAANNNN'T--
--HEAR YOU!
I'M GLAD YOU DIDN'T HEAR THE LAST C.
DON'T TELL ME! I DON'T WANNA KNOW.

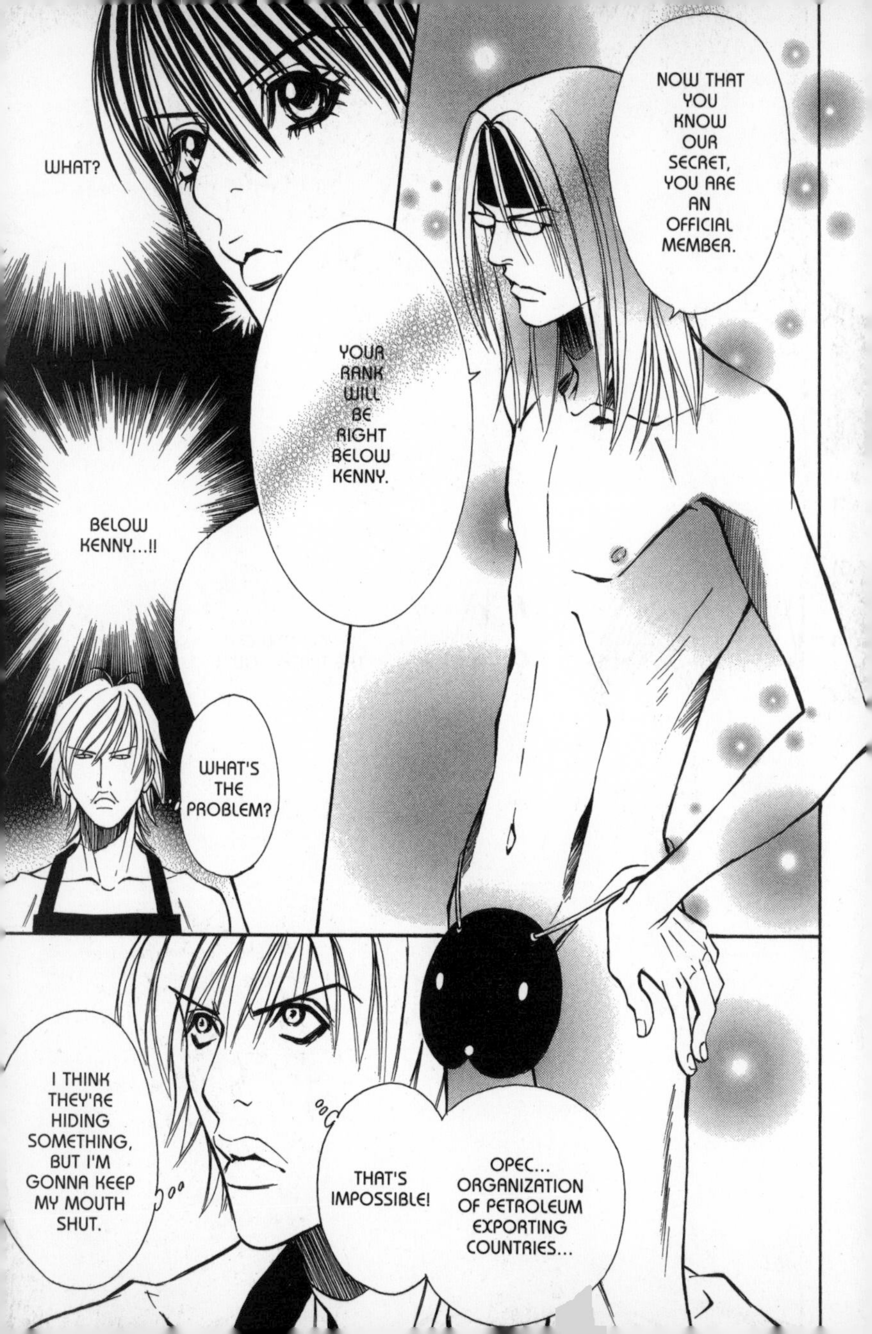
NOW THAT YOU KNOW OUR SECRET, YOU ARE AN OFFICIAL MEMBER.
YOUR RANK WILL BE RIGHT BELOW KENNY.
WHAT?
BELOW KENNY...!!
WHAT'S THE PROBLEM?
OPEC... ORGANIZATION OF PETROLEUM EXPORTING COUNTRIES...
THAT'S IMPOSSIBLE!
I THINK THEY'RE HIDING SOMETHING, BUT I'M GONNA KEEP MY MOUTH SHUT.

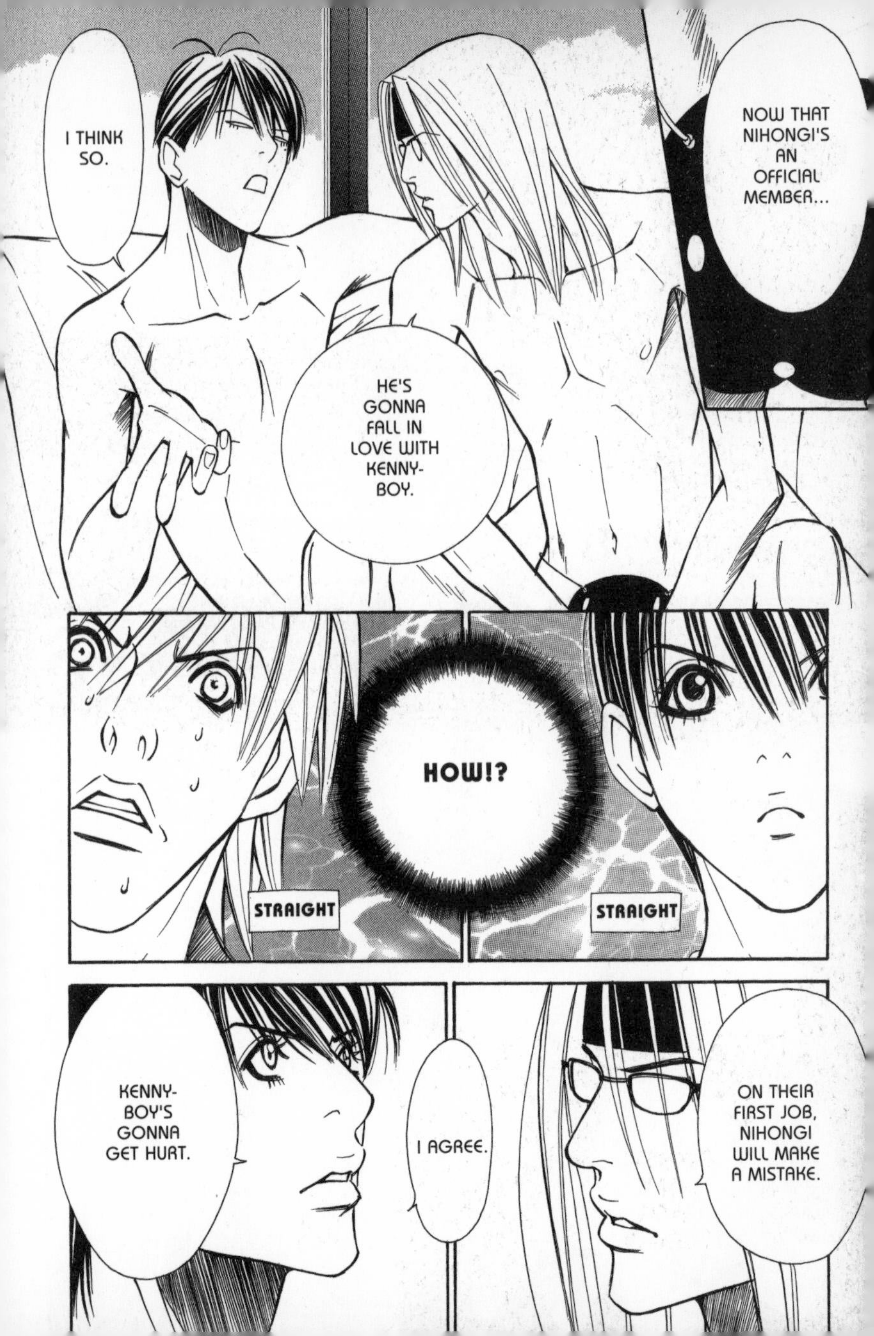
NOW THAT NIHONGI'S AN OFFICIAL MEMBER...
HE'S GONNA FALL IN LOVE WITH KENNY-BOY.
I THINK SO.
HOW!?
STRAIGHT
STRAIGHT
ON THEIR FIRST JOB, NIHONGI WILL MAKE A MISTAKE.
I AGREE.
KENNY-BOY'S GONNA GET HURT.

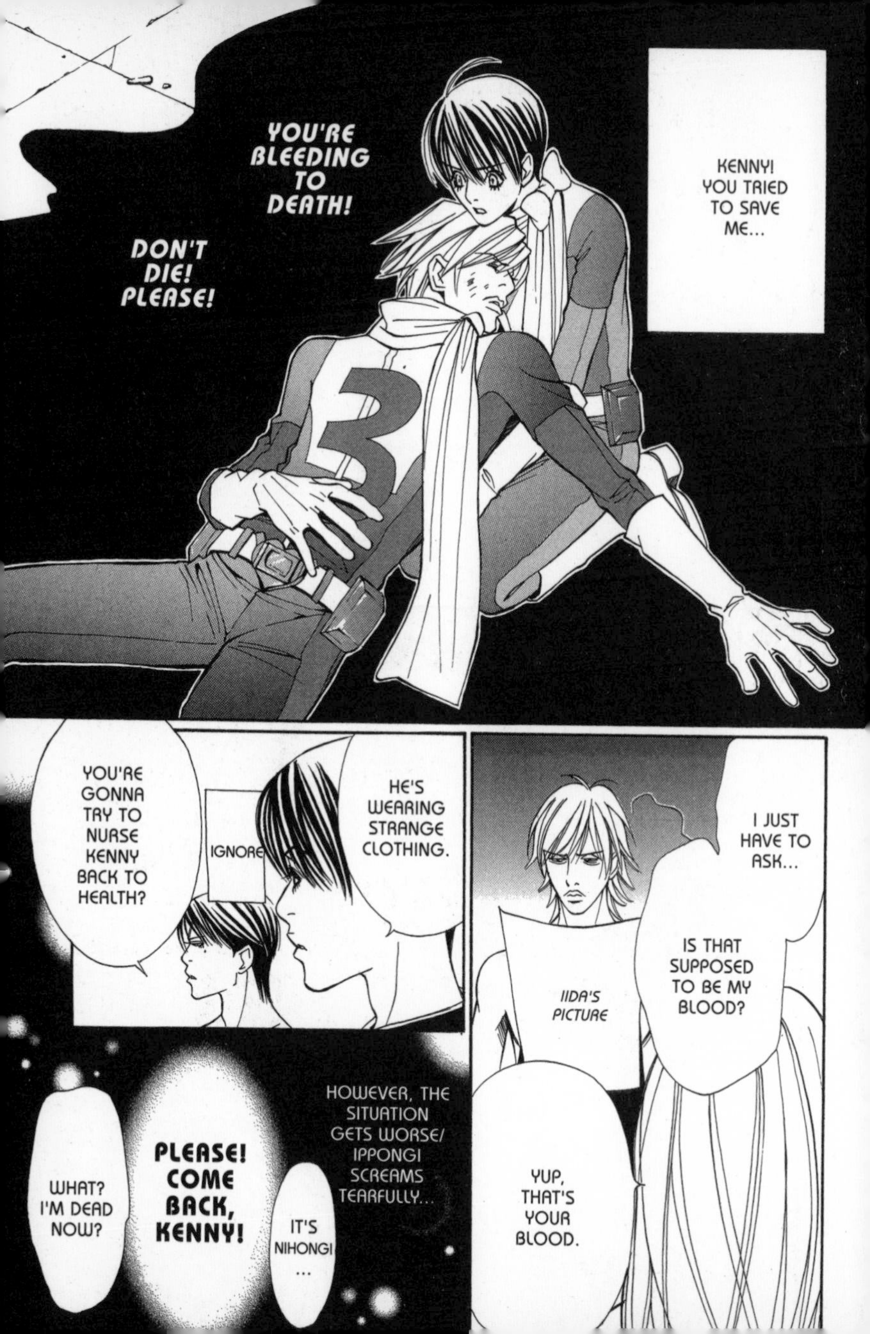
KENNY! YOU TRIED TO SAVE ME...
YOU'RE BLEEDING TO DEATH!
DON'T DIE! PLEASE!
I JUST HAVE TO ASK...
IS THAT SUPPOSED TO BE MY BLOOD?
IIDA'S PICTURE
YUP, THAT'S YOUR BLOOD.
HE'S WEARING STRANGE CLOTHING.
IGNORE
YOU'RE GONNA TRY TO NURSE KENNY BACK TO HEALTH?
HOWEVER, THE SITUATION GETS WORSE/ IPPONGI SCREAMS TEARFULLY...
IT'S NIHONGI ...
PLEASE! COME BACK, KENNY!
WHAT? I'M DEAD NOW?

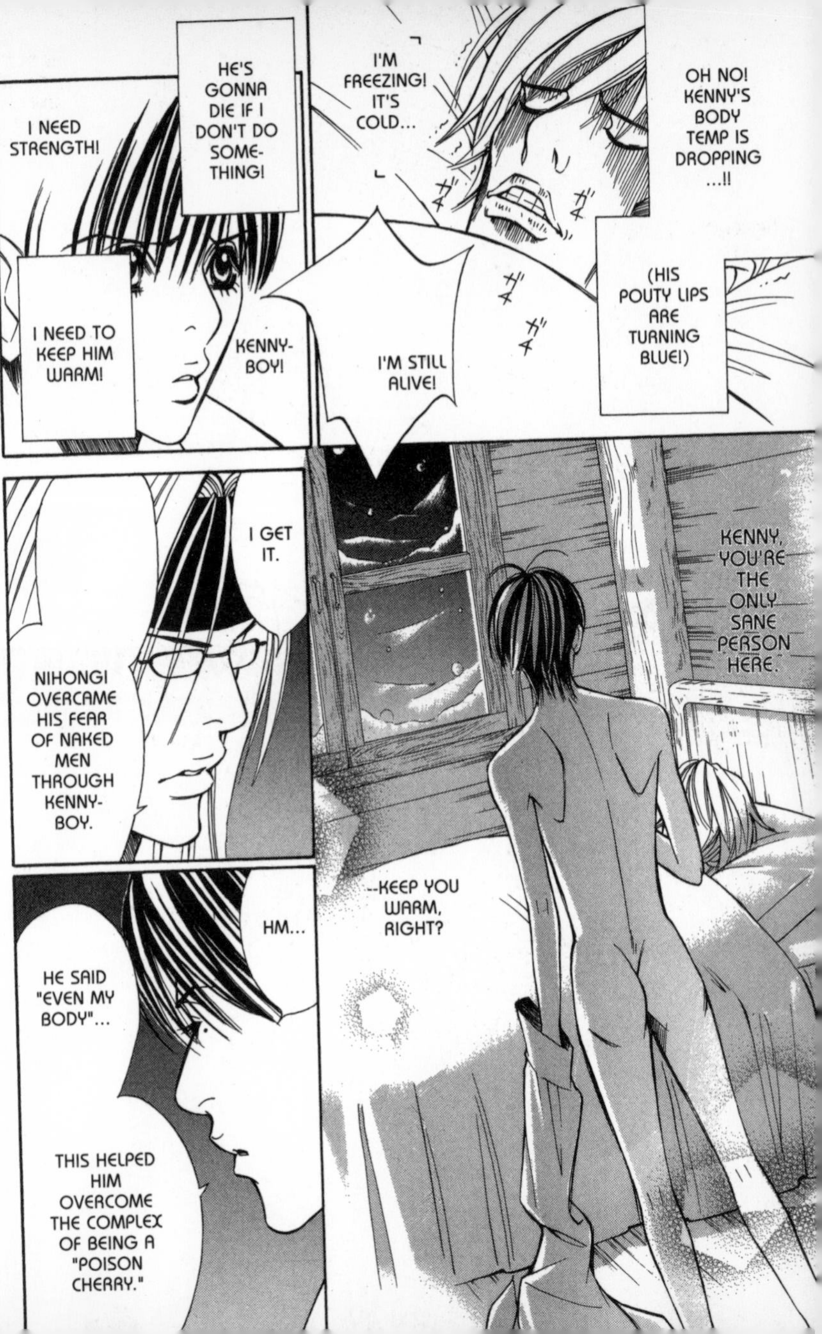
OH NO! KENNY'S BODY TEMP IS DROPPING ...!!
I'M FREEZING! IT'S COLD...
(HIS POUTY LIPS ARE TURNING BLUE!)
I'M STILL ALIVE!
HE'S GONNA DIE IF I DON'T DO SOME-THING!
I NEED STRENGTH!
KENNY-BOY!
I NEED TO KEEP HIM WARM!
KENNY, YOU'RE THE ONLY SANE PERSON HERE.
--KEEP YOU WARM, RIGHT?
I GET IT.
NIHONGI OVERCAME HIS FEAR OF NAKED MEN THROUGH KENNY-BOY.
HM...
HE SAID "EVEN MY BODY"...
THIS HELPED HIM OVERCOME THE COMPLEX OF BEING A "POISON CHERRY."

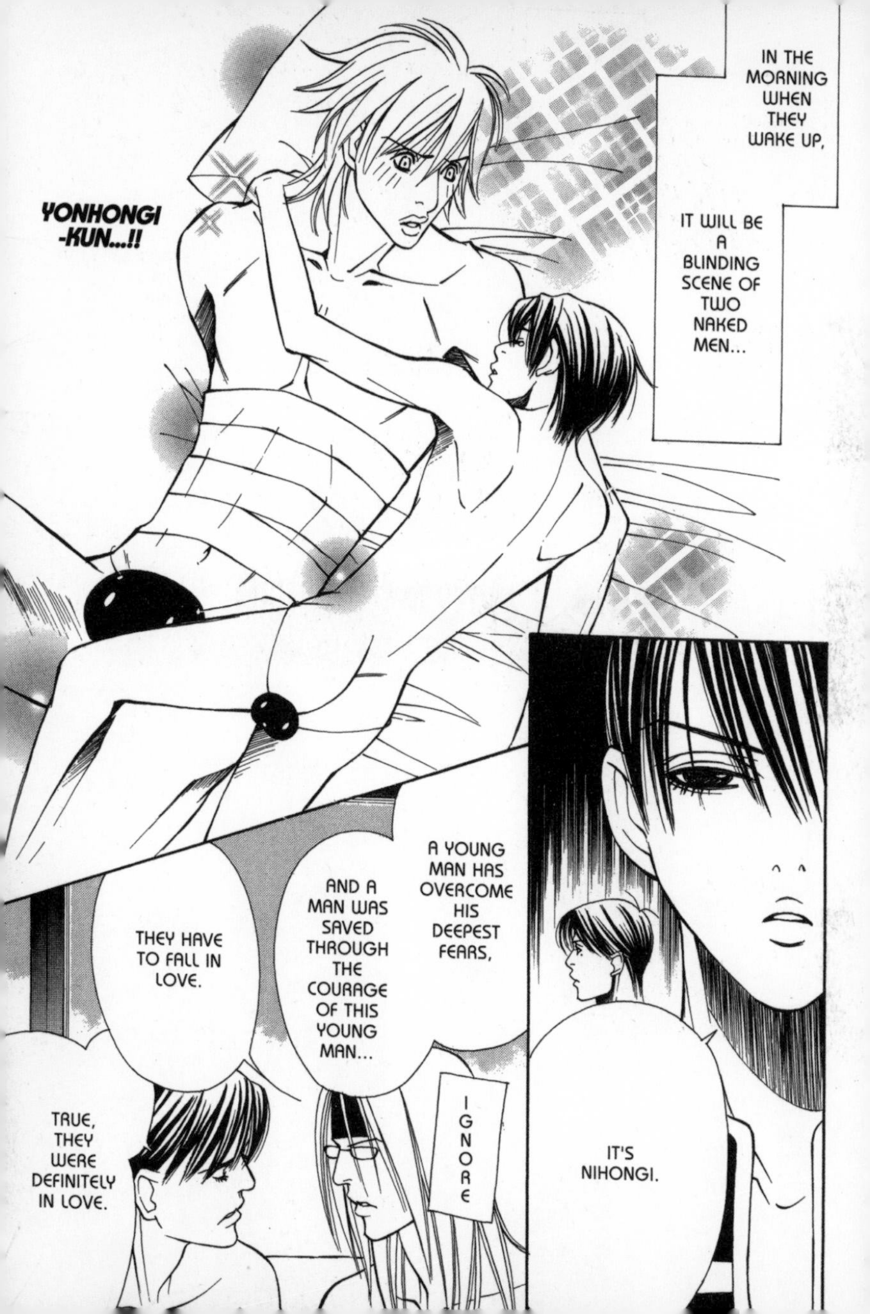
IN THE MORNING WHEN THEY WAKE UP,
IT WILL BE A BLINDING SCENE OF TWO NAKED MEN...
YONHONGI -KUN...!!
IT'S NIHONGI.
A YOUNG MAN HAS OVERCOME HIS DEEPEST FEARS,
AND A MAN WAS SAVED THROUGH THE COURAGE OF THIS YOUNG MAN...
THEY HAVE TO FALL IN LOVE.
IGNORE
TRUE, THEY WERE DEFINITELY IN LOVE.

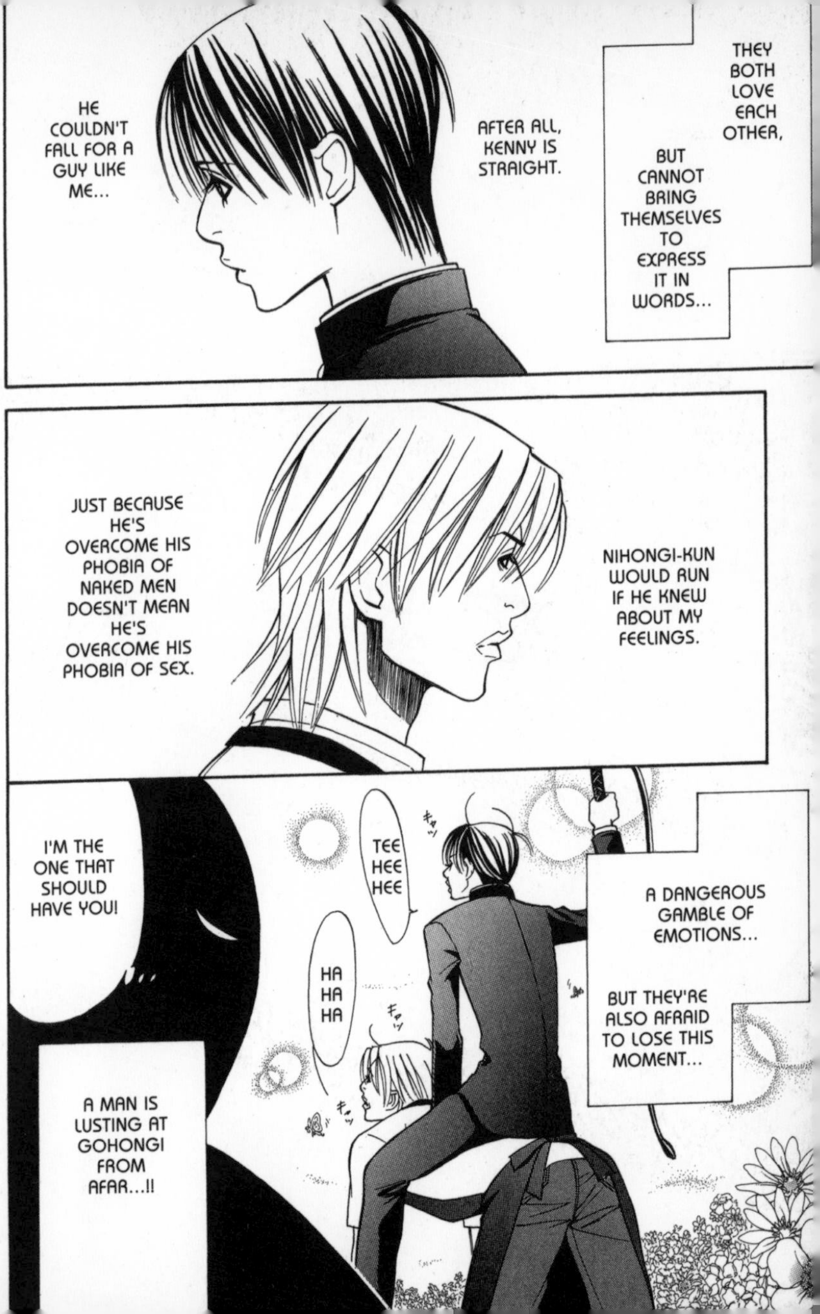
THEY BOTH LOVE EACH OTHER,
BUT CANNOT BRING THEMSELVES TO EXPRESS IT IN WORDS...
AFTER ALL, KENNY IS STRAIGHT.
HE COULDN'T FALL FOR A GUY LIKE ME...
NIHONGI-KUN WOULD RUN IF HE KNEW ABOUT MY FEELINGS.
JUST BECAUSE HE'S OVERCOME HIS PHOBIA OF NAKED MEN DOESN'T MEAN HE'S OVERCOME HIS PHOBIA OF SEX.
A DANGEROUS GAMBLE OF EMOTIONS...
BUT THEY'RE ALSO AFRAID TO LOSE THIS MOMENT...
TEE HEE HEE
HA HA HA
I'M THE ONE THAT SHOULD HAVE YOU!
A MAN IS LUSTING AT GOHONGI FROM AFAR...!!

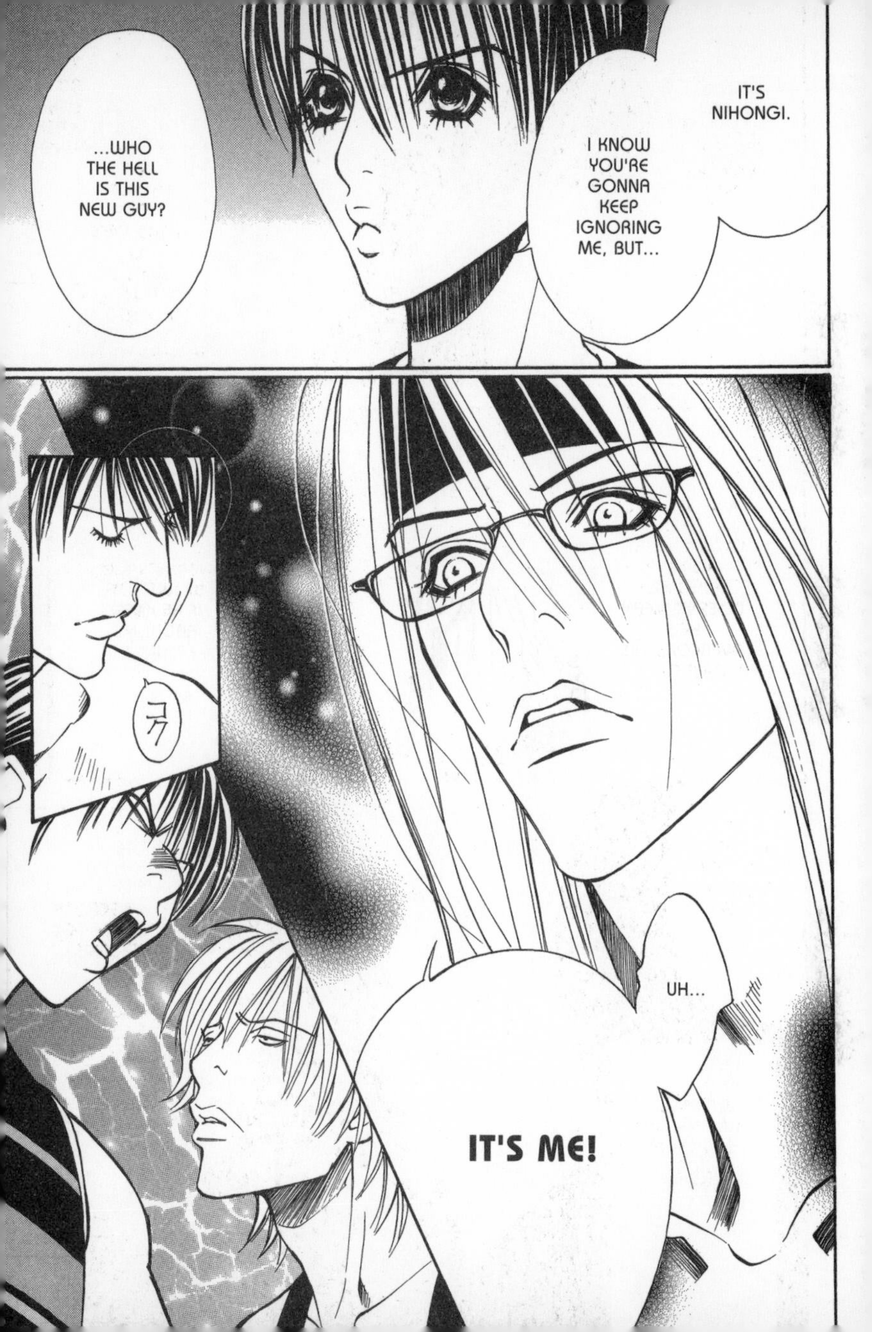
IT'S NIHONGI.
I KNOW YOU'RE GONNA KEEP IGNORING ME, BUT...
...WHO THE HELL IS THIS NEW GUY?
UH...
IT'S ME!
コク

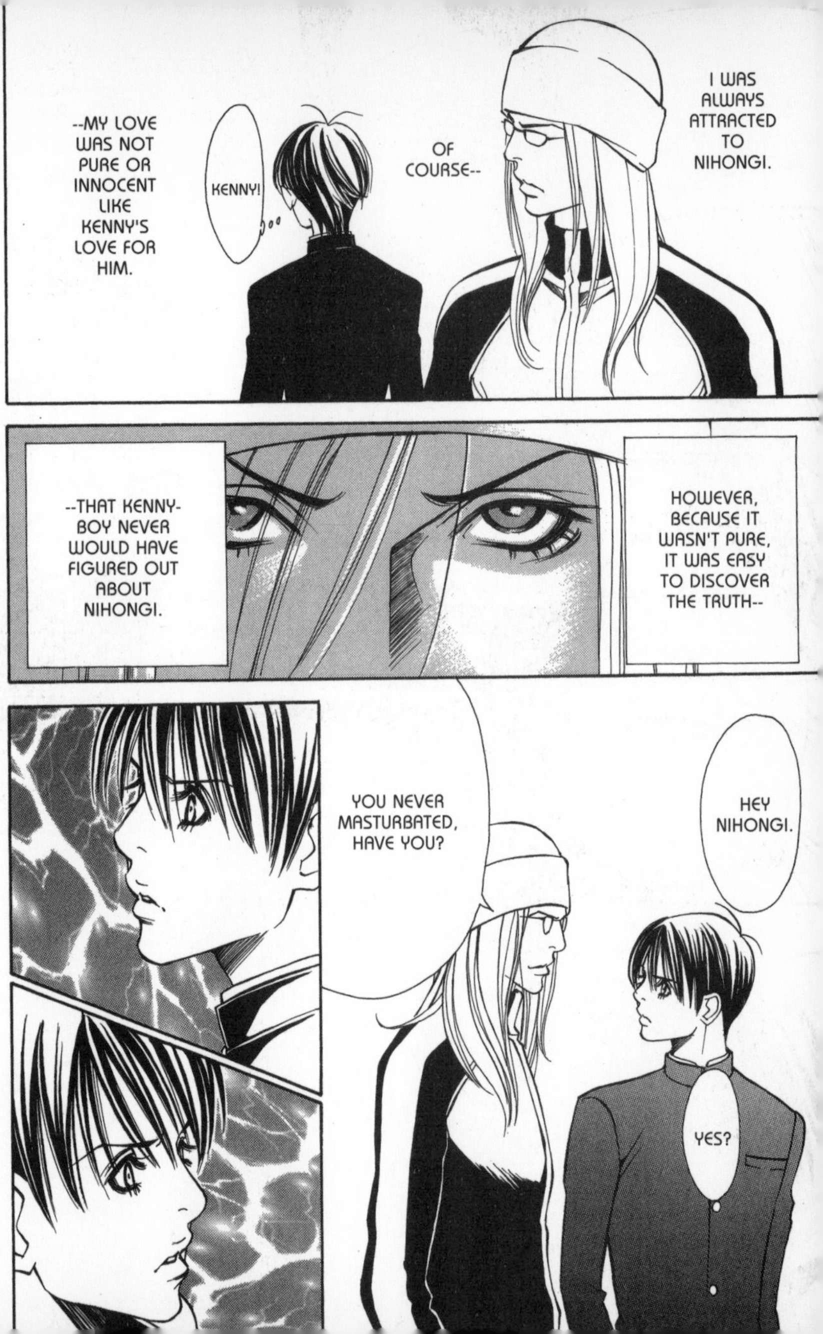
I WAS ALWAYS ATTRACTED TO NIHONGI.
OF COURSE--
KENNY!
--MY LOVE WAS NOT PURE OR INNOCENT LIKE KENNY'S LOVE FOR HIM.
HOWEVER, BECAUSE IT WASN'T PURE, IT WAS EASY TO DISCOVER THE TRUTH--
--THAT KENNY-BOY NEVER WOULD HAVE FIGURED OUT ABOUT NIHONGI.
HEY NIHONGI.
YES?
YOU NEVER MASTURBATED, HAVE YOU?

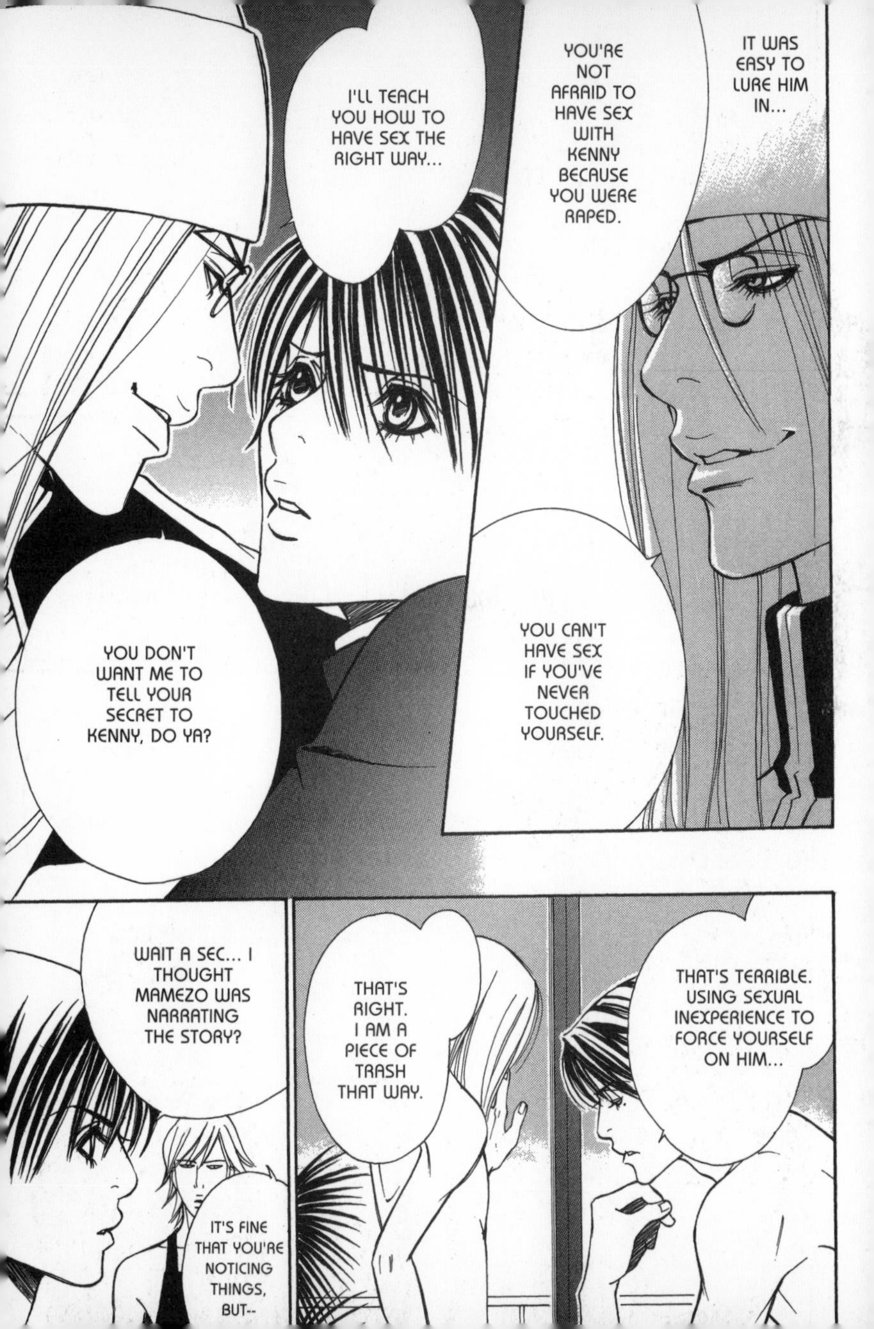
IT WAS EASY TO LURE HIM IN...
YOU'RE NOT AFRAID TO HAVE SEX WITH KENNY BECAUSE YOU WERE RAPED.
YOU CAN'T HAVE SEX IF YOU'VE NEVER TOUCHED YOURSELF.
I'LL TEACH YOU HOW TO HAVE SEX THE RIGHT WAY...
YOU DON'T WANT ME TO TELL YOUR SECRET TO KENNY, DO YA?
THAT'S TERRIBLE. USING SEXUAL INEXPERIENCE TO FORCE YOURSELF ON HIM...
THAT'S RIGHT. I AM A PIECE OF TRASH THAT WAY.
WAIT A SEC... I THOUGHT MAMEZO WAS NARRATING THE STORY?
IT'S FINE THAT YOU'RE NOTICING THINGS, BUT--

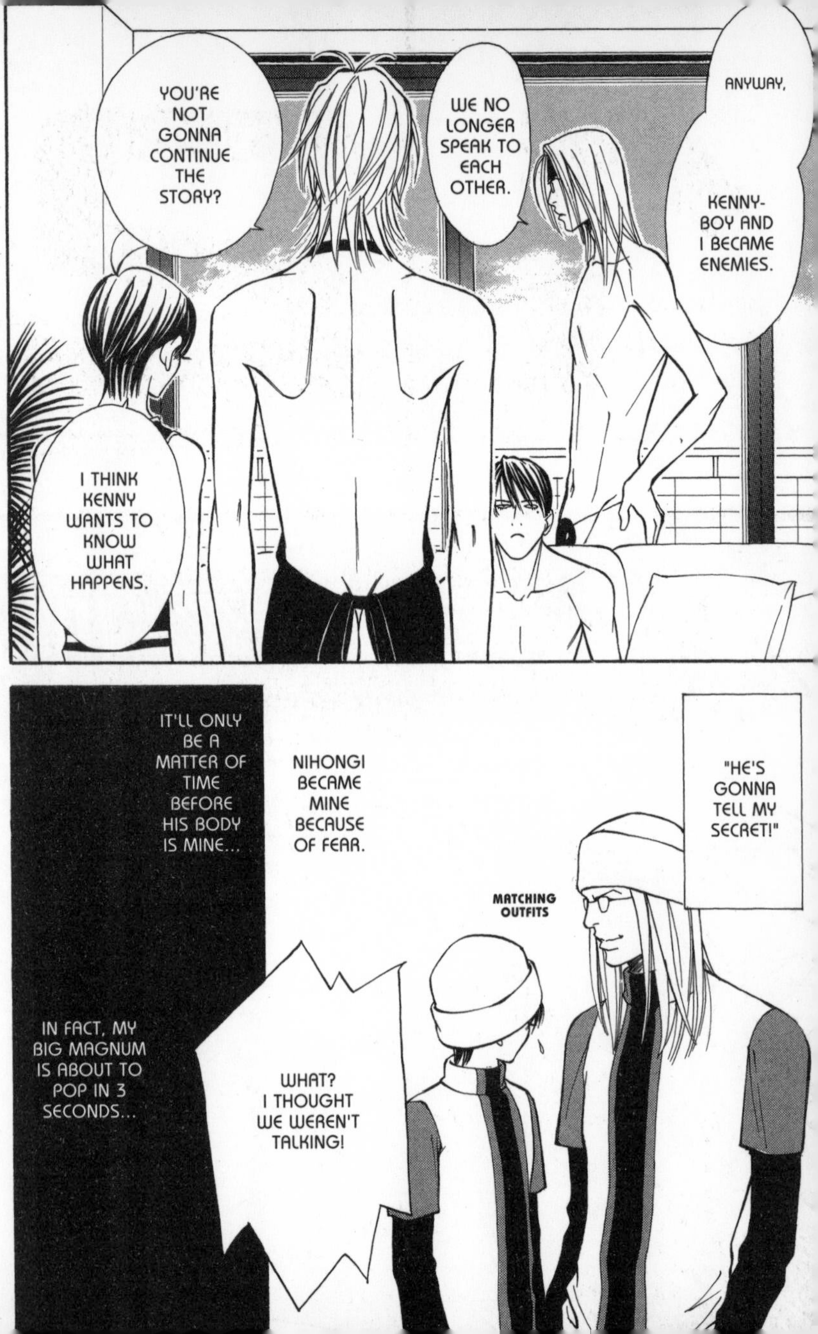
ANYWAY,
KENNY-BOY AND I BECAME ENEMIES.
WE NO LONGER SPEAK TO EACH OTHER.
YOU'RE NOT GONNA CONTINUE THE STORY?
I THINK KENNY WANTS TO KNOW WHAT HAPPENS.
"HE'S GONNA TELL MY SECRET!"
NIHONGI BECAME MINE BECAUSE OF FEAR.
IT'LL ONLY BE A MATTER OF TIME BEFORE HIS BODY IS MINE...
MATCHING OUTFITS
IN FACT, MY BIG MAGNUM IS ABOUT TO POP IN 3 SECONDS...
WHAT? I THOUGHT WE WEREN'T TALKING!

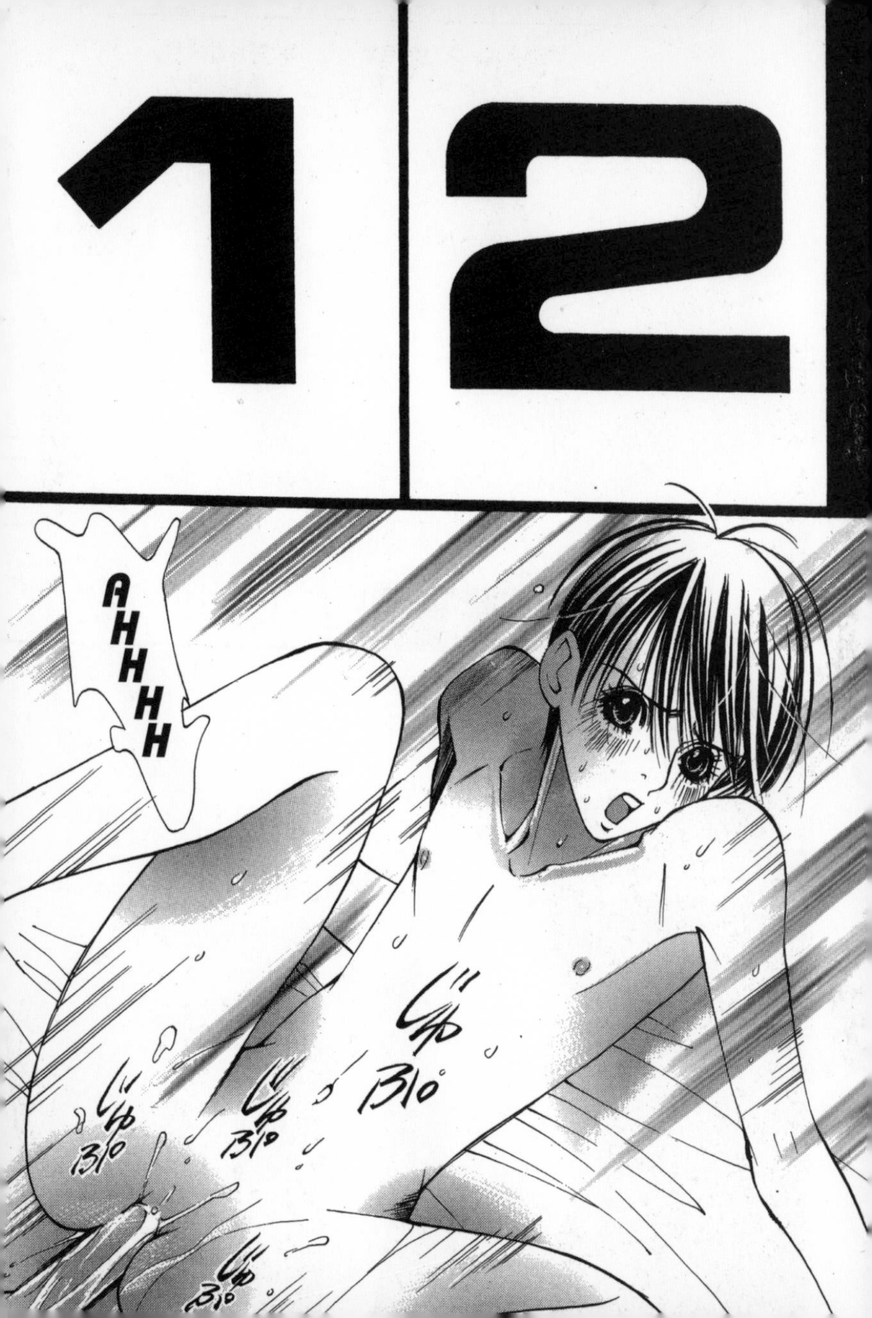
1
2
AHHHHH
じゅぶ
じゅぶ
じゅぶ
じゅぶ

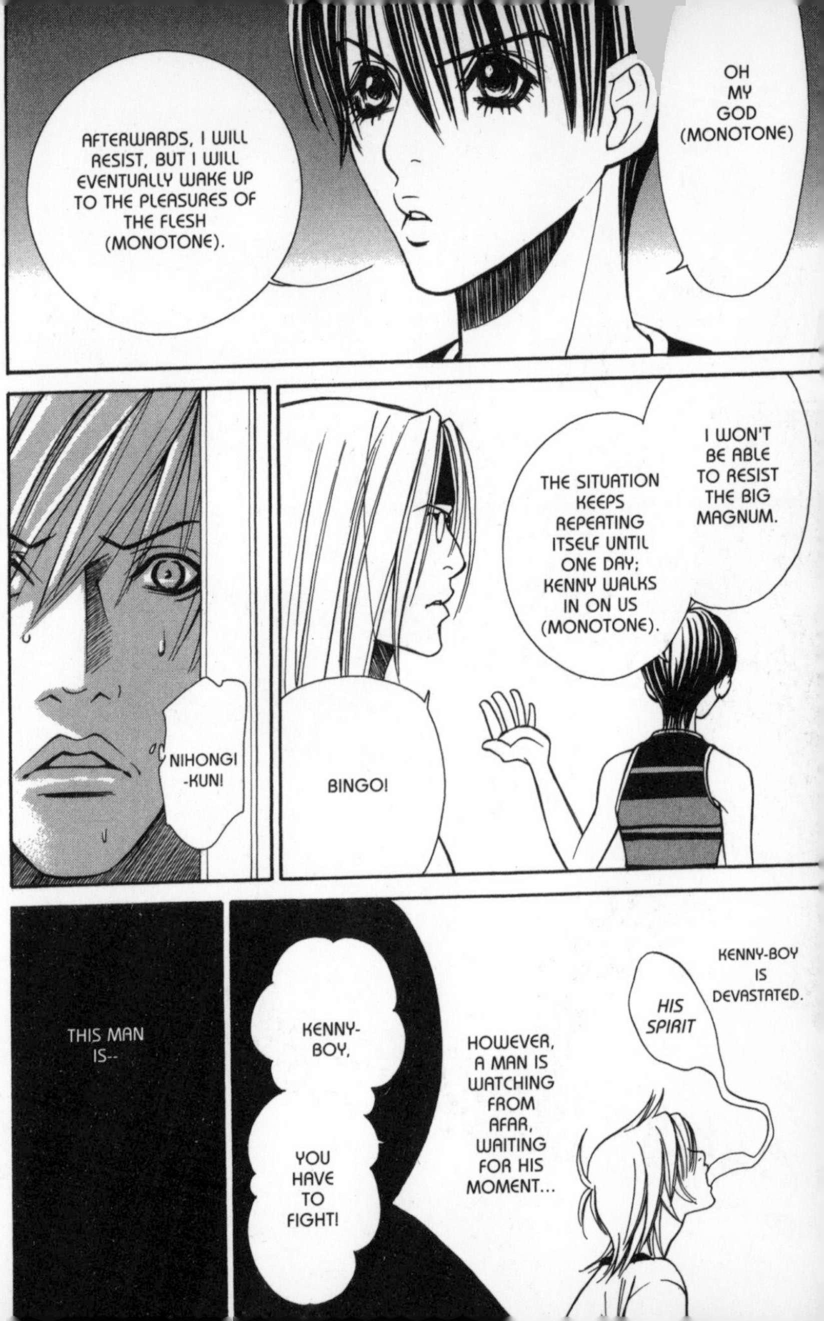
OH MY GOD (MONOTONE)
AFTERWARDS, I WILL RESIST, BUT I WILL EVENTUALLY WAKE UP TO THE PLEASURES OF THE FLESH (MONOTONE).
I WON'T BE ABLE TO RESIST THE BIG MAGNUM.
THE SITUATION KEEPS REPEATING ITSELF UNTIL ONE DAY; KENNY WALKS IN ON US (MONOTONE).
BINGO!
NIHONGI -KUN!
KENNY-BOY IS DEVASTATED.
HIS SPIRIT
HOWEVER, A MAN IS WATCHING FROM AFAR, WAITING FOR HIS MOMENT...
KENNY-BOY,
YOU HAVE TO FIGHT!
THIS MAN IS--

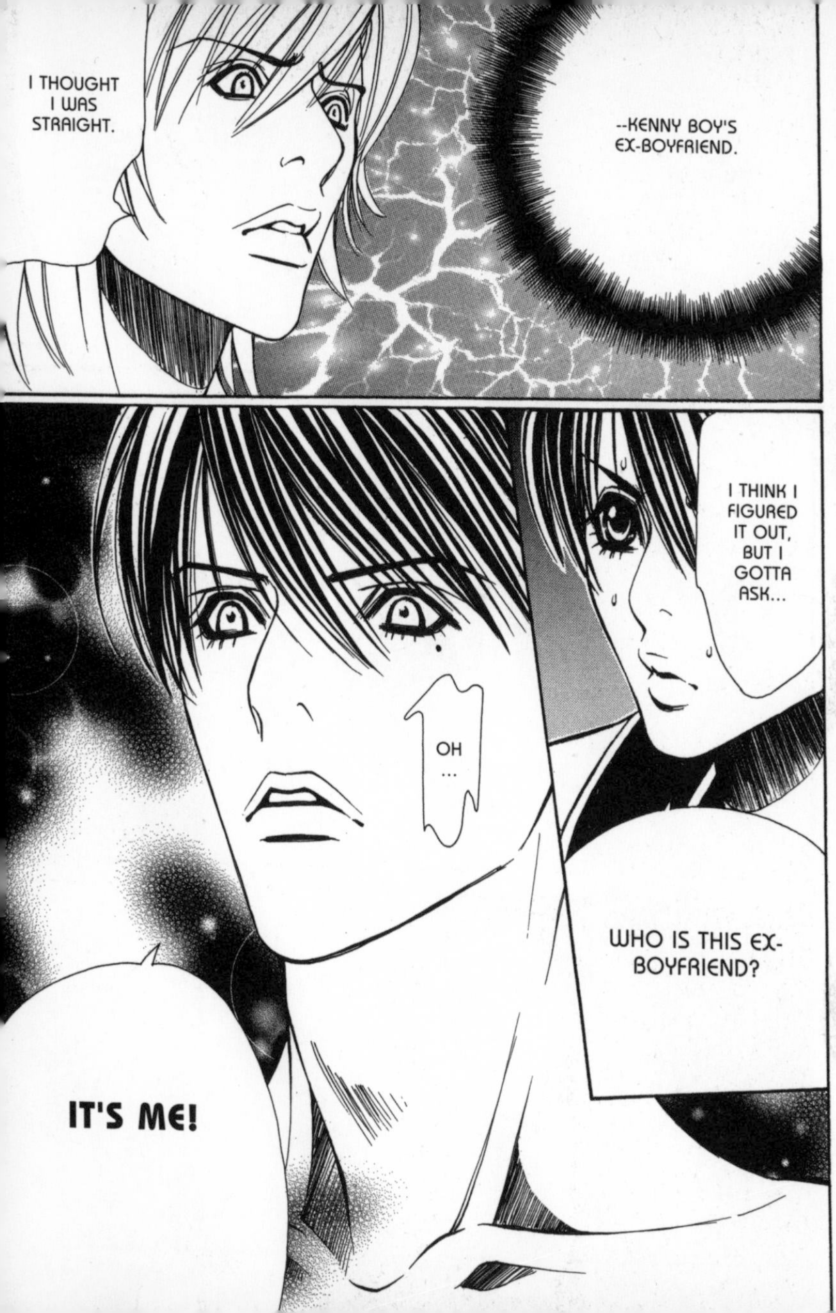
I THOUGHT I WAS STRAIGHT.
--KENNY BOY'S EX-BOYFRIEND.
I THINK I FIGURED IT OUT, BUT I GOTTA ASK...
WHO IS THIS EX-BOYFRIEND?
OH ...
IT'S ME!

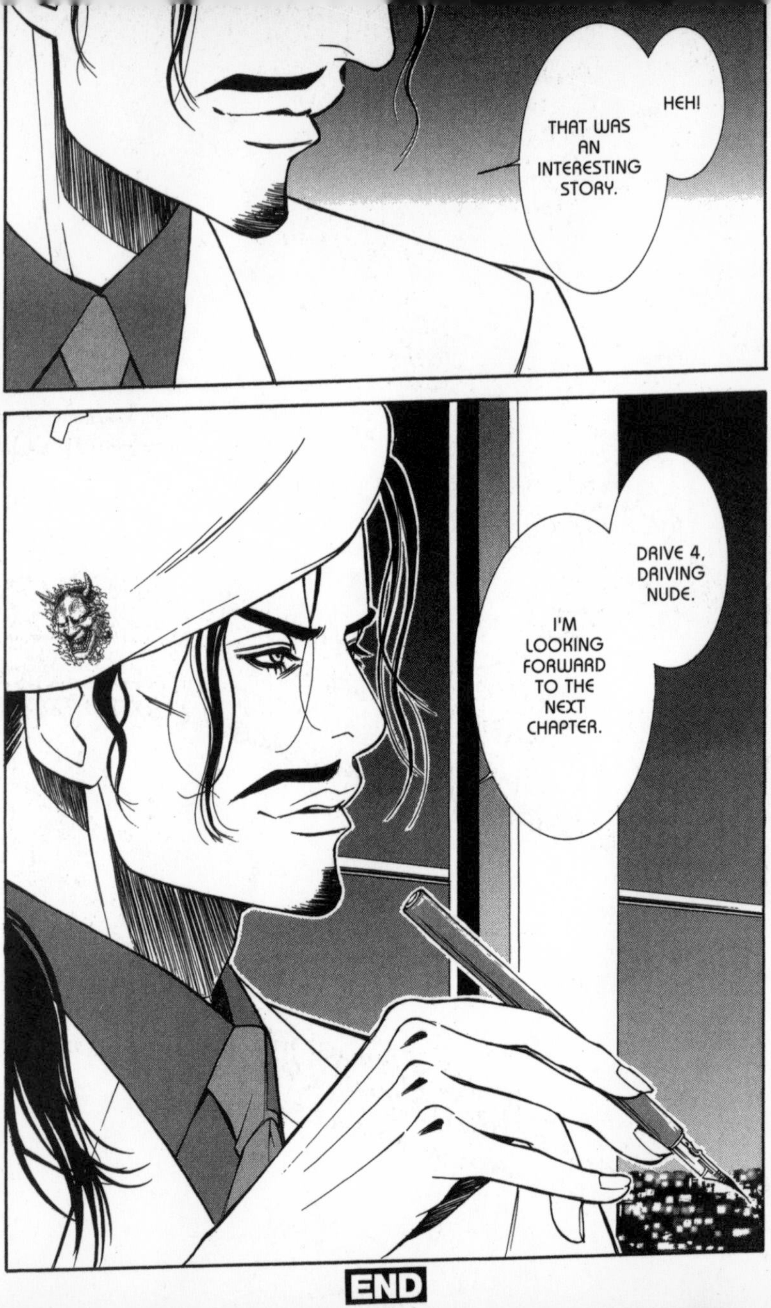
HEH!
THAT WAS AN INTERESTING STORY.
DRIVE 4, DRIVING NUDE.
I'M LOOKING FORWARD TO THE NEXT CHAPTER.

END

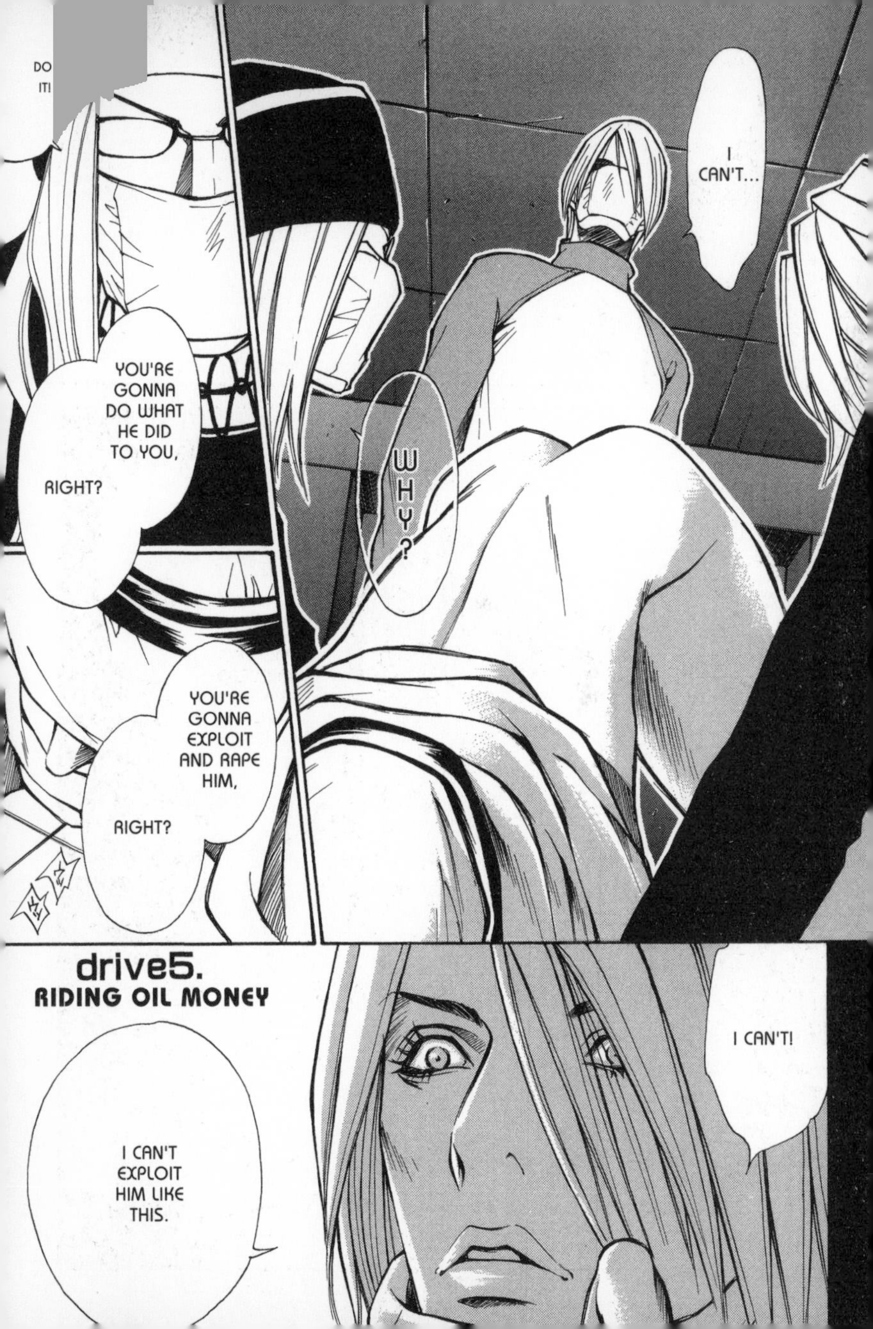
DO IT!
I CAN'T...
YOU'RE GONNA DO WHAT HE DID TO YOU, RIGHT?
WHY?
YOU'RE GONNA EXPLOIT AND RAPE HIM, RIGHT?
drive5.
RIDING OIL MONEY
I CAN'T!
I CAN'T EXPLOIT HIM LIKE THIS.

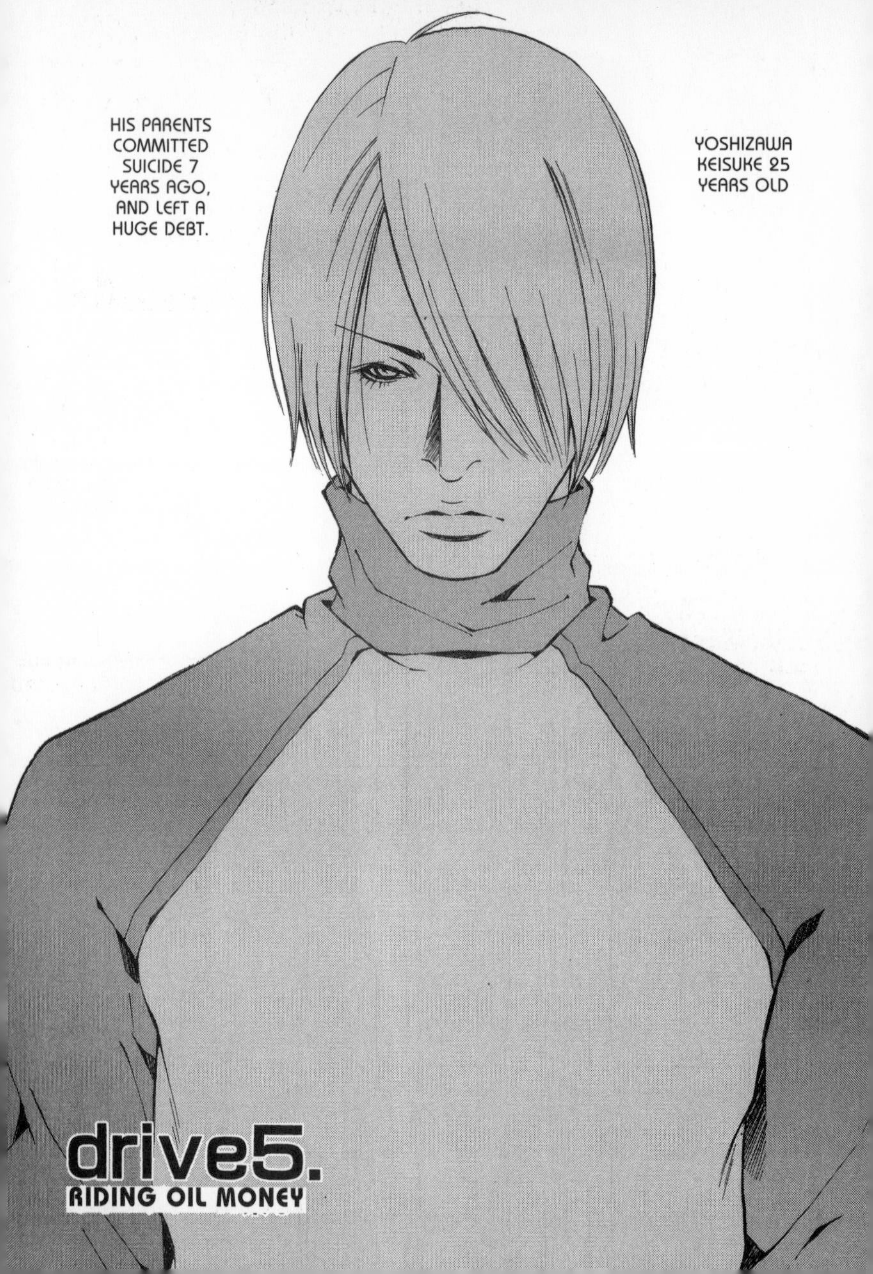
HIS PARENTS COMMITTED SUICIDE 7 YEARS AGO, AND LEFT A HUGE DEBT.
YOSHIZAWA KEISUKE 25 YEARS OLD
drive5.
RIDING OIL MONEY

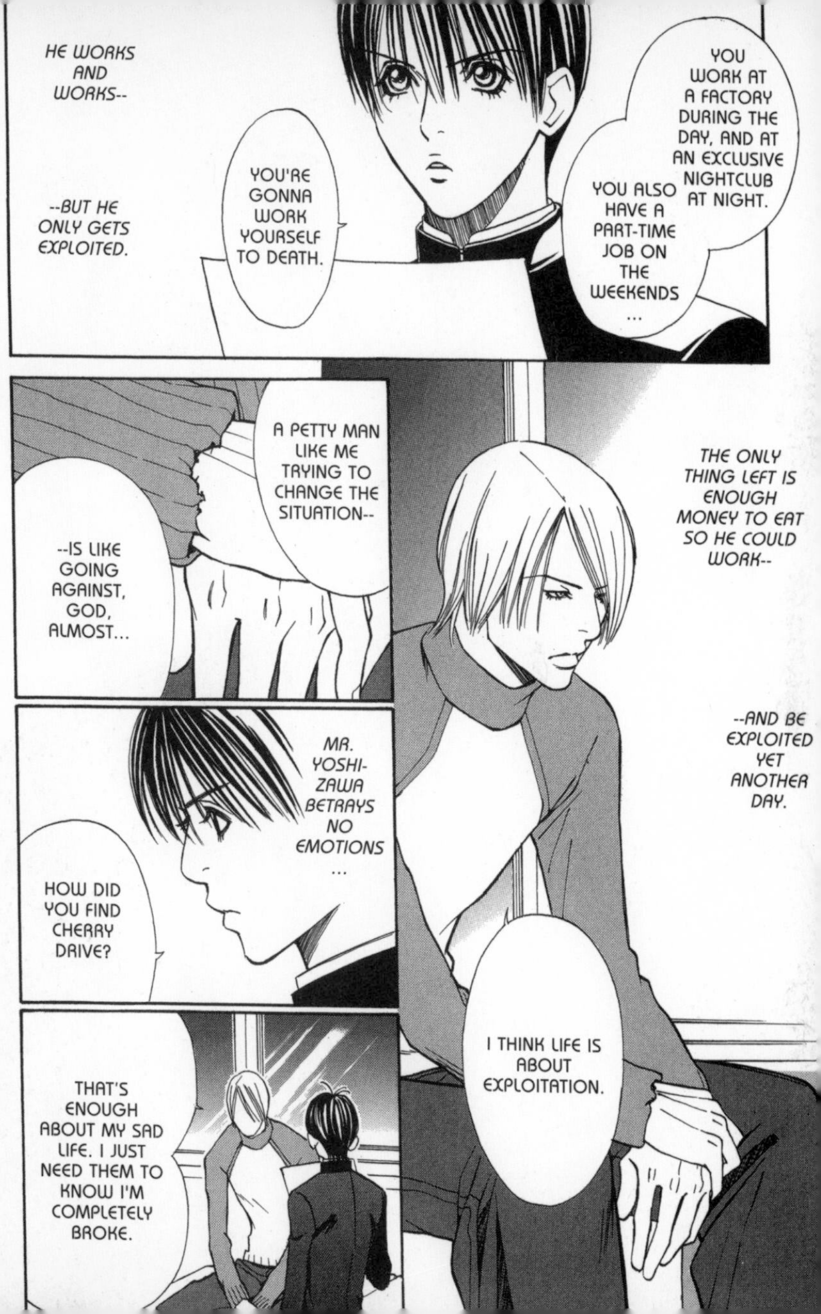
YOU WORK AT A FACTORY DURING THE DAY, AND AT AN EXCLUSIVE NIGHTCLUB AT NIGHT.
YOU ALSO HAVE A PART-TIME JOB ON THE WEEKENDS...
YOU'RE GONNA WORK YOURSELF TO DEATH.
HE WORKS AND WORKS--
--BUT HE ONLY GETS EXPLOITED.
THE ONLY THING LEFT IS ENOUGH MONEY TO EAT SO HE COULD WORK--
--AND BE EXPLOITED YET ANOTHER DAY.
A PETTY MAN LIKE ME TRYING TO CHANGE THE SITUATION--
--IS LIKE GOING AGAINST, GOD, ALMOST...
I THINK LIFE IS ABOUT EXPLOITATION.
MR. YOSHI-ZAWA BETRAYS NO EMOTIONS...
HOW DID YOU FIND CHERRY DRIVE?
THAT'S ENOUGH ABOUT MY SAD LIFE. I JUST NEED THEM TO KNOW I'M COMPLETELY BROKE.

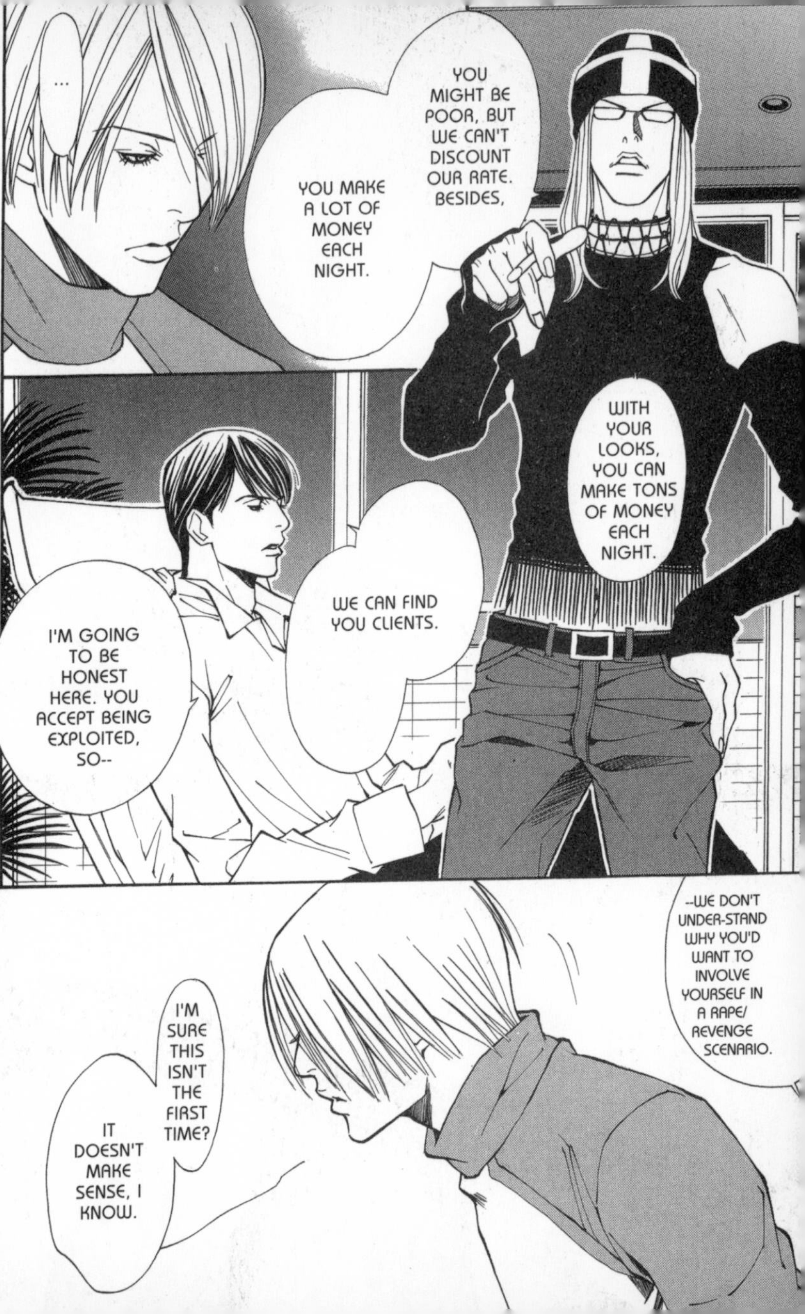
YOU MIGHT BE POOR, BUT WE CAN'T DISCOUNT OUR RATE. BESIDES,
YOU MAKE A LOT OF MONEY EACH NIGHT.
...
WITH YOUR LOOKS, YOU CAN MAKE TONS OF MONEY EACH NIGHT.
WE CAN FIND YOU CLIENTS.
I'M GOING TO BE HONEST HERE. YOU ACCEPT BEING EXPLOITED, SO--
--WE DON'T UNDER-STAND WHY YOU'D WANT TO INVOLVE YOURSELF IN A RAPE/ REVENGE SCENARIO.
I'M SURE THIS ISN'T THE FIRST TIME?
IT DOESN'T MAKE SENSE, I KNOW.

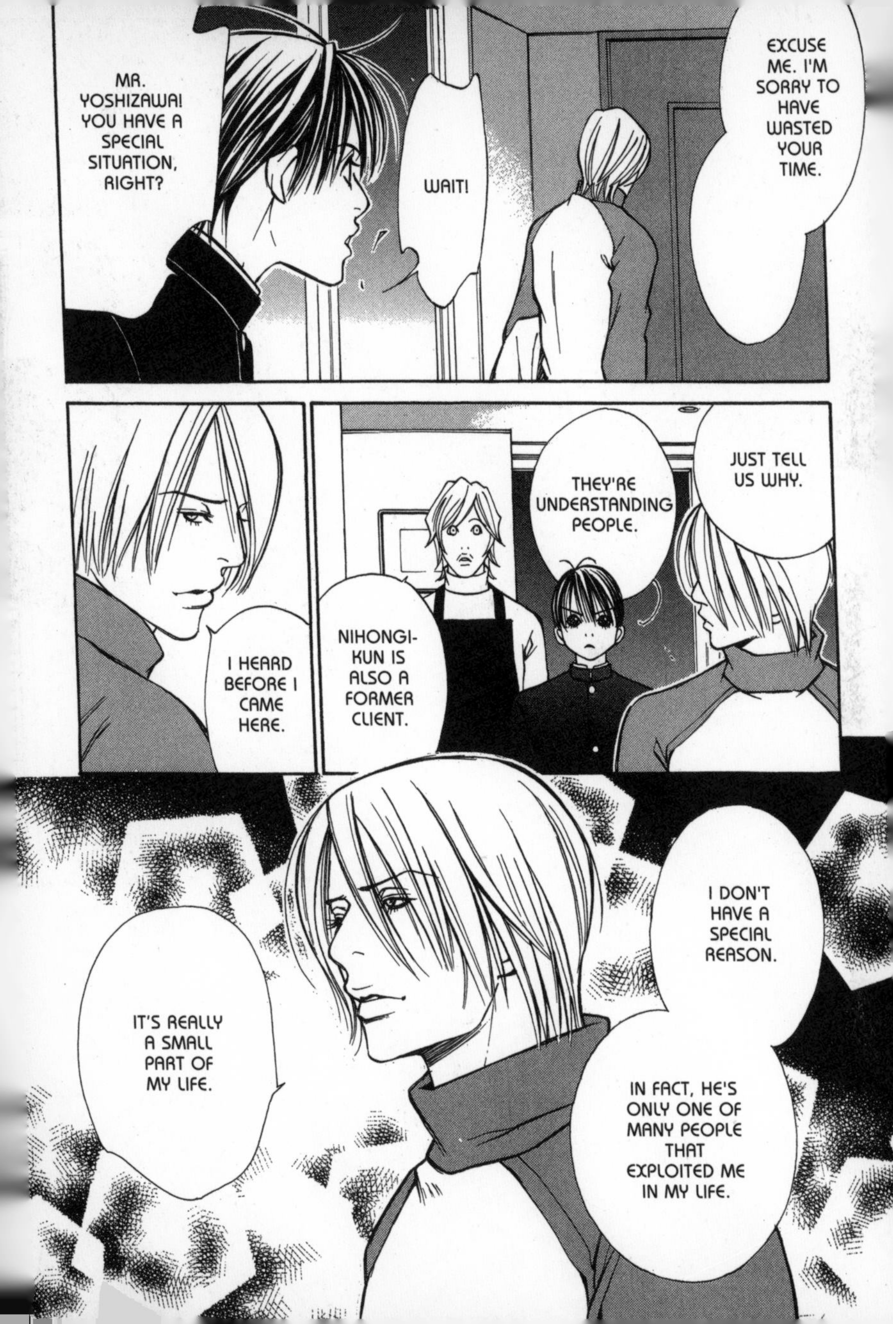
EXCUSE ME. I'M SORRY TO HAVE WASTED YOUR TIME.
WAIT!
MR. YOSHIZAWA! YOU HAVE A SPECIAL SITUATION, RIGHT?
JUST TELL US WHY.
THEY'RE UNDERSTANDING PEOPLE.
NIHONGI-KUN IS ALSO A FORMER CLIENT.
I HEARD BEFORE I CAME HERE.
I DON'T HAVE A SPECIAL REASON.
IN FACT, HE'S ONLY ONE OF MANY PEOPLE THAT EXPLOITED ME IN MY LIFE.
IT'S REALLY A SMALL PART OF MY LIFE.

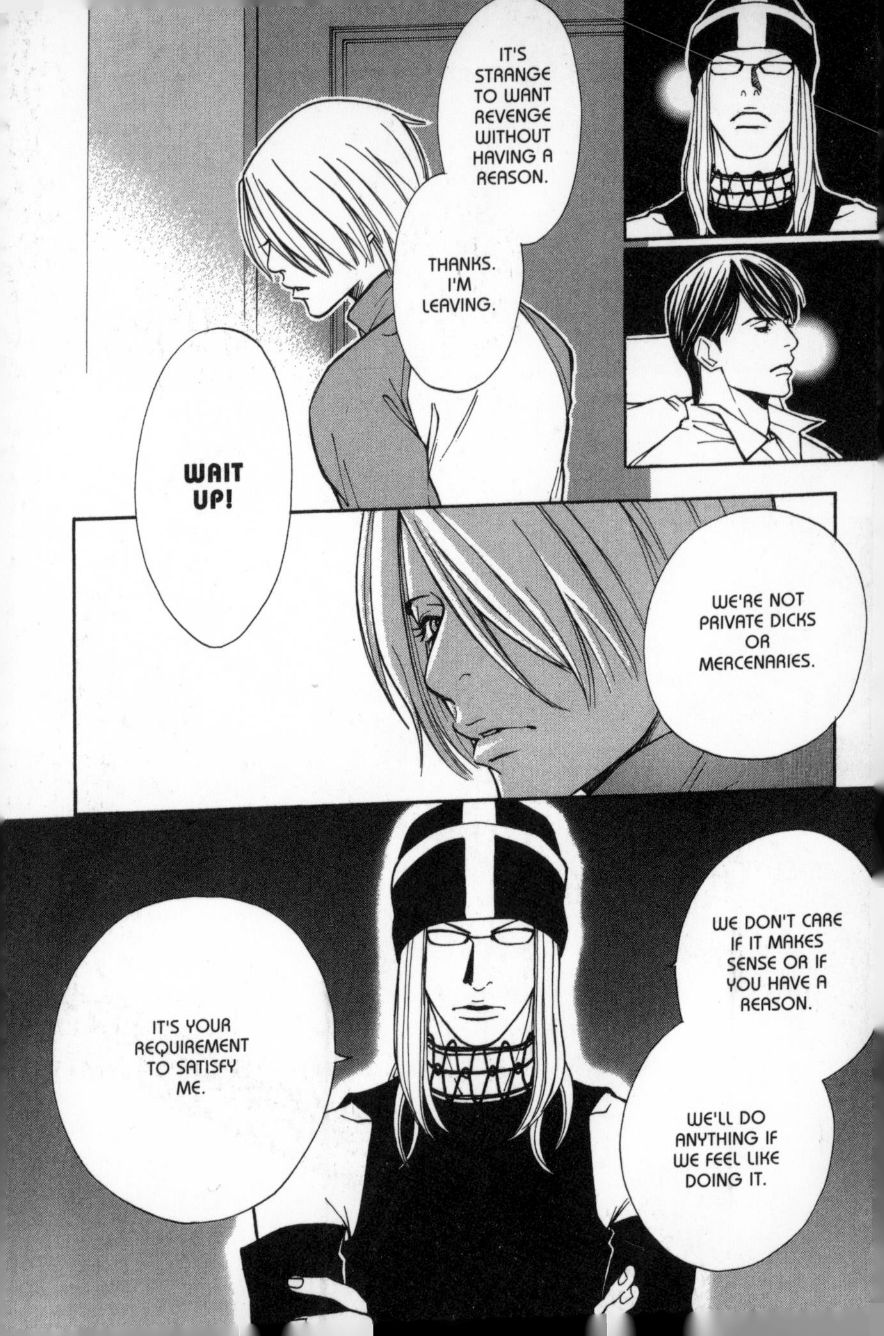
IT'S STRANGE TO WANT REVENGE WITHOUT HAVING A REASON.
THANKS. I'M LEAVING.
WAIT UP!
WE'RE NOT PRIVATE DICKS OR MERCENARIES.
WE DON'T CARE IF IT MAKES SENSE OR IF YOU HAVE A REASON.
WE'LL DO ANYTHING IF WE FEEL LIKE DOING IT.
IT'S YOUR REQUIREMENT TO SATISFY ME.

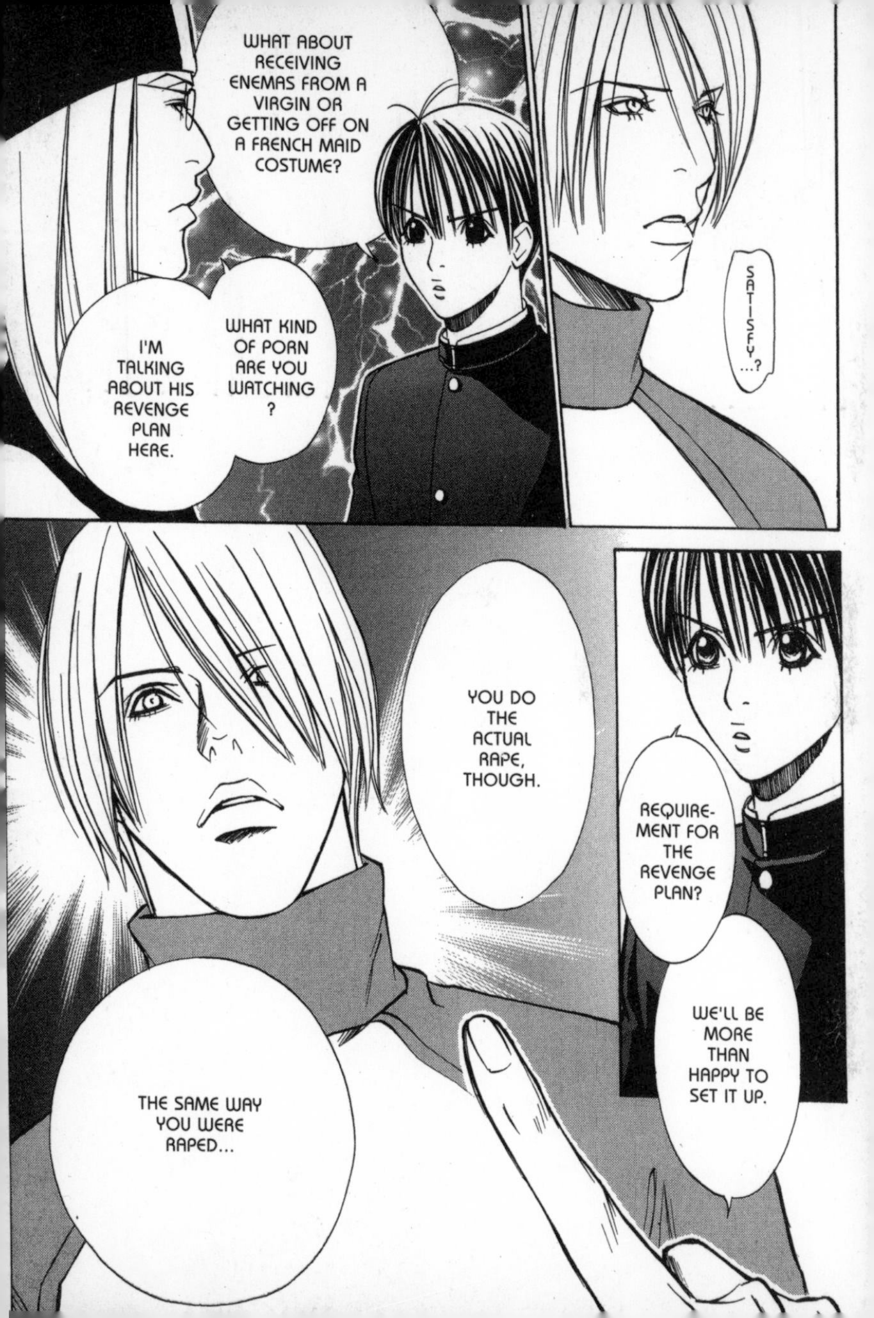
SATISFY...?
WHAT ABOUT RECEIVING ENEMAS FROM A VIRGIN OR GETTING OFF ON A FRENCH MAID COSTUME?
WHAT KIND OF PORN ARE YOU WATCHING?
I'M TALKING ABOUT HIS REVENGE PLAN HERE.
REQUIREMENT FOR THE REVENGE PLAN?
WE'LL BE MORE THAN HAPPY TO SET IT UP.
YOU DO THE ACTUAL RAPE, THOUGH.
THE SAME WAY YOU WERE RAPED...

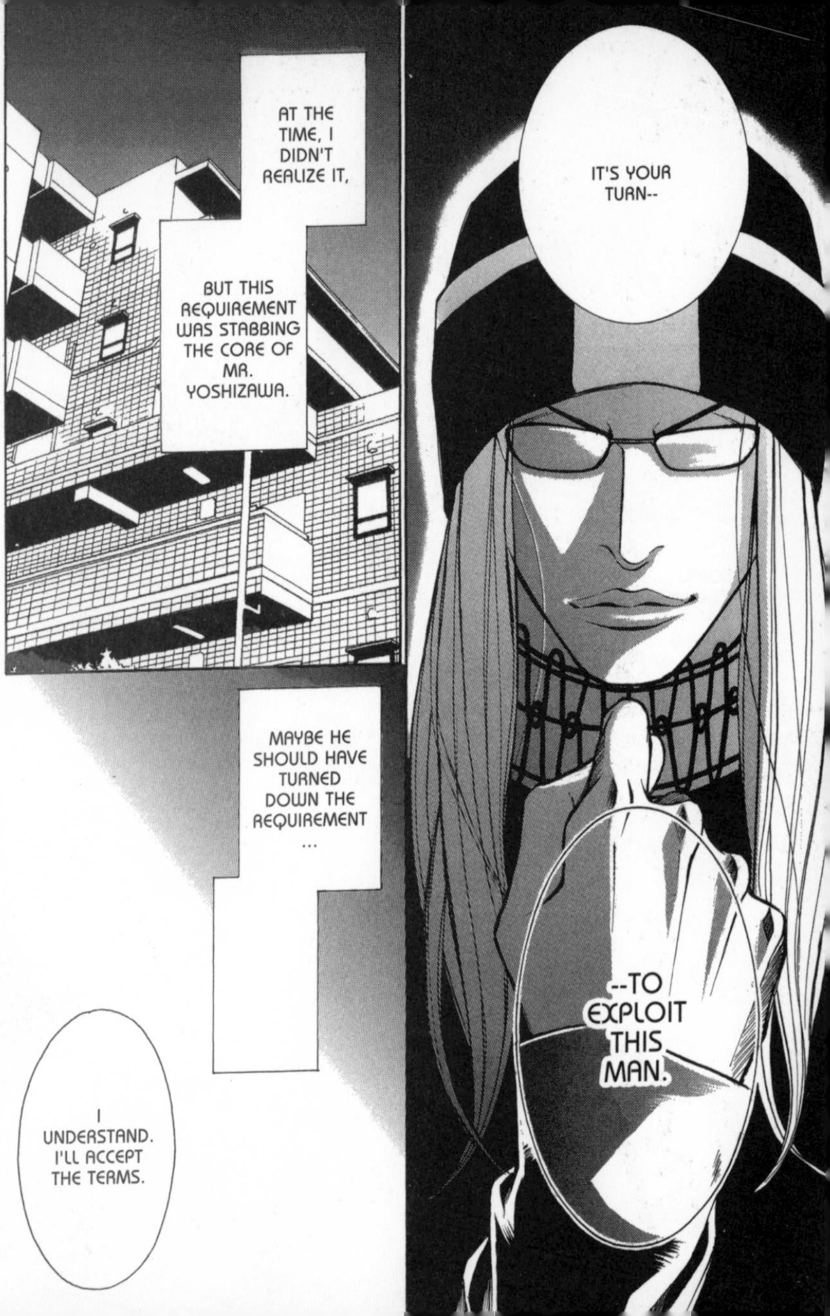
IT'S YOUR TURN--
--TO EXPLOIT THIS MAN.
AT THE TIME, I DIDN'T REALIZE IT,
BUT THIS REQUIREMENT WAS STABBING THE CORE OF MR. YOSHIZAWA.
MAYBE HE SHOULD HAVE TURNED DOWN THE REQUIREMENT ...
I UNDERSTAND. I'LL ACCEPT THE TERMS.

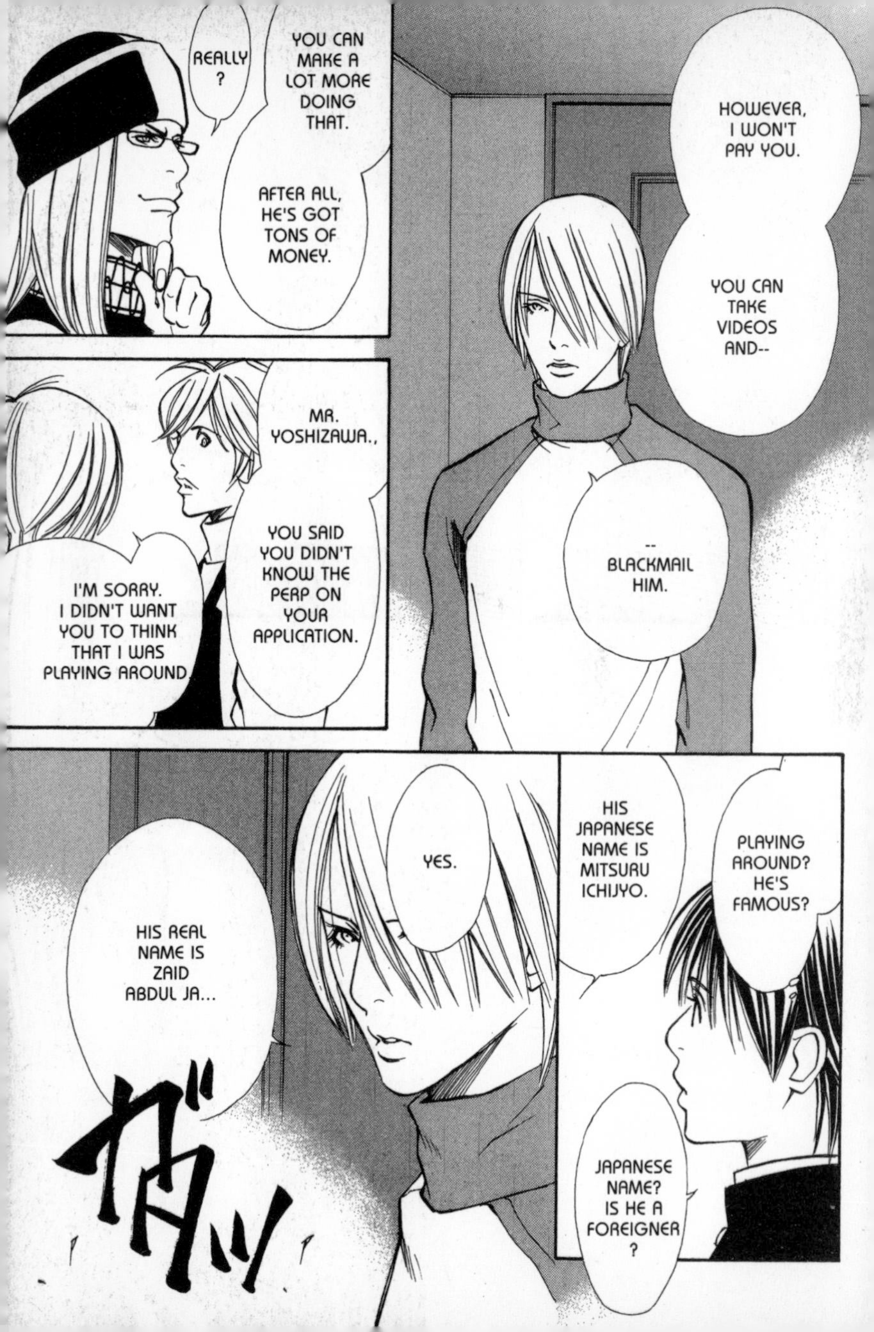
HOWEVER, I WON'T PAY YOU.
YOU CAN TAKE VIDEOS AND--
-- BLACKMAIL HIM.
REALLY ?
YOU CAN MAKE A LOT MORE DOING THAT.
AFTER ALL, HE'S GOT TONS OF MONEY.
MR. YOSHIZAWA.,
YOU SAID YOU DIDN'T KNOW THE PERP ON YOUR APPLICATION.
I'M SORRY. I DIDN'T WANT YOU TO THINK THAT I WAS PLAYING AROUND.
PLAYING AROUND? HE'S FAMOUS?
HIS JAPANESE NAME IS MITSURU ICHIJYO.
JAPANESE NAME? IS HE A FOREIGNER ?
YES.
HIS REAL NAME IS ZAID ABDUL JA...
ガバッ

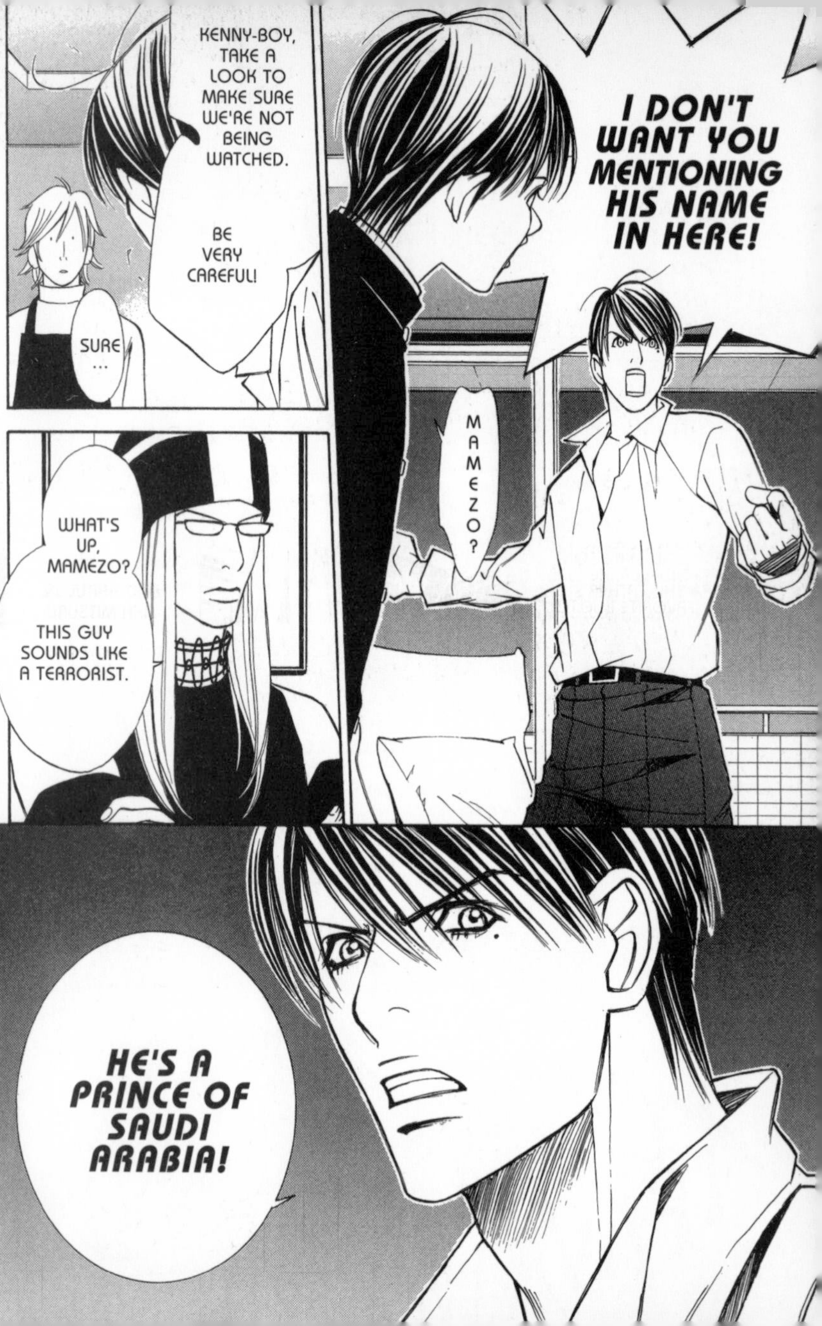
I DON'T WANT YOU MENTIONING HIS NAME IN HERE!
MAMEZO?
KENNY-BOY, TAKE A LOOK TO MAKE SURE WE'RE NOT BEING WATCHED.
BE VERY CAREFUL!
SURE ...
WHAT'S UP, MAMEZO?
THIS GUY SOUNDS LIKE A TERRORIST.
HE'S A PRINCE OF SAUDI ARABIA!

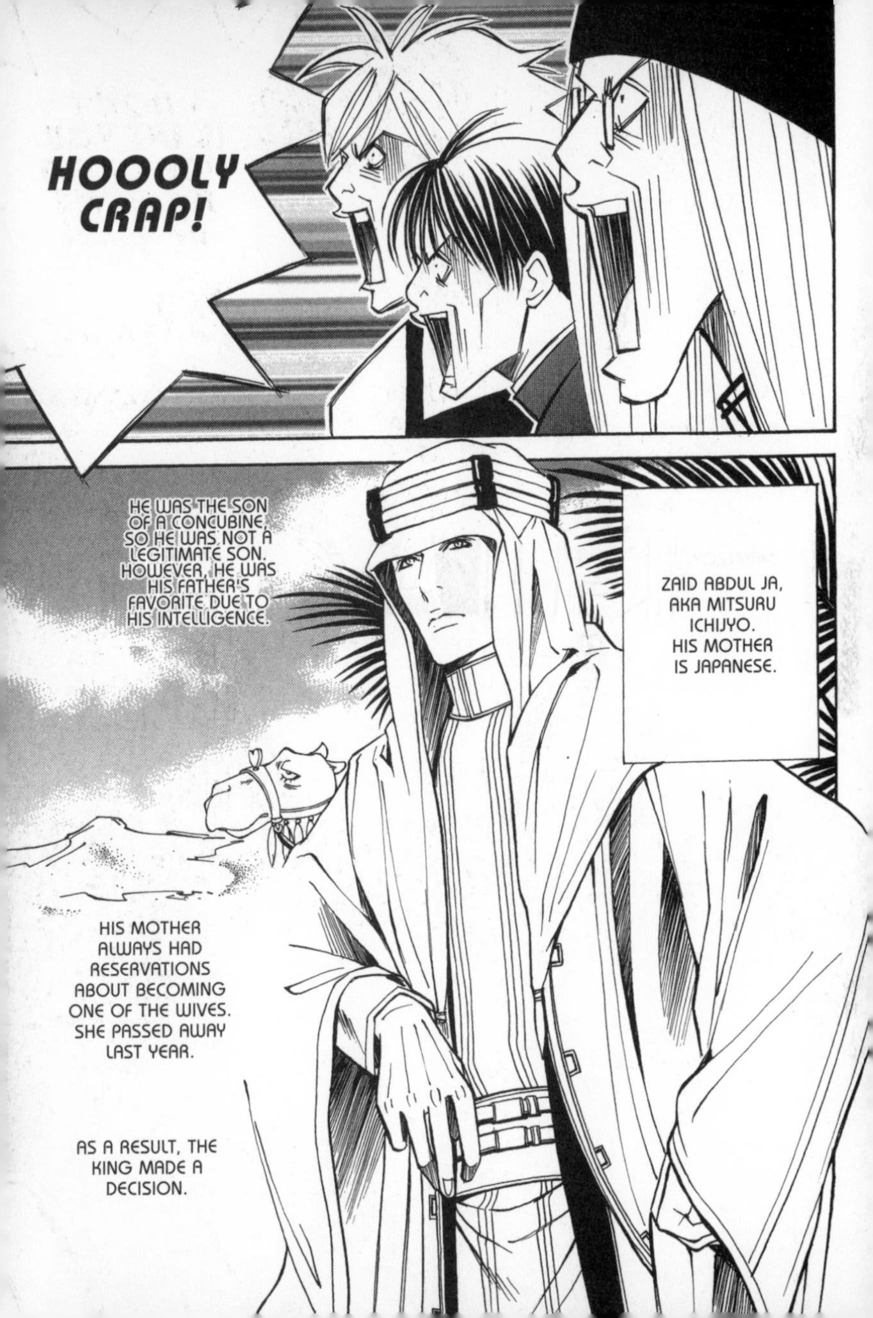
HOOOLY CRAP!
ZAID ABDUL JA, AKA MITSURU ICHIJYO. HIS MOTHER IS JAPANESE.
HE WAS THE SON OF A CONCUBINE, SO HE WAS NOT A LEGITIMATE SON. HOWEVER, HE WAS HIS FATHER'S FAVORITE DUE TO HIS INTELLIGENCE.
HIS MOTHER ALWAYS HAD RESERVATIONS ABOUT BECOMING ONE OF THE WIVES. SHE PASSED AWAY LAST YEAR.
AS A RESULT, THE KING MADE A DECISION.

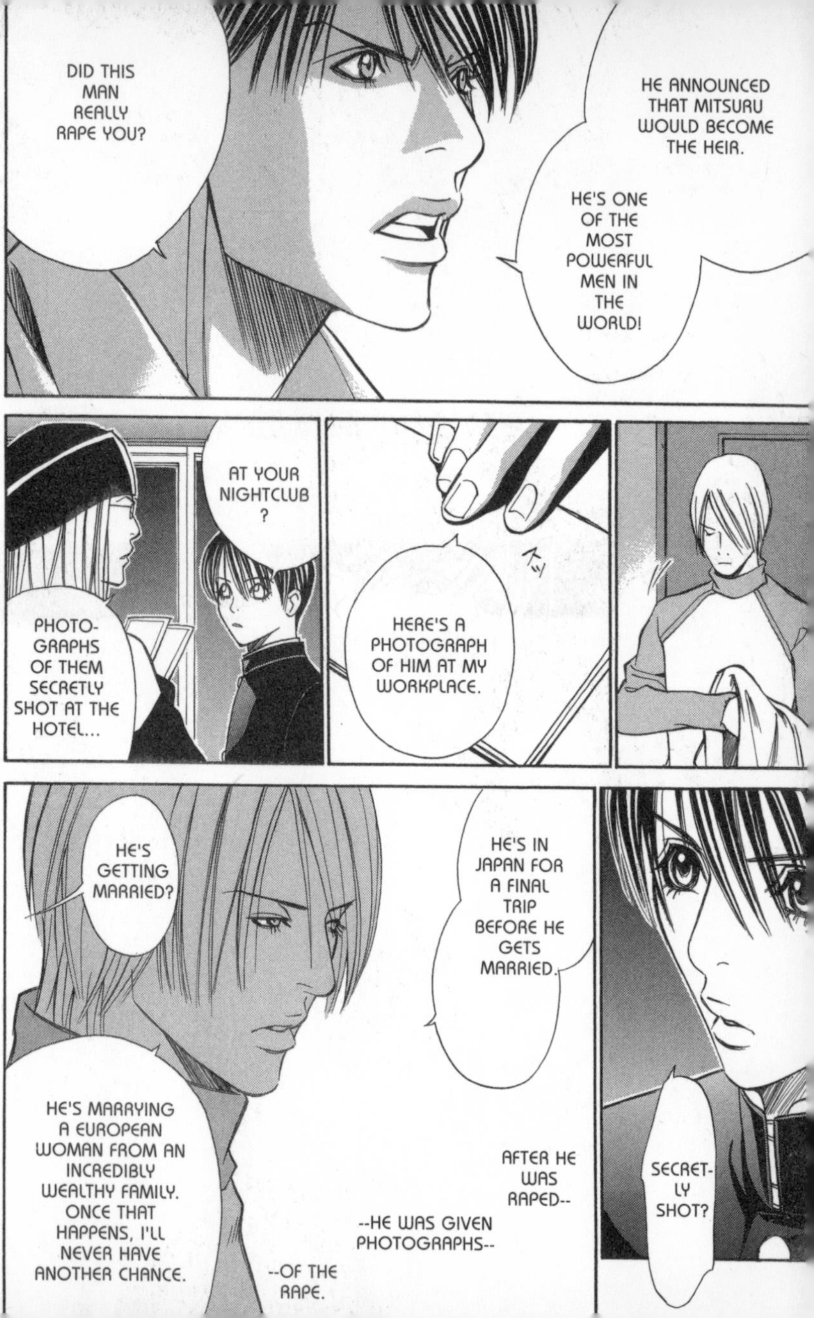
HE ANNOUNCED THAT MITSURU WOULD BECOME THE HEIR.
HE'S ONE OF THE MOST POWERFUL MEN IN THE WORLD!
DID THIS MAN REALLY RAPE YOU?
HERE'S A PHOTOGRAPH OF HIM AT MY WORKPLACE.
AT YOUR NIGHTCLUB?
PHOTOGRAPHS OF THEM SECRETLY SHOT AT THE HOTEL...
SECRETLY SHOT?
HE'S IN JAPAN FOR A FINAL TRIP BEFORE HE GETS MARRIED.
HE'S GETTING MARRIED?
HE'S MARRYING A EUROPEAN WOMAN FROM AN INCREDIBLY WEALTHY FAMILY. ONCE THAT HAPPENS, I'LL NEVER HAVE ANOTHER CHANCE.
AFTER HE WAS RAPED--
--HE WAS GIVEN PHOTOGRAPHS--
--OF THE RAPE.

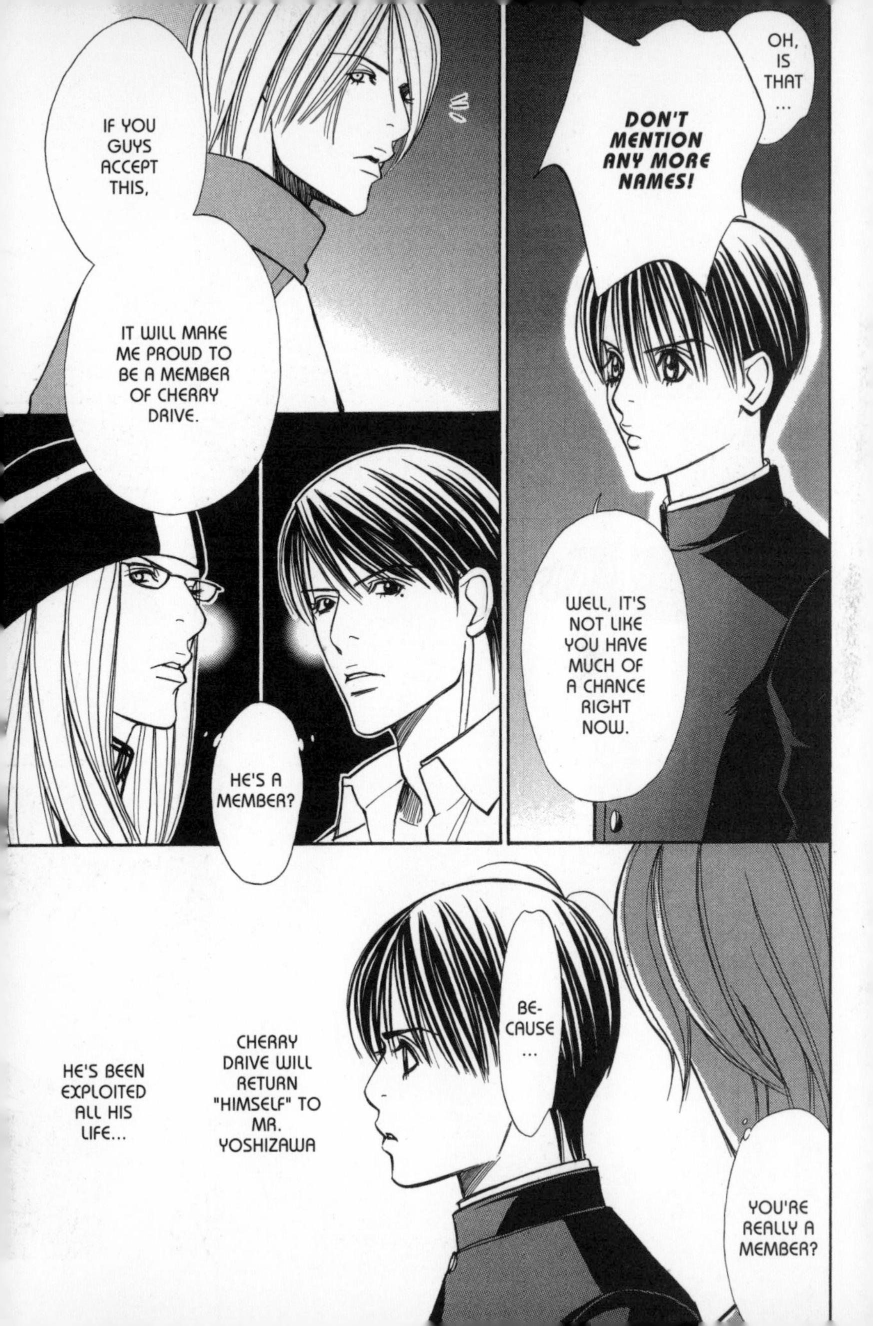
OH, IS THAT ...
DON'T MENTION ANY MORE NAMES!
WELL, IT'S NOT LIKE YOU HAVE MUCH OF A CHANCE RIGHT NOW.
IF YOU GUYS ACCEPT THIS,
IT WILL MAKE ME PROUD TO BE A MEMBER OF CHERRY DRIVE.
HE'S A MEMBER?
YOU'RE REALLY A MEMBER?
BE-CAUSE ...
CHERRY DRIVE WILL RETURN "HIMSELF" TO MR. YOSHIZAWA
HE'S BEEN EXPLOITED ALL HIS LIFE...

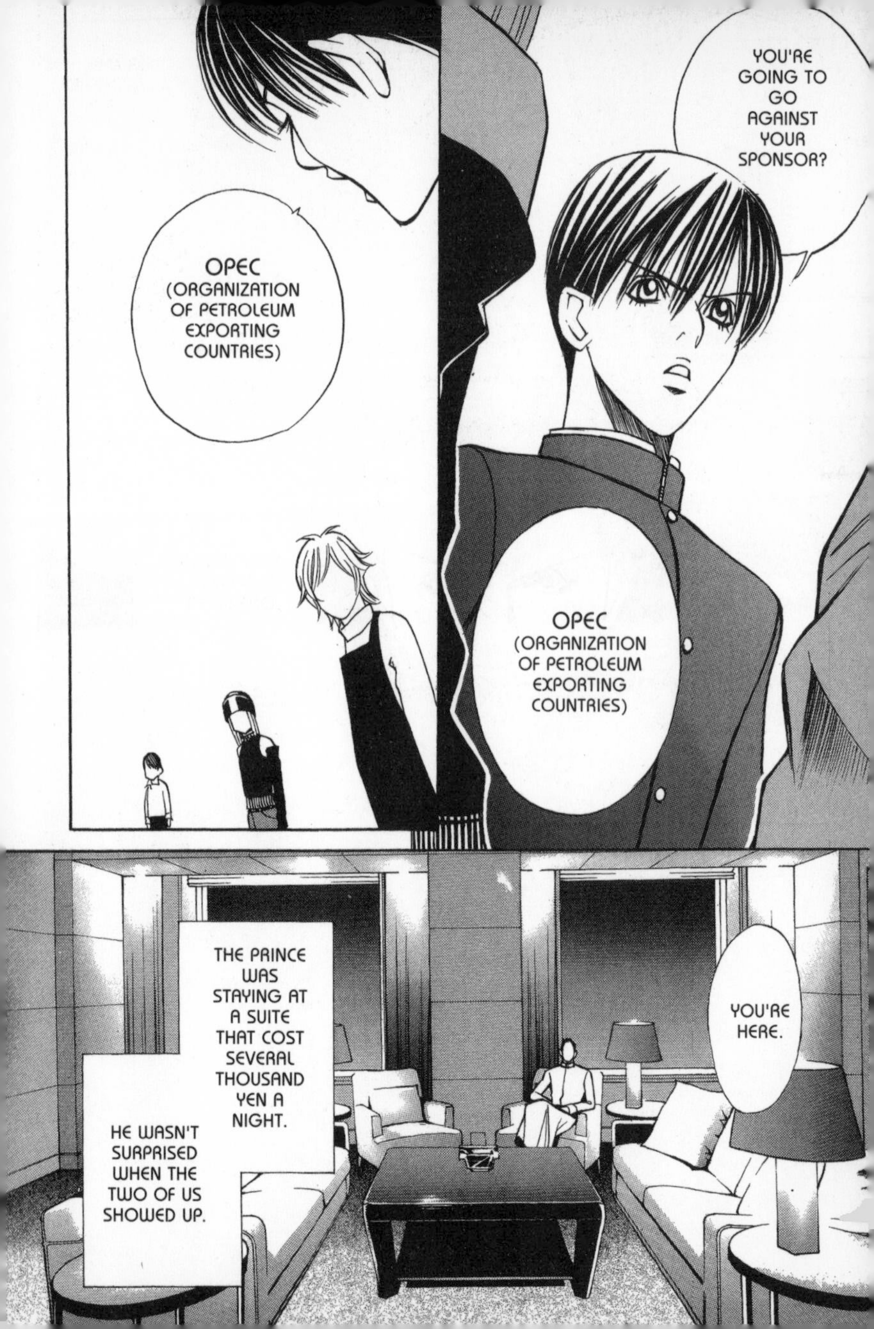
YOU'RE GOING TO GO AGAINST YOUR SPONSOR?
OPEC (ORGANIZATION OF PETROLEUM EXPORTING COUNTRIES)
OPEC (ORGANIZATION OF PETROLEUM EXPORTING COUNTRIES)
THE PRINCE WAS STAYING AT A SUITE THAT COST SEVERAL THOUSAND YEN A NIGHT.
HE WASN'T SURPRISED WHEN THE TWO OF US SHOWED UP.
YOU'RE HERE.

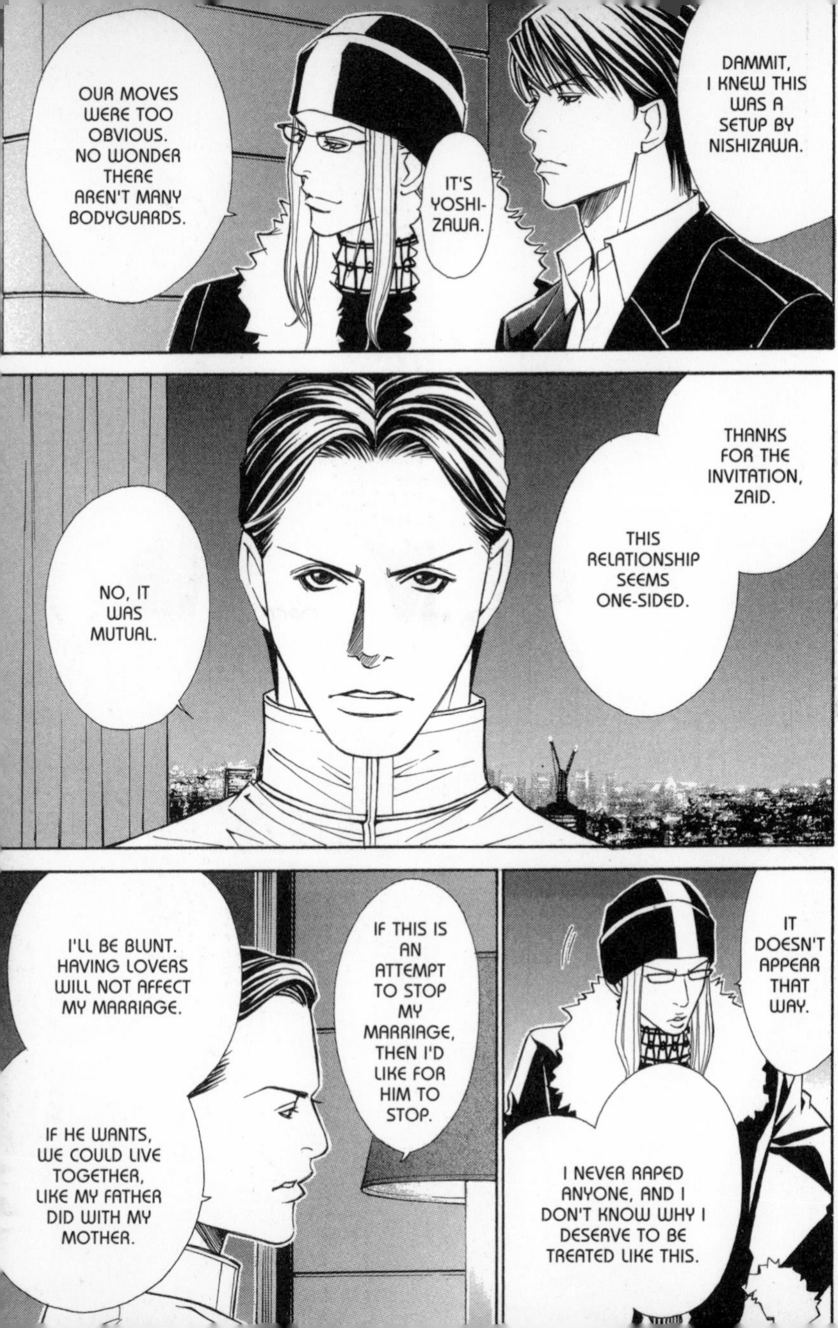
DAMMIT, I KNEW THIS WAS A SETUP BY NISHIZAWA.
IT'S YOSHI-ZAWA.
OUR MOVES WERE TOO OBVIOUS. NO WONDER THERE AREN'T MANY BODYGUARDS.
THANKS FOR THE INVITATION, ZAID.
THIS RELATIONSHIP SEEMS ONE-SIDED.
NO, IT WAS MUTUAL.
IT DOESN'T APPEAR THAT WAY.
I NEVER RAPED ANYONE, AND I DON'T KNOW WHY I DESERVE TO BE TREATED LIKE THIS.
IF THIS IS AN ATTEMPT TO STOP MY MARRIAGE, THEN I'D LIKE FOR HIM TO STOP.
I'LL BE BLUNT. HAVING LOVERS WILL NOT AFFECT MY MARRIAGE.
IF HE WANTS, WE COULD LIVE TOGETHER, LIKE MY FATHER DID WITH MY MOTHER.

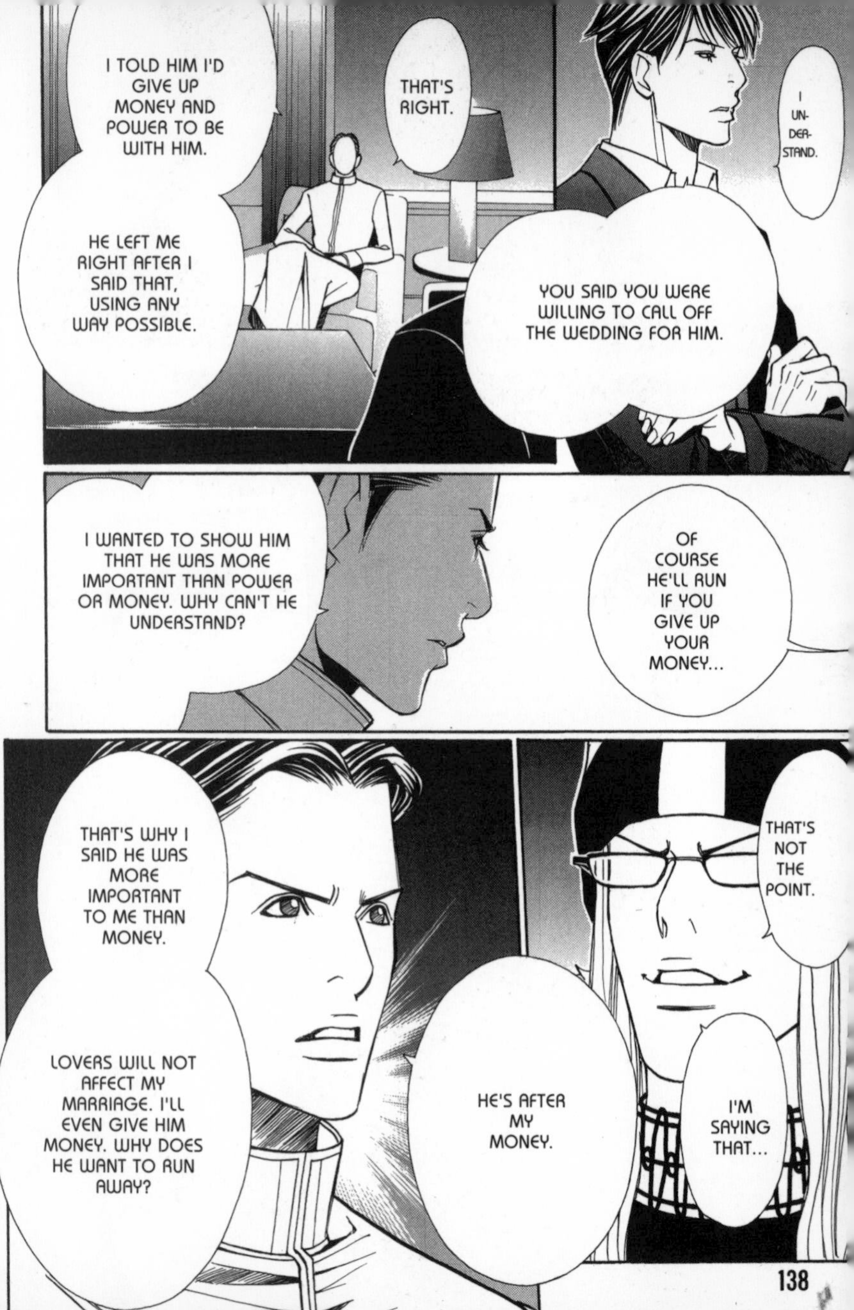
I UN-DER-STAND.
YOU SAID YOU WERE WILLING TO CALL OFF THE WEDDING FOR HIM.
THAT'S RIGHT.
I TOLD HIM I'D GIVE UP MONEY AND POWER TO BE WITH HIM.
HE LEFT ME RIGHT AFTER I SAID THAT, USING ANY WAY POSSIBLE.
OF COURSE HE'LL RUN IF YOU GIVE UP YOUR MONEY...
I WANTED TO SHOW HIM THAT HE WAS MORE IMPORTANT THAN POWER OR MONEY. WHY CAN'T HE UNDERSTAND?
THAT'S NOT THE POINT.
I'M SAYING THAT...
HE'S AFTER MY MONEY.
THAT'S WHY I SAID HE WAS MORE IMPORTANT TO ME THAN MONEY.
LOVERS WILL NOT AFFECT MY MARRIAGE. I'LL EVEN GIVE HIM MONEY. WHY DOES HE WANT TO RUN AWAY?

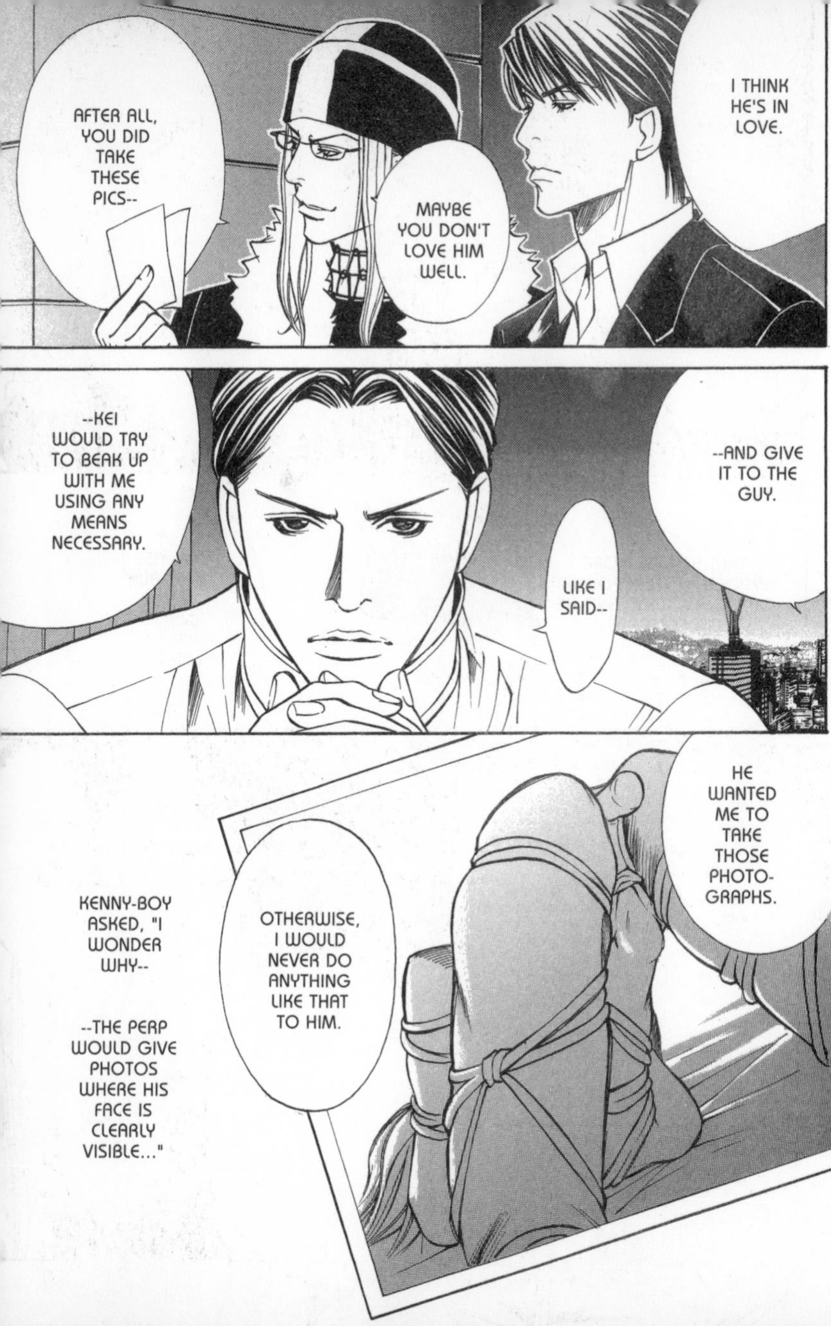
I THINK HE'S IN LOVE.
MAYBE YOU DON'T LOVE HIM WELL.
AFTER ALL, YOU DID TAKE THESE PICS--
--AND GIVE IT TO THE GUY.
LIKE I SAID--
--KEI WOULD TRY TO BEAK UP WITH ME USING ANY MEANS NECESSARY.
HE WANTED ME TO TAKE THOSE PHOTO-GRAPHS.
OTHERWISE, I WOULD NEVER DO ANYTHING LIKE THAT TO HIM.
KENNY-BOY ASKED, "I WONDER WHY--
--THE PERP WOULD GIVE PHOTOS WHERE HIS FACE IS CLEARLY VISIBLE..."

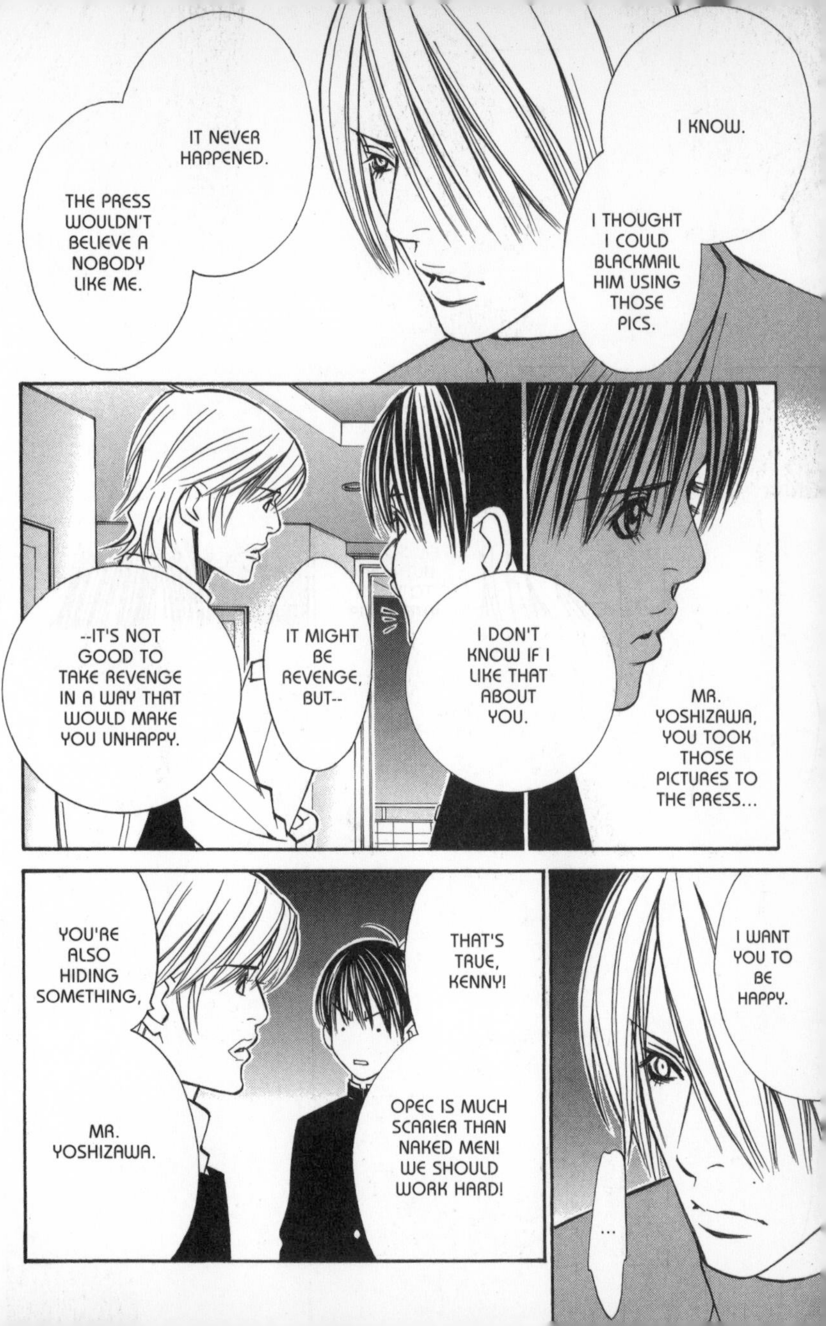
I KNOW.
I THOUGHT I COULD BLACKMAIL HIM USING THOSE PICS.
IT NEVER HAPPENED.
THE PRESS WOULDN'T BELIEVE A NOBODY LIKE ME.
MR. YOSHIZAWA, YOU TOOK THOSE PICTURES TO THE PRESS...
I DON'T KNOW IF I LIKE THAT ABOUT YOU.
IT MIGHT BE REVENGE, BUT--
--IT'S NOT GOOD TO TAKE REVENGE IN A WAY THAT WOULD MAKE YOU UNHAPPY.
I WANT YOU TO BE HAPPY.
...
THAT'S TRUE, KENNY!
OPEC IS MUCH SCARIER THAN NAKED MEN! WE SHOULD WORK HARD!
YOU'RE ALSO HIDING SOMETHING,
MR. YOSHIZAWA.

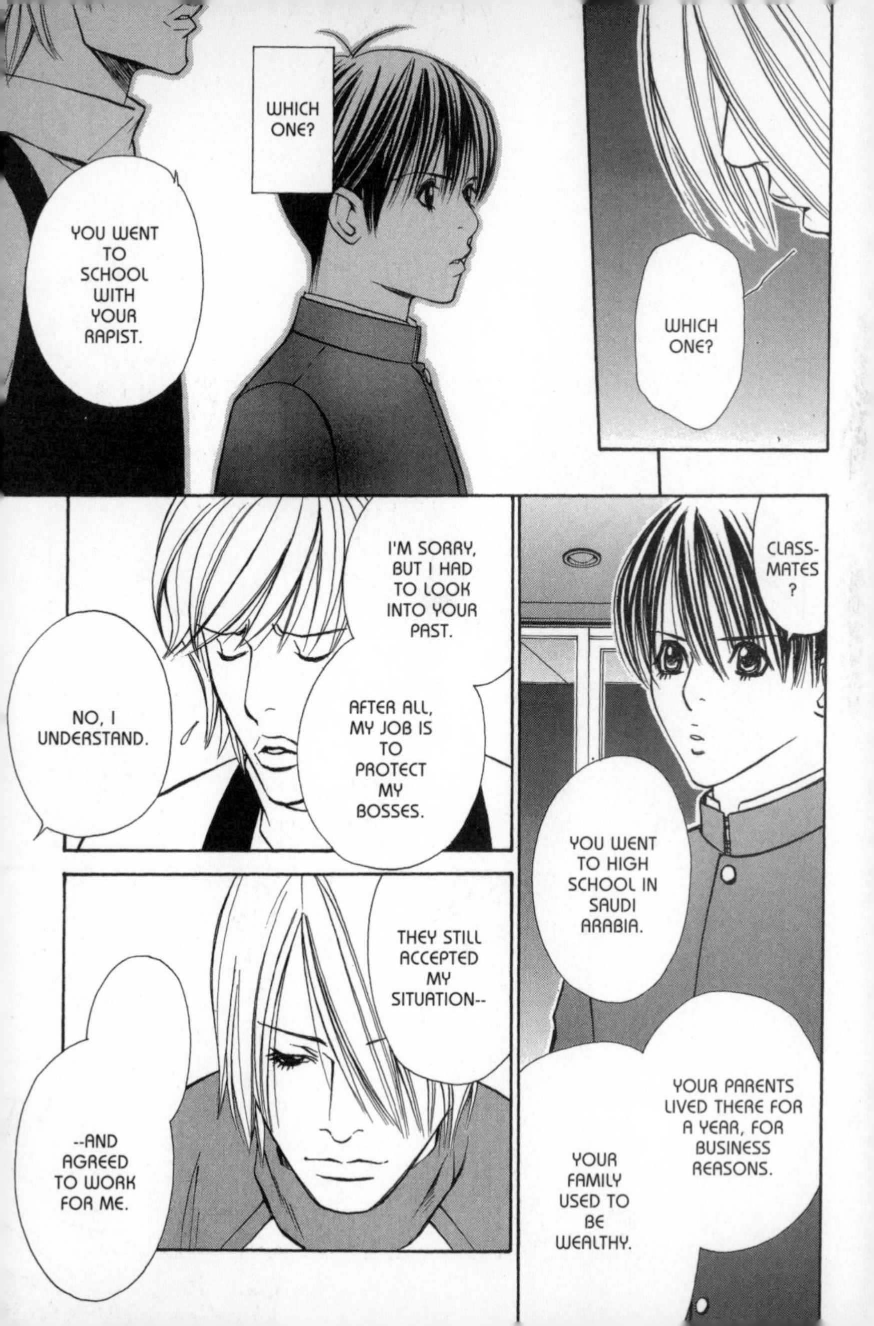
WHICH ONE?
WHICH ONE?
YOU WENT TO SCHOOL WITH YOUR RAPIST.
CLASS-MATES?
YOU WENT TO HIGH SCHOOL IN SAUDI ARABIA.
YOUR PARENTS LIVED THERE FOR A YEAR, FOR BUSINESS REASONS.
YOUR FAMILY USED TO BE WEALTHY.
I'M SORRY, BUT I HAD TO LOOK INTO YOUR PAST.
AFTER ALL, MY JOB IS TO PROTECT MY BOSSES.
NO, I UNDERSTAND.
THEY STILL ACCEPTED MY SITUATION--
--AND AGREED TO WORK FOR ME.

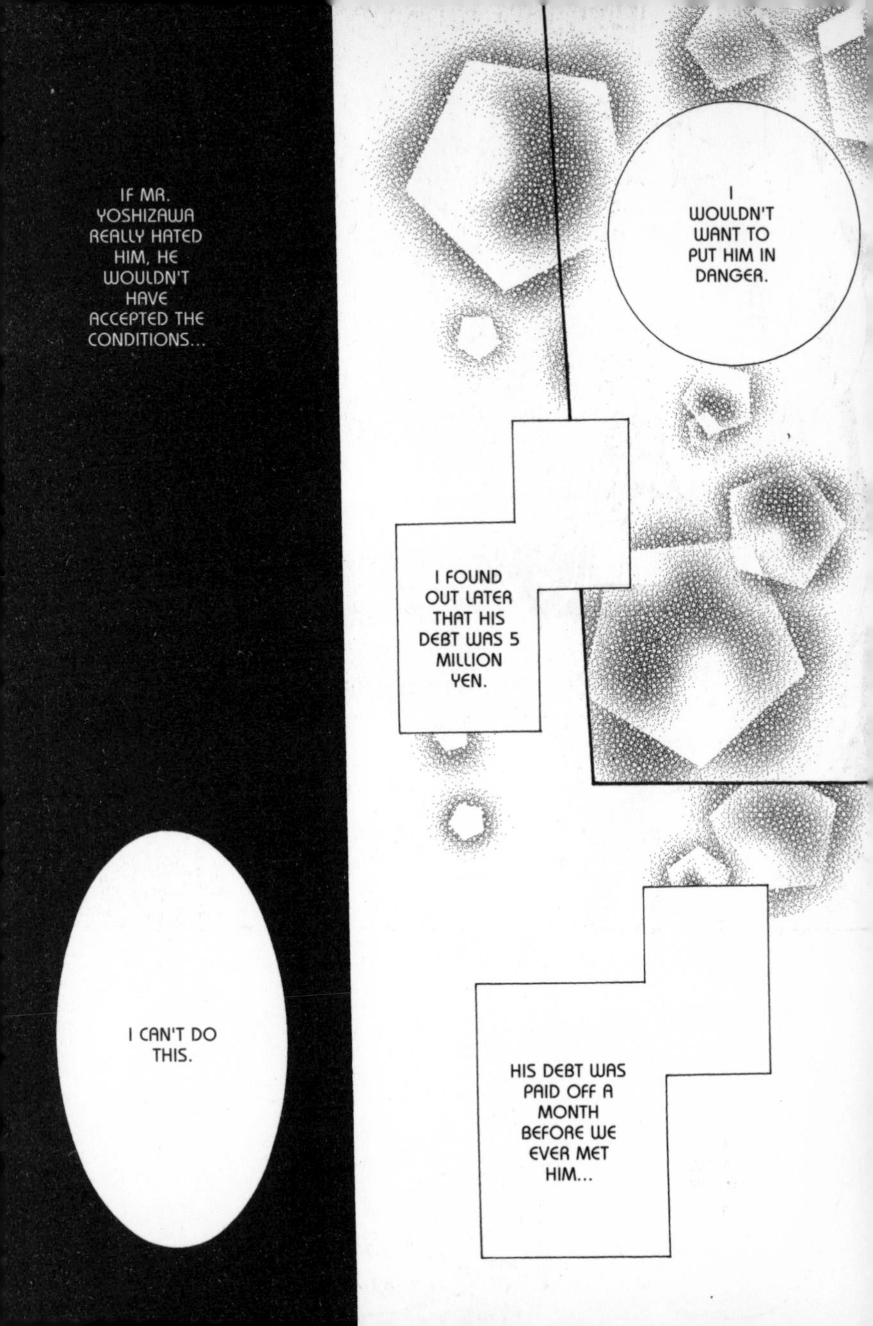
I WOULDN'T WANT TO PUT HIM IN DANGER.
I FOUND OUT LATER THAT HIS DEBT WAS 5 MILLION YEN.
HIS DEBT WAS PAID OFF A MONTH BEFORE WE EVER MET HIM...
IF MR. YOSHIZAWA REALLY HATED HIM, HE WOULDN'T HAVE ACCEPTED THE CONDITIONS...
I CAN'T DO THIS.

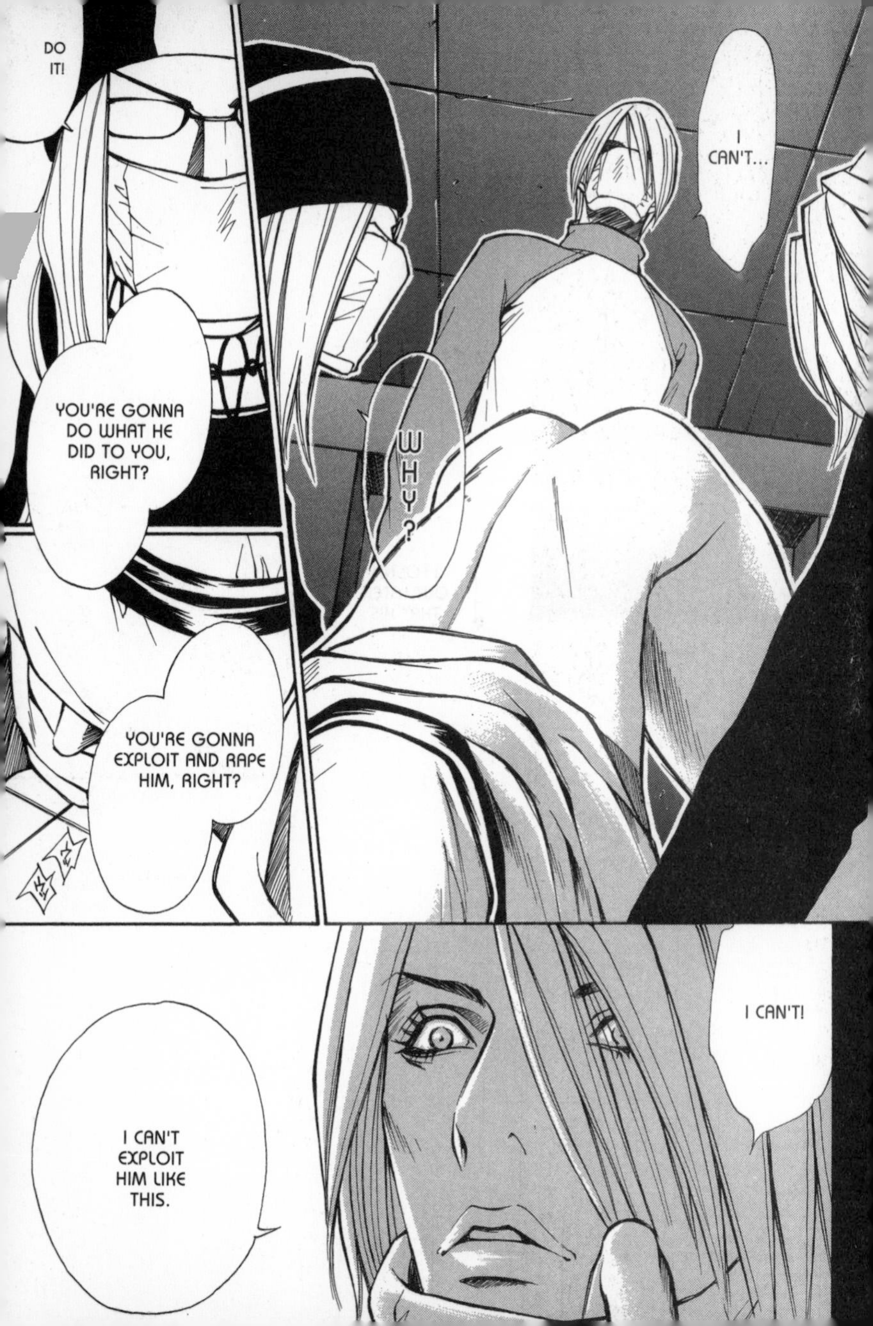
I CAN'T...
WHY?
DO IT!
YOU'RE GONNA DO WHAT HE DID TO YOU, RIGHT?
YOU'RE GONNA EXPLOIT AND RAPE HIM, RIGHT?
I CAN'T!
I CAN'T EXPLOIT HIM LIKE THIS.

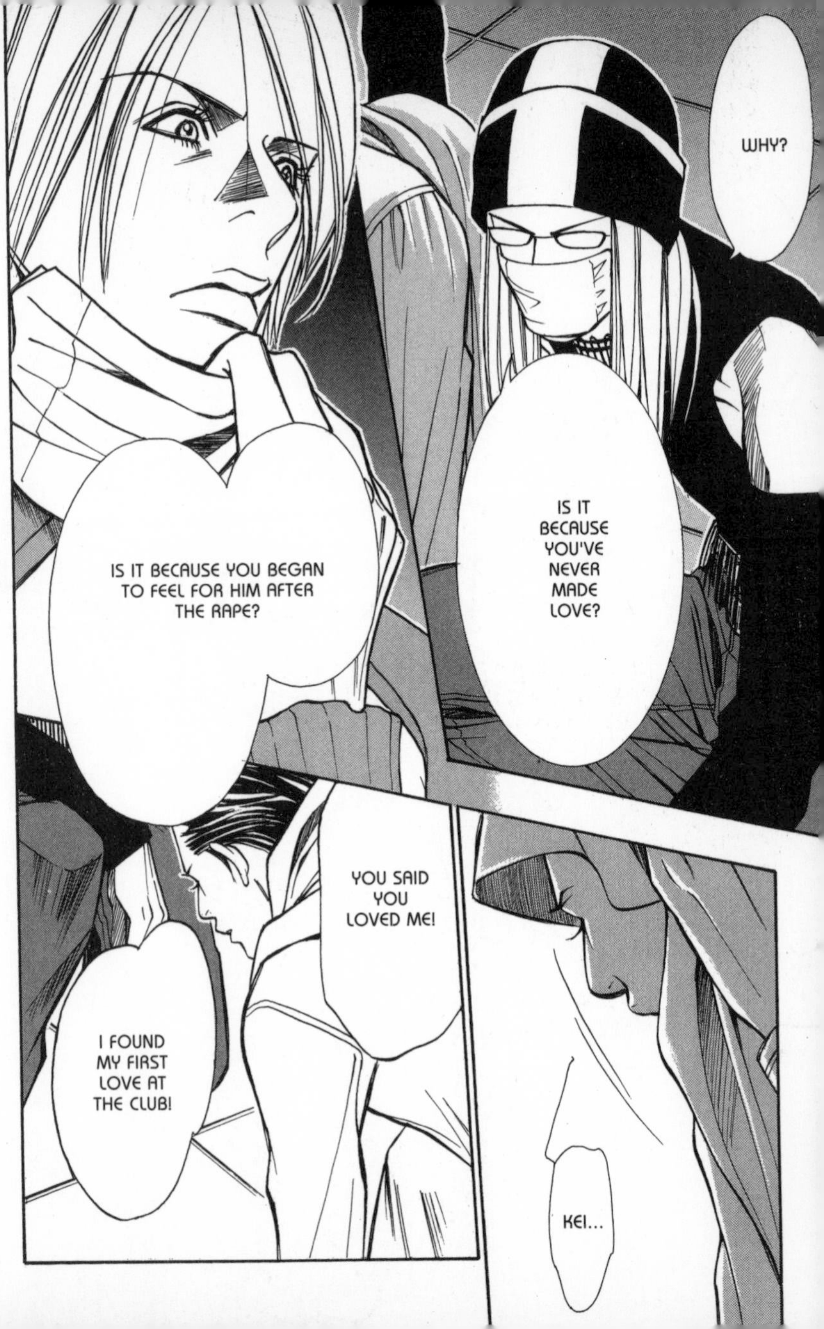
WHY?
IS IT BECAUSE YOU'VE NEVER MADE LOVE?
IS IT BECAUSE YOU BEGAN TO FEEL FOR HIM AFTER THE RAPE?
KEI...
YOU SAID YOU LOVED ME!
I FOUND MY FIRST LOVE AT THE CLUB!

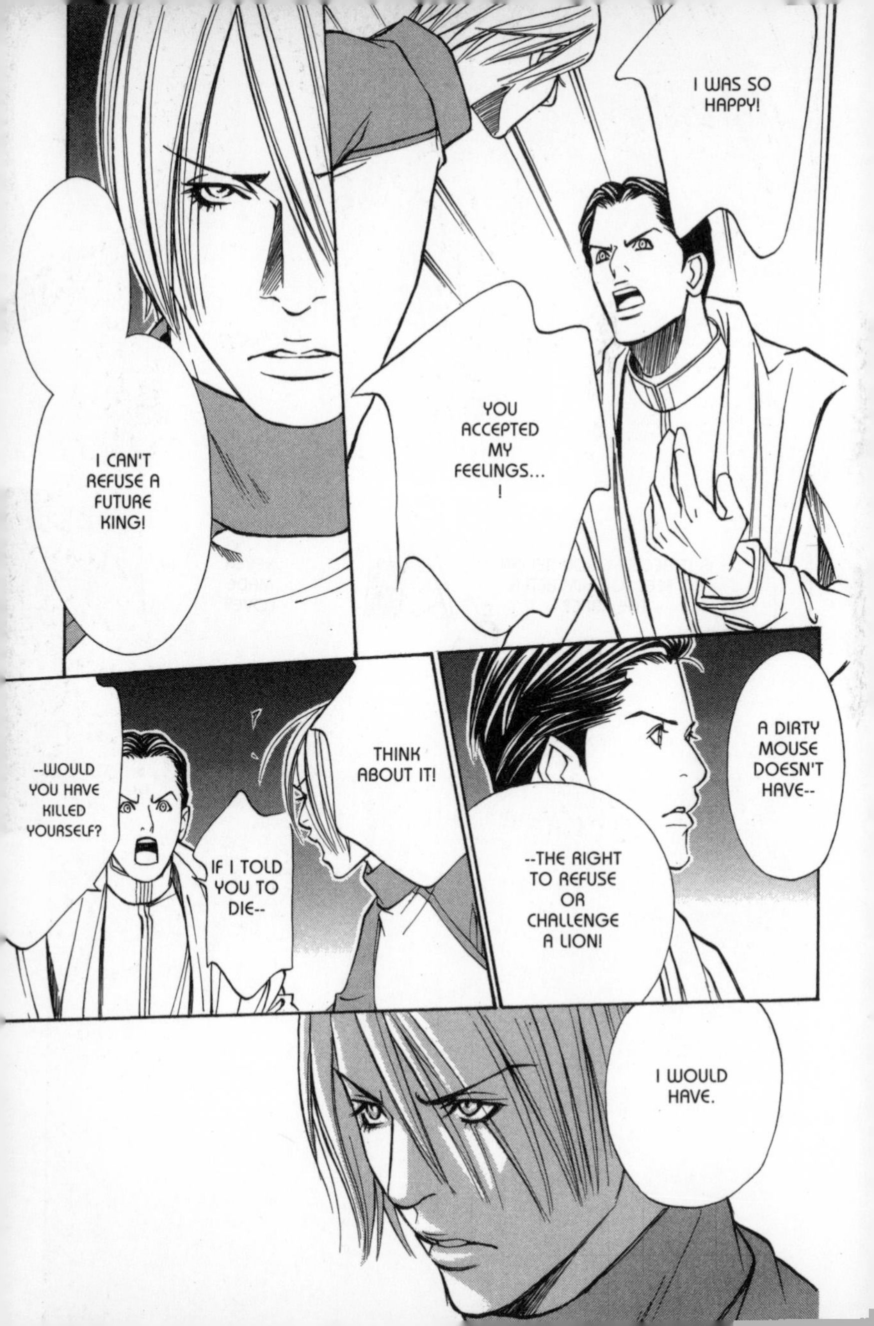
I WAS SO HAPPY!
YOU ACCEPTED MY FEELINGS...!
I CAN'T REFUSE A FUTURE KING!
A DIRTY MOUSE DOESN'T HAVE--
--THE RIGHT TO REFUSE OR CHALLENGE A LION!
THINK ABOUT IT!
IF I TOLD YOU TO DIE--
--WOULD YOU HAVE KILLED YOURSELF?
I WOULD HAVE.

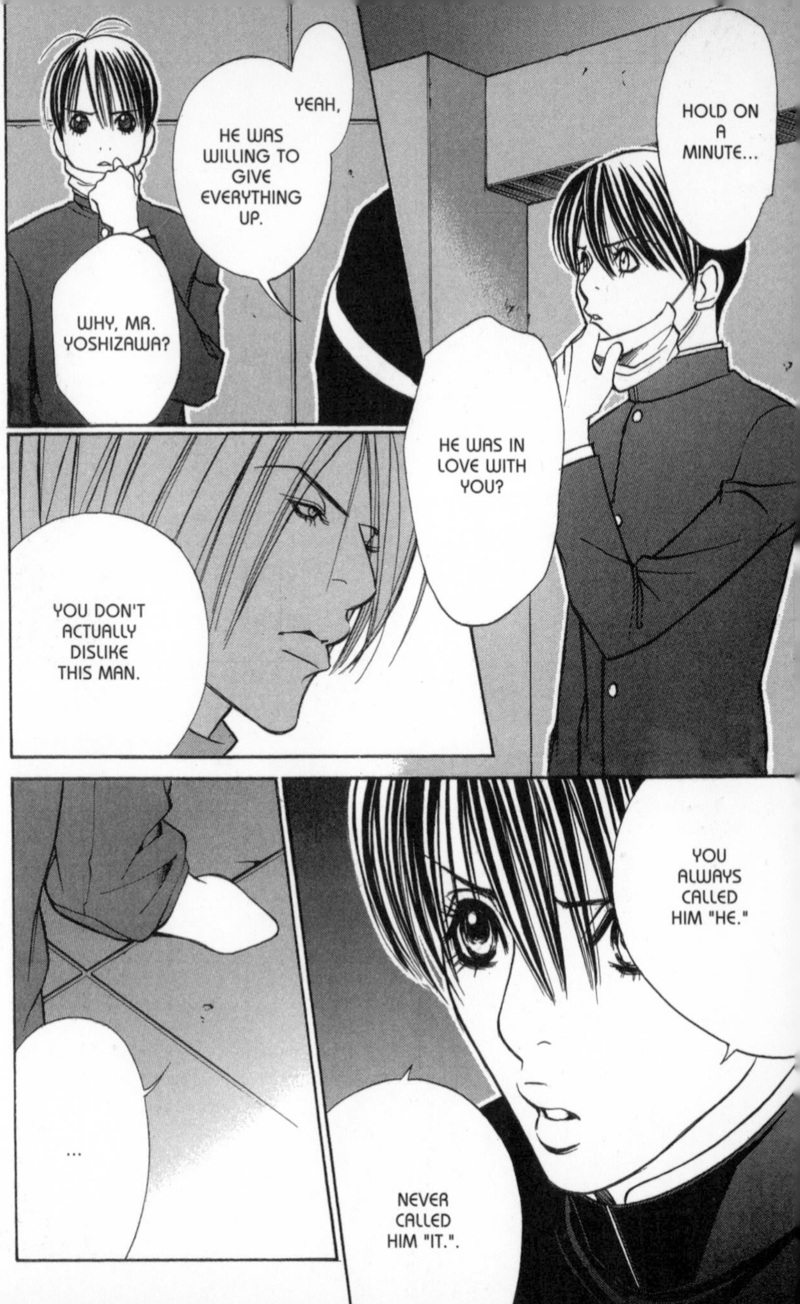
HOLD ON A MINUTE...
HE WAS IN LOVE WITH YOU?
YEAH,
HE WAS WILLING TO GIVE EVERYTHING UP.
WHY, MR. YOSHIZAWA?
YOU DON'T ACTUALLY DISLIKE THIS MAN.
YOU ALWAYS CALLED HIM "HE."
NEVER CALLED HIM "IT.".
...

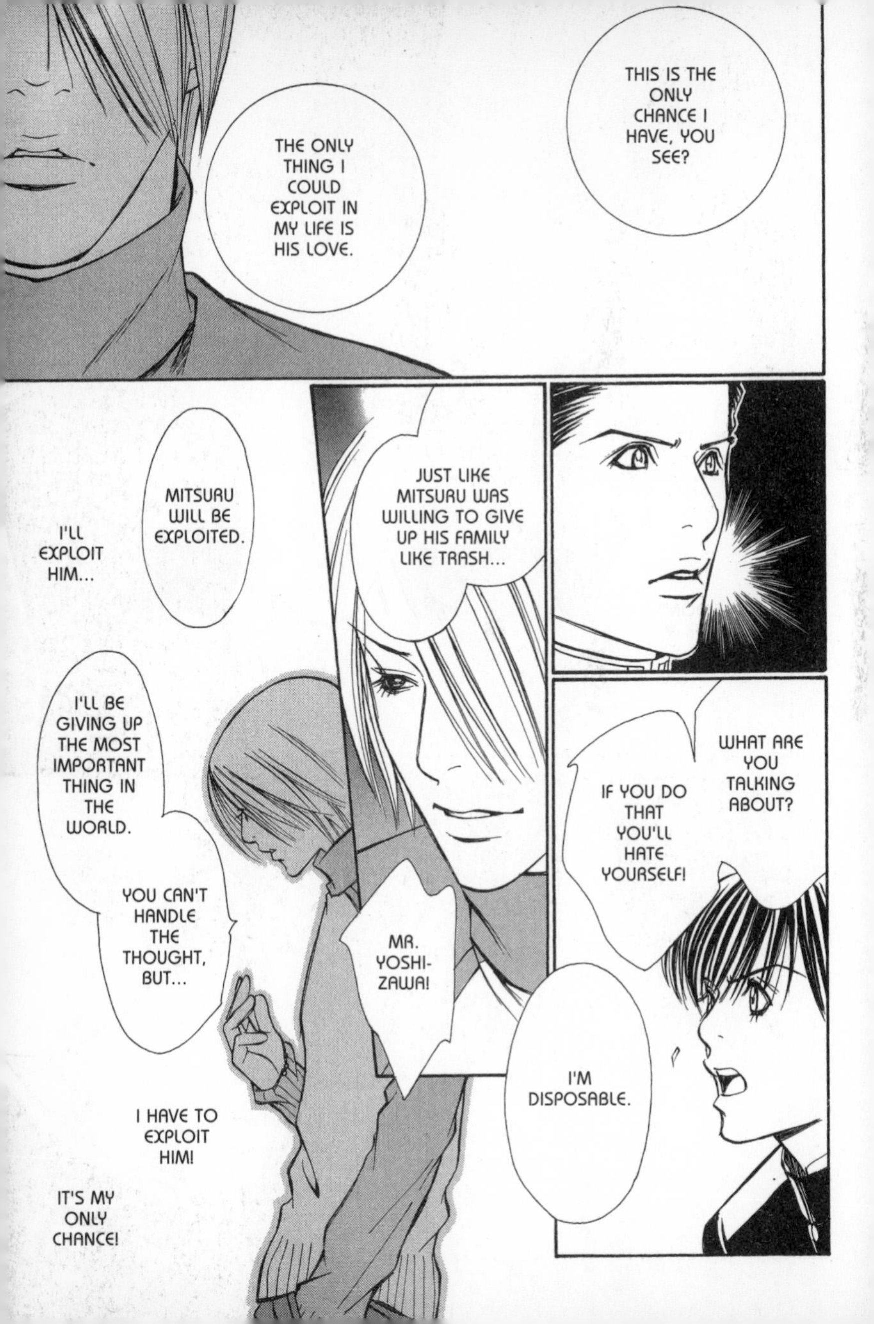
THIS IS THE ONLY CHANCE I HAVE, YOU SEE?
THE ONLY THING I COULD EXPLOIT IN MY LIFE IS HIS LOVE.
JUST LIKE MITSURU WAS WILLING TO GIVE UP HIS FAMILY LIKE TRASH...
MITSURU WILL BE EXPLOITED.
I'LL EXPLOIT HIM...
WHAT ARE YOU TALKING ABOUT?
IF YOU DO THAT YOU'LL HATE YOURSELF!
I'M DISPOSABLE.
MR. YOSHI-ZAWA!
I'LL BE GIVING UP THE MOST IMPORTANT THING IN THE WORLD.
YOU CAN'T HANDLE THE THOUGHT, BUT...
I HAVE TO EXPLOIT HIM!
IT'S MY ONLY CHANCE!

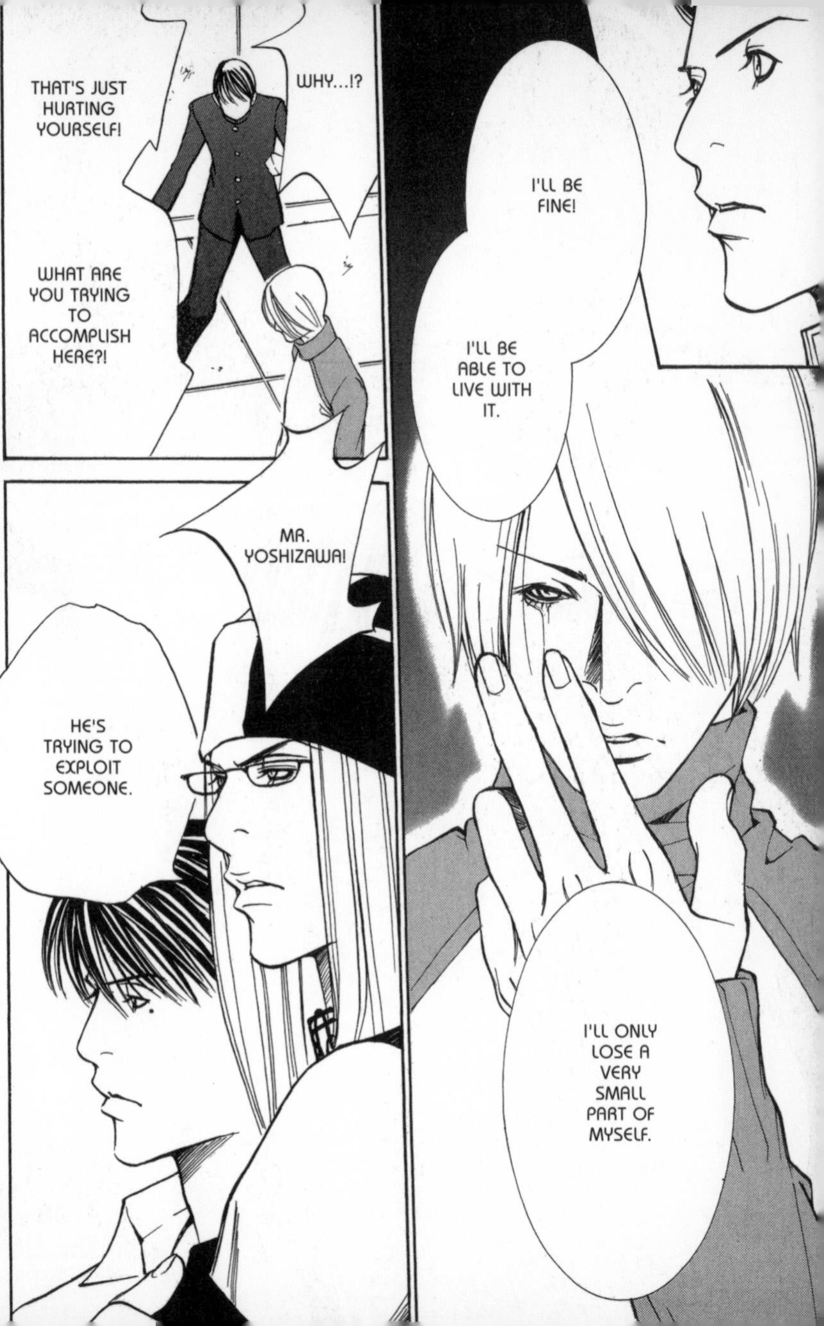
I'LL BE FINE!
I'LL BE ABLE TO LIVE WITH IT.
I'LL ONLY LOSE A VERY SMALL PART OF MYSELF.
WHY...!?
THAT'S JUST HURTING YOURSELF!
WHAT ARE YOU TRYING TO ACCOMPLISH HERE?!
MR. YOSHIZAWA!
HE'S TRYING TO EXPLOIT SOMEONE.

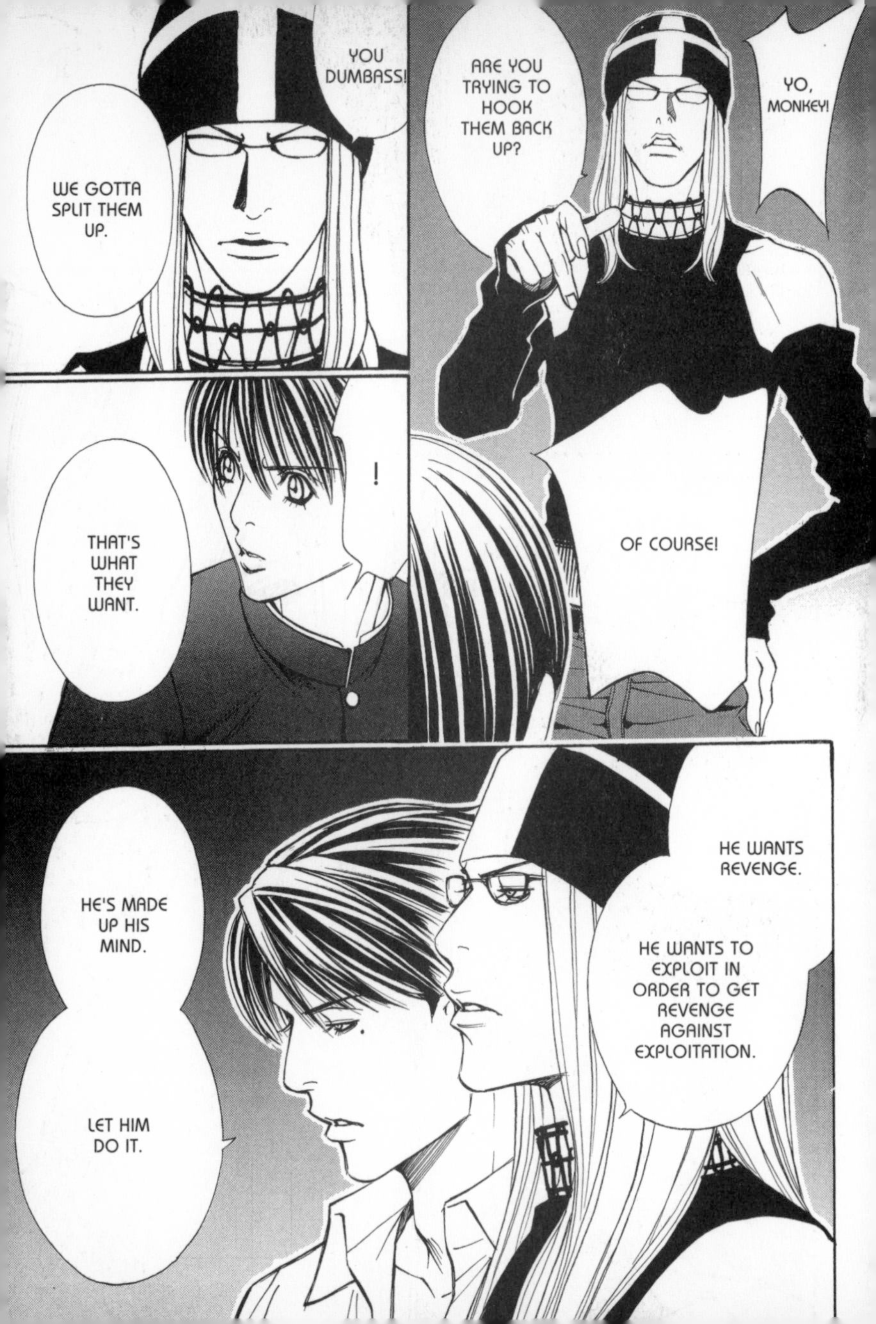
YO, MONKEY!
ARE YOU TRYING TO HOOK THEM BACK UP?
OF COURSE!
YOU DUMBASS!
WE GOTTA SPLIT THEM UP.
!
THAT'S WHAT THEY WANT.
HE WANTS REVENGE.
HE WANTS TO EXPLOIT IN ORDER TO GET REVENGE AGAINST EXPLOITATION.
HE'S MADE UP HIS MIND.
LET HIM DO IT.

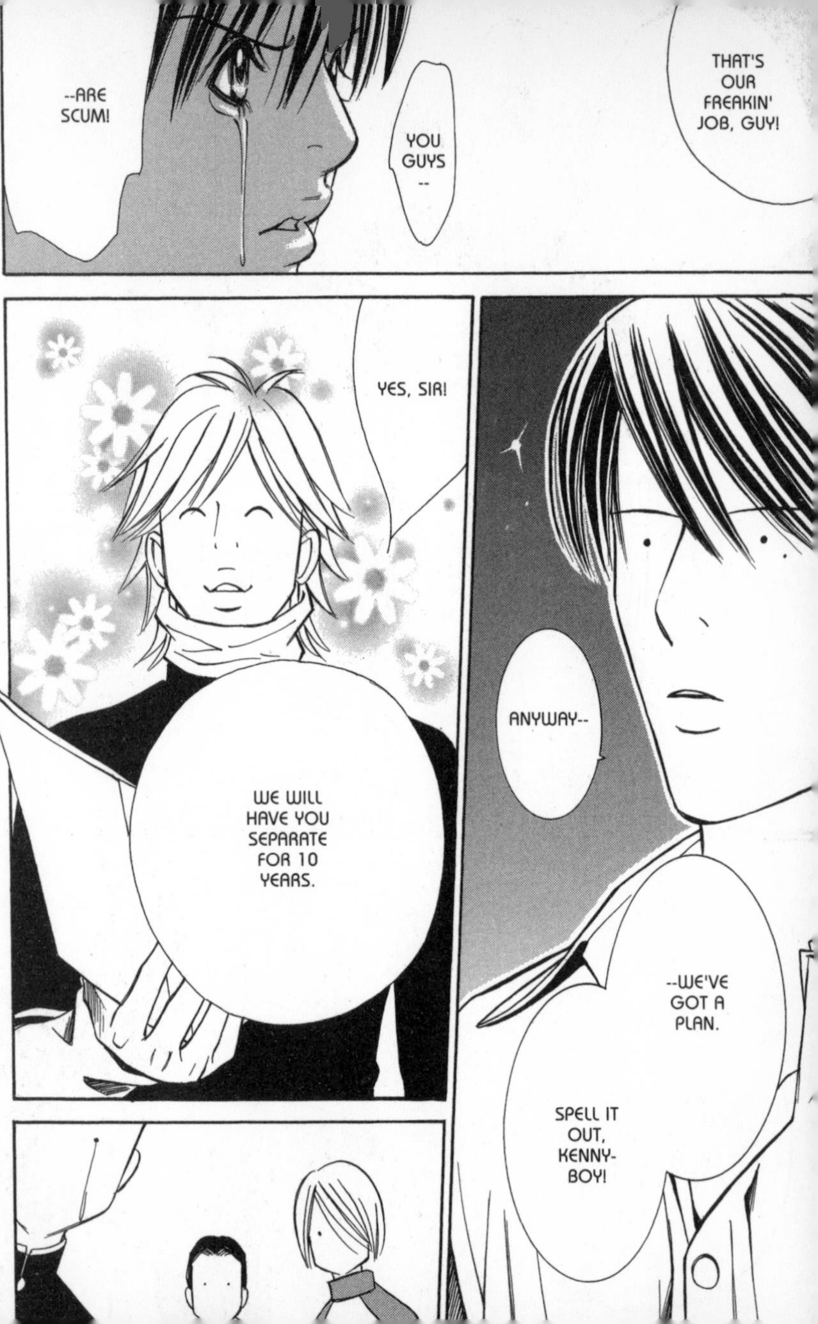

THAT'S OUR FREAKIN' JOB, GUY!
YOU GUYS --
--ARE SCUM!
ANYWAY--
--WE'VE GOT A PLAN.
SPELL IT OUT, KENNY-BOY!
YES, SIR!
WE WILL HAVE YOU SEPARATE FOR 10 YEARS.

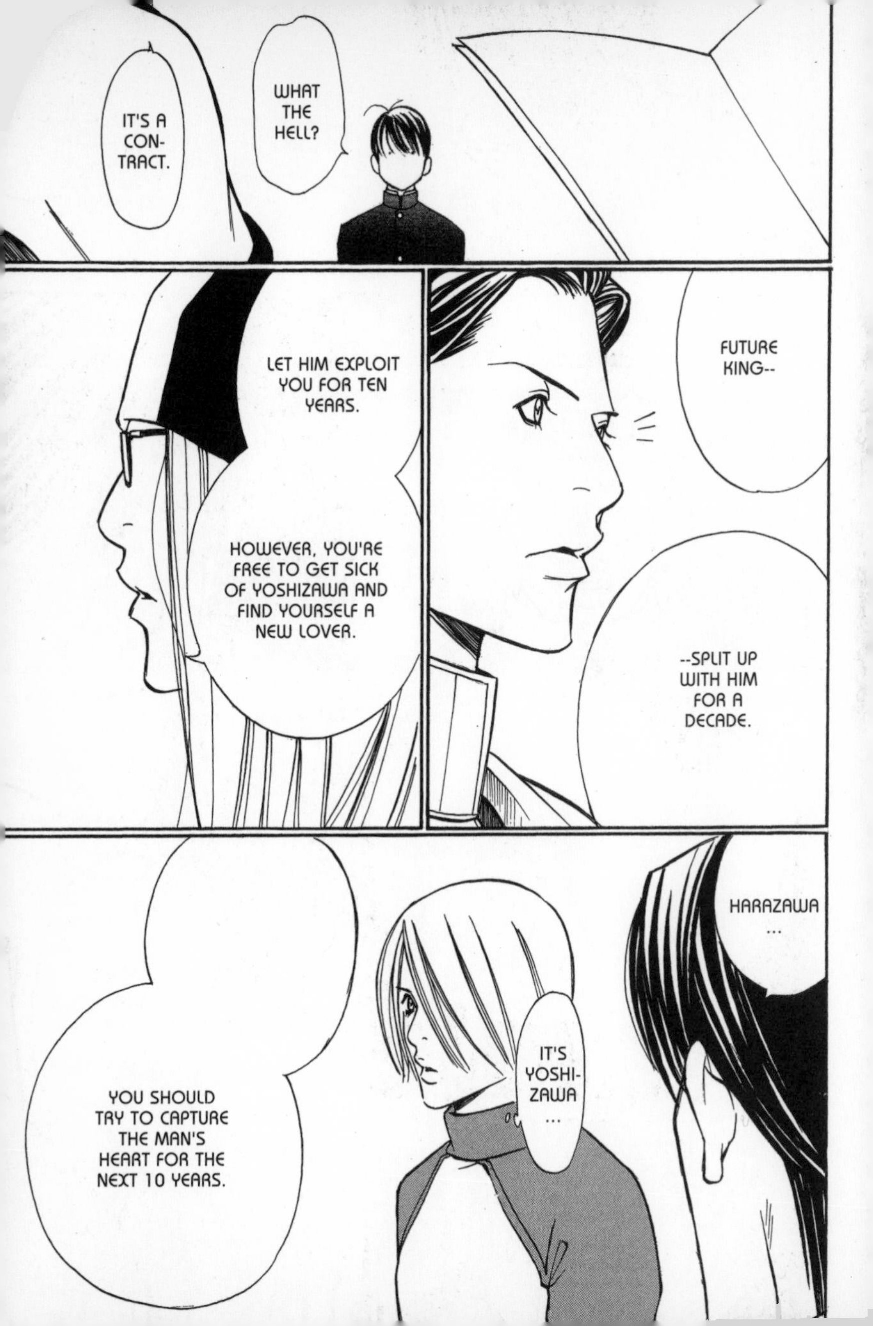
WHAT THE HELL?
IT'S A CONTRACT.
FUTURE KING--
--SPLIT UP WITH HIM FOR A DECADE.
LET HIM EXPLOIT YOU FOR TEN YEARS.
HOWEVER, YOU'RE FREE TO GET SICK OF YOSHIZAWA AND FIND YOURSELF A NEW LOVER.
HARAZAWA ...
IT'S YOSHIZAWA ...
YOU SHOULD TRY TO CAPTURE THE MAN'S HEART FOR THE NEXT 10 YEARS.

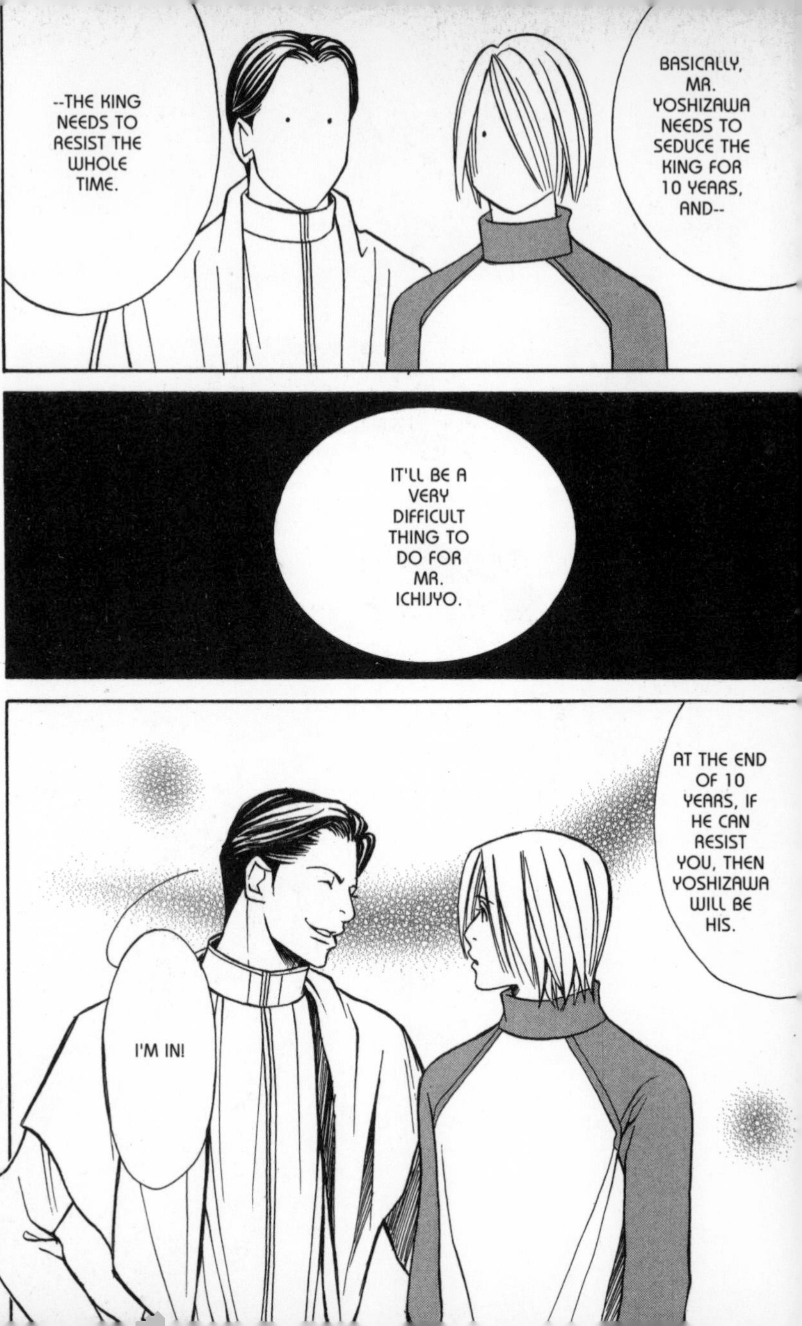
BASICALLY, MR. YOSHIZAWA NEEDS TO SEDUCE THE KING FOR 10 YEARS, AND--
--THE KING NEEDS TO RESIST THE WHOLE TIME.
IT'LL BE A VERY DIFFICULT THING TO DO FOR MR. ICHIJYO.
AT THE END OF 10 YEARS, IF HE CAN RESIST YOU, THEN YOSHIZAWA WILL BE HIS.
I'M IN!

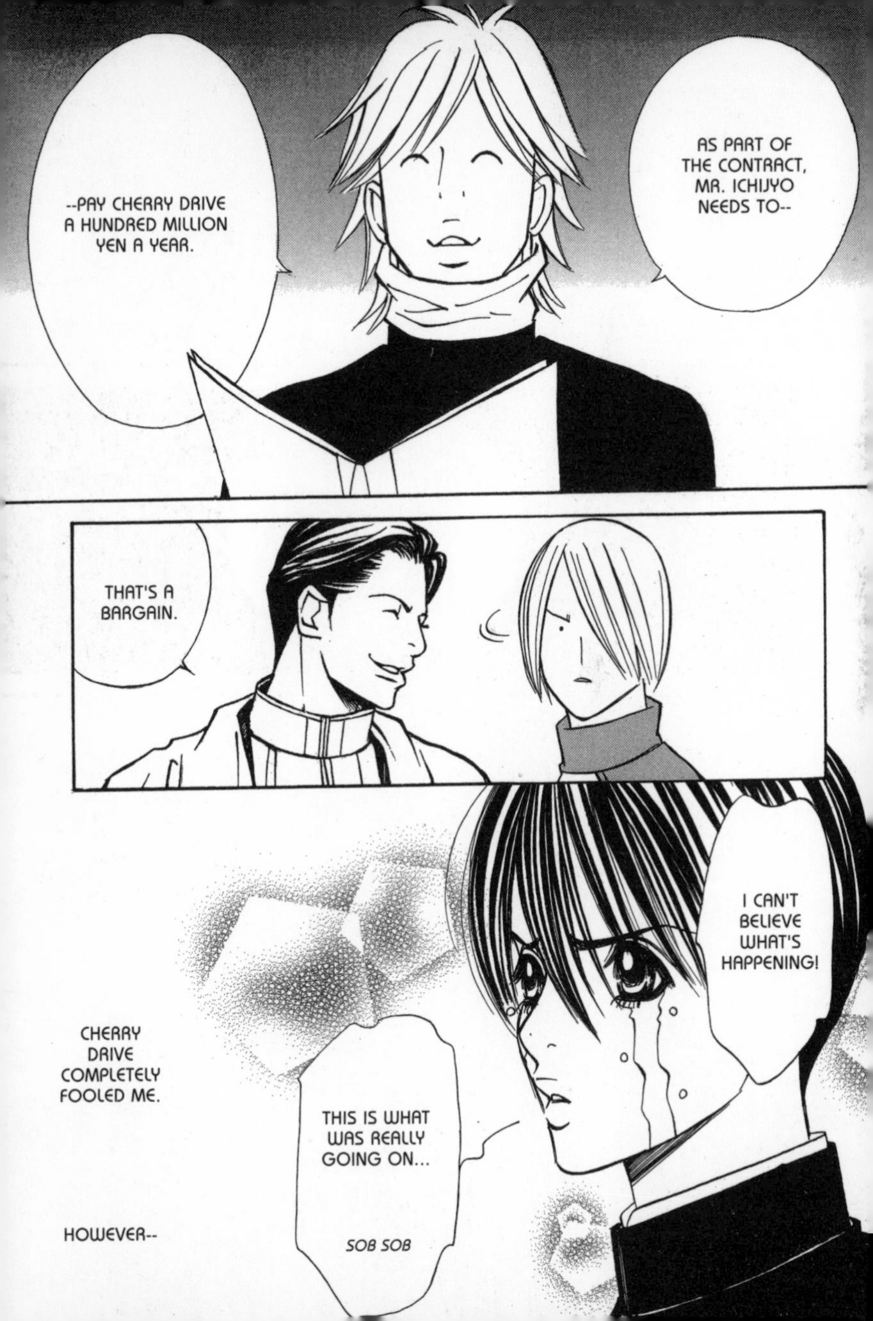
AS PART OF THE CONTRACT, MR. ICHIJYO NEEDS TO--
--PAY CHERRY DRIVE A HUNDRED MILLION YEN A YEAR.
THAT'S A BARGAIN.
I CAN'T BELIEVE WHAT'S HAPPENING!
THIS IS WHAT WAS REALLY GOING ON...
SOB SOB
CHERRY DRIVE COMPLETELY FOOLED ME.
HOWEVER--

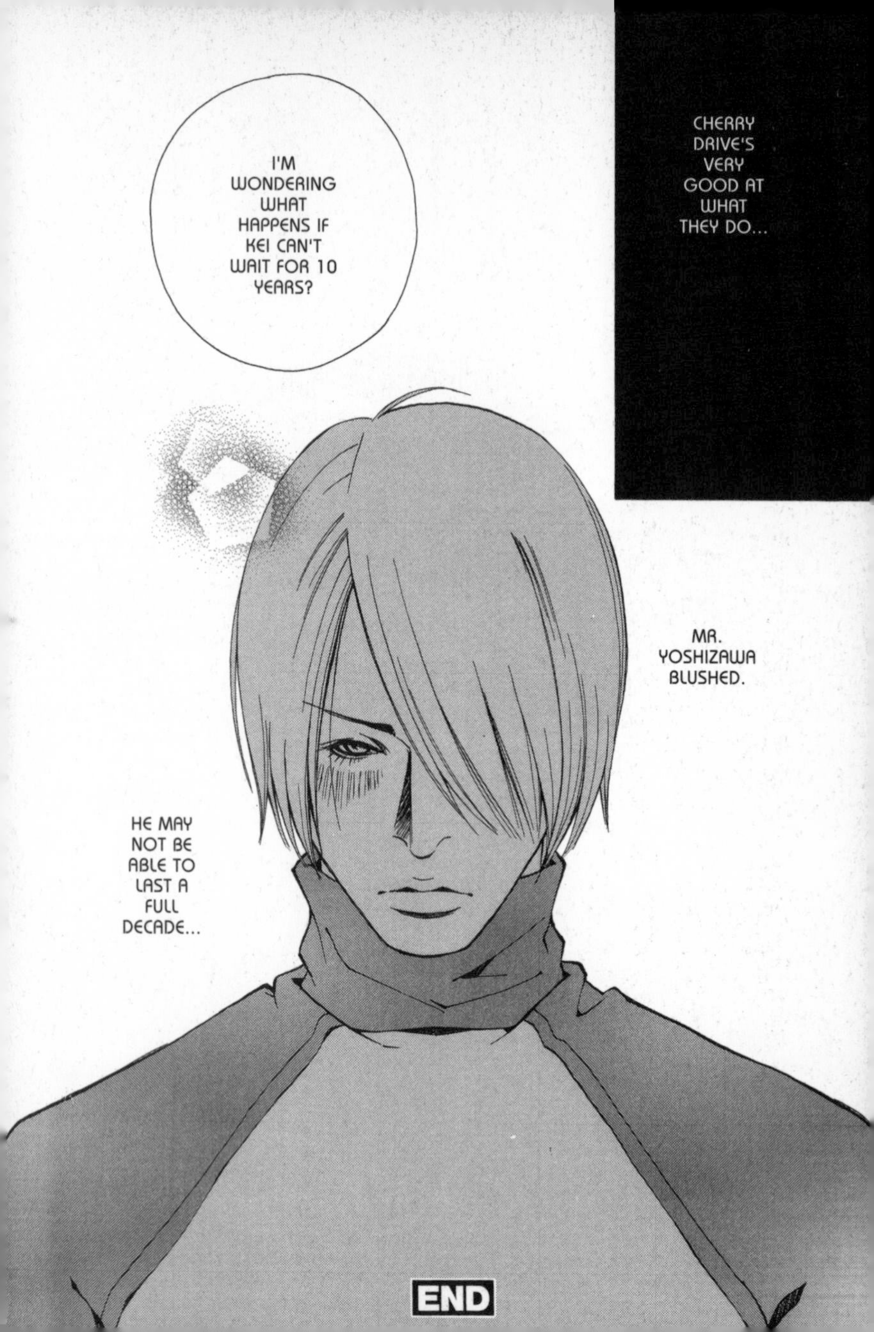
CHERRY DRIVE'S VERY GOOD AT WHAT THEY DO...
I'M WONDERING WHAT HAPPENS IF KEI CAN'T WAIT FOR 10 YEARS?
MR. YOSHIZAWA BLUSHED.
HE MAY NOT BE ABLE TO LAST A FULL DECADE...
END

POSTSCRIPT

ポイズン・チェリー・ドライブ

Poison Cherry Drive

drive 2. PASSIONATE DRIVER NAMING MEETING

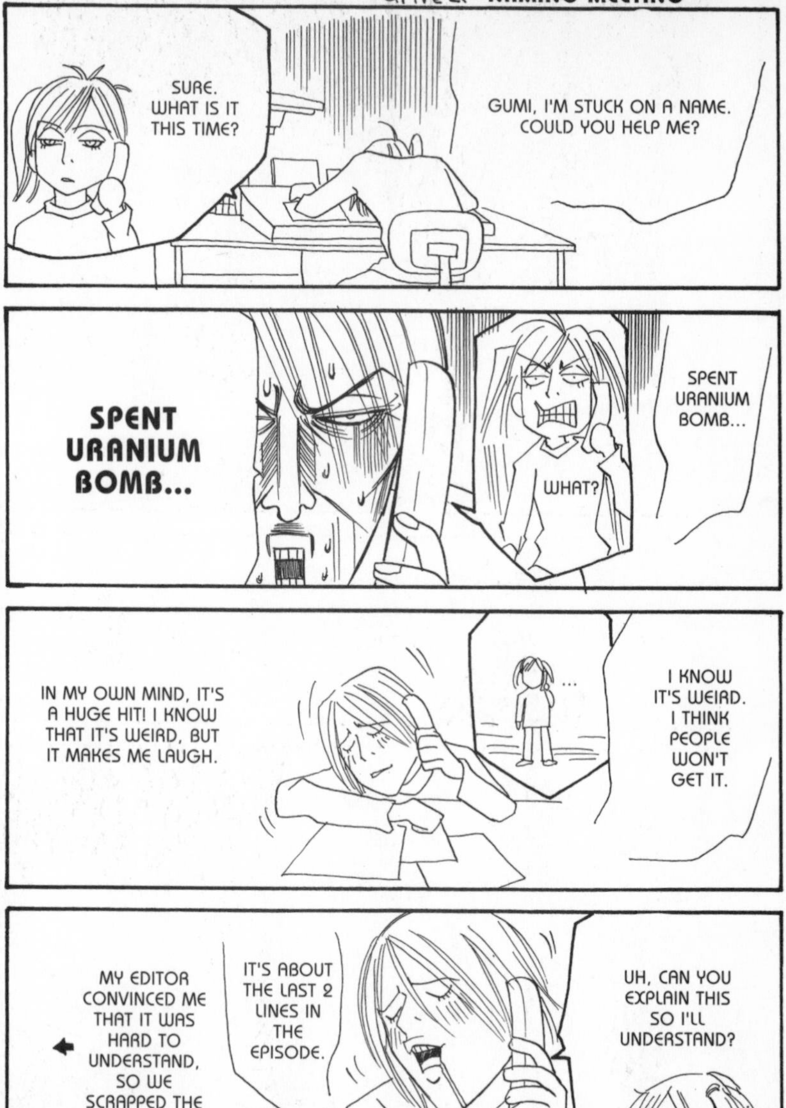
GUMI, I'M STUCK ON A NAME. COULD YOU HELP ME?
SURE. WHAT IS IT THIS TIME?
SPENT URANIUM BOMB...
WHAT?
SPENT URANIUM BOMB...
I KNOW IT'S WEIRD. I THINK PEOPLE WON'T GET IT.
...
IN MY OWN MIND, IT'S A HUGE HIT! I KNOW THAT IT'S WEIRD, BUT IT MAKES ME LAUGH.
UH, CAN YOU EXPLAIN THIS SO I'LL UNDERSTAND?
IT'S ABOUT THE LAST 2 LINES IN THE EPISODE.
MY EDITOR CONVINCED ME THAT IT WAS HARD TO UNDERSTAND, SO WE SCRAPPED THE NAME.

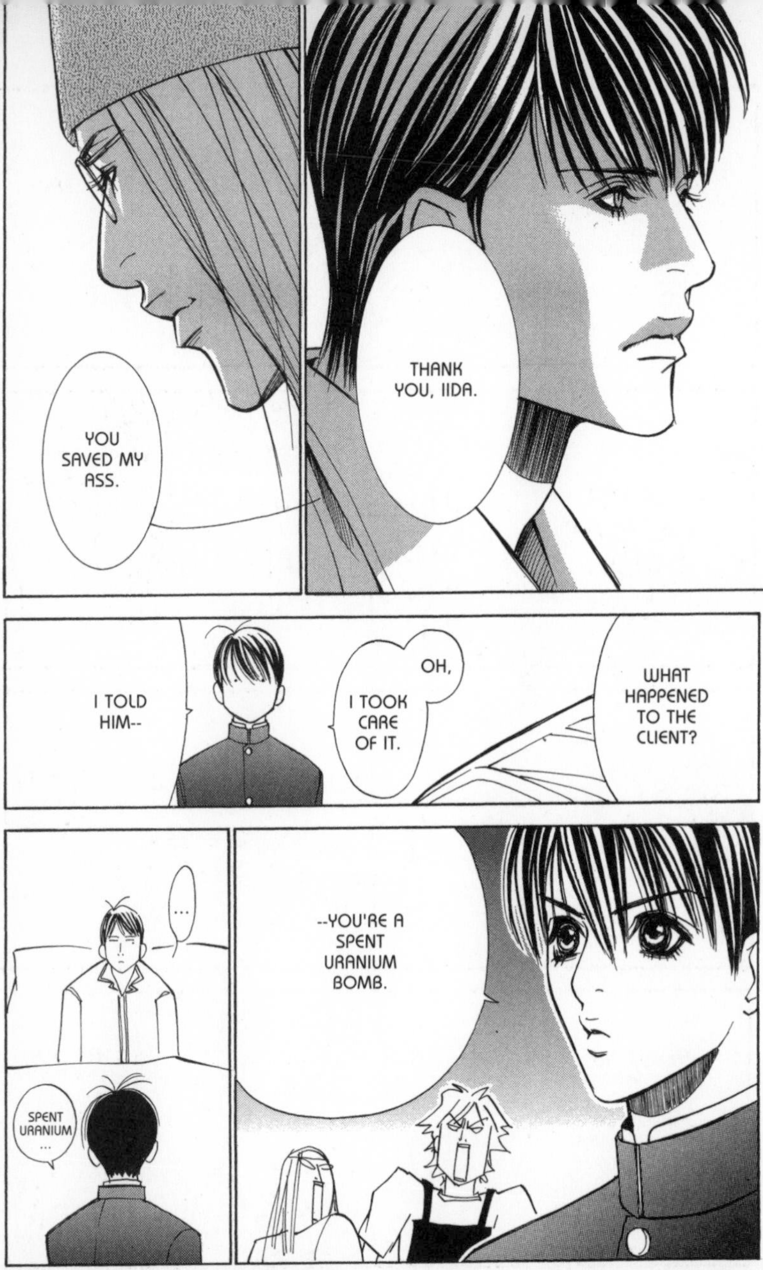
THANK YOU, IIDA.
YOU SAVED MY ASS.
WHAT HAPPENED TO THE CLIENT?
OH, I TOOK CARE OF IT.
I TOLD HIM--
--YOU'RE A SPENT URANIUM BOMB.
...
SPENT URANIUM ...

drive5、RIDING OIL MONEY NAMING COMMITTEE

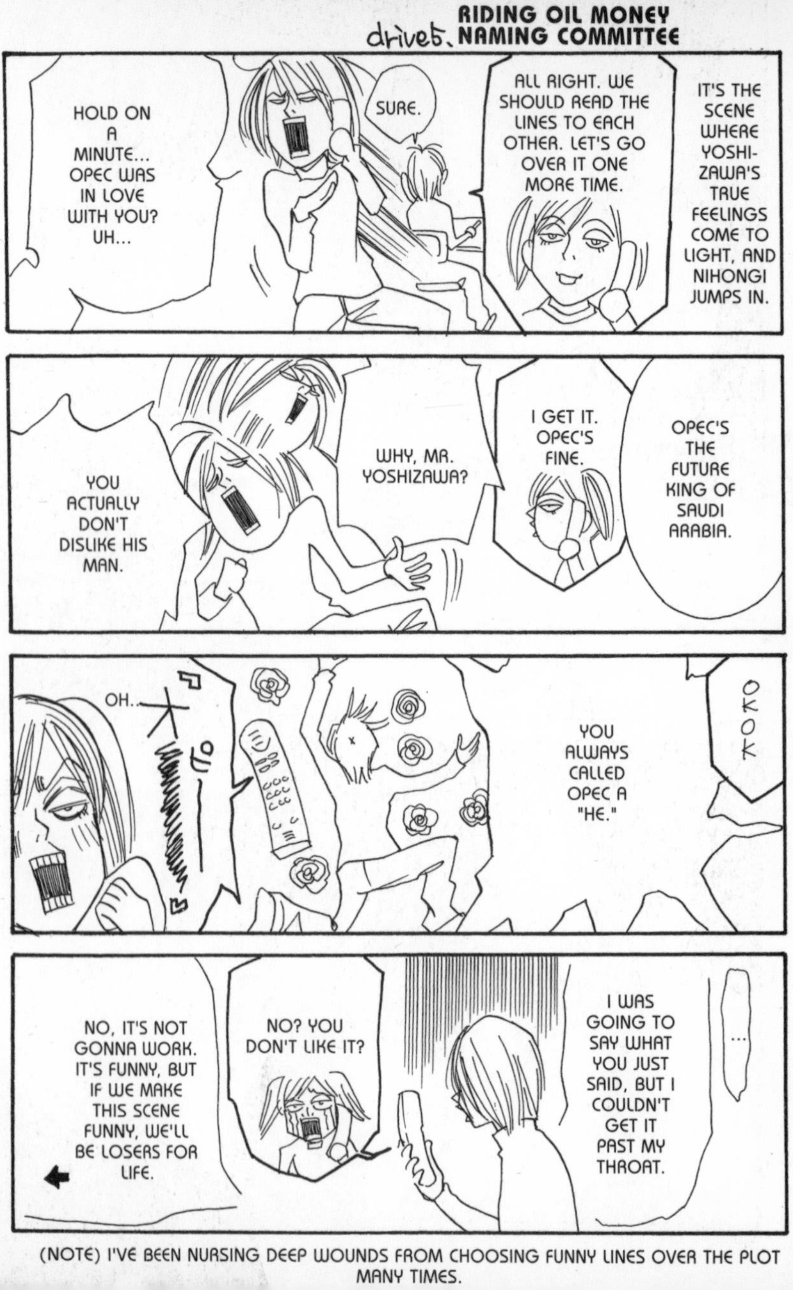
IT'S THE SCENE WHERE YOSHIZAWA'S TRUE FEELINGS COME TO LIGHT, AND NIHONGI JUMPS IN.
ALL RIGHT. WE SHOULD READ THE LINES TO EACH OTHER. LET'S GO OVER IT ONE MORE TIME.
SURE.
HOLD ON A MINUTE... OPEC WAS IN LOVE WITH YOU? UH...
OPEC'S THE FUTURE KING OF SAUDI ARABIA.
I GET IT. OPEC'S FINE.
WHY, MR. YOSHIZAWA?
YOU ACTUALLY DON'T DISLIKE HIS MAN.
OKOK
YOU ALWAYS CALLED OPEC A "HE."
OH..
...
I WAS GOING TO SAY WHAT YOU JUST SAID, BUT I COULDN'T GET IT PAST MY THROAT.
NO? YOU DON'T LIKE IT?
NO, IT'S NOT GONNA WORK. IT'S FUNNY, BUT IF WE MAKE THIS SCENE FUNNY, WE'LL BE LOSERS FOR LIFE.

(NOTE) I'VE BEEN NURSING DEEP WOUNDS FROM CHOOSING FUNNY LINES OVER THE PLOT MANY TIMES.

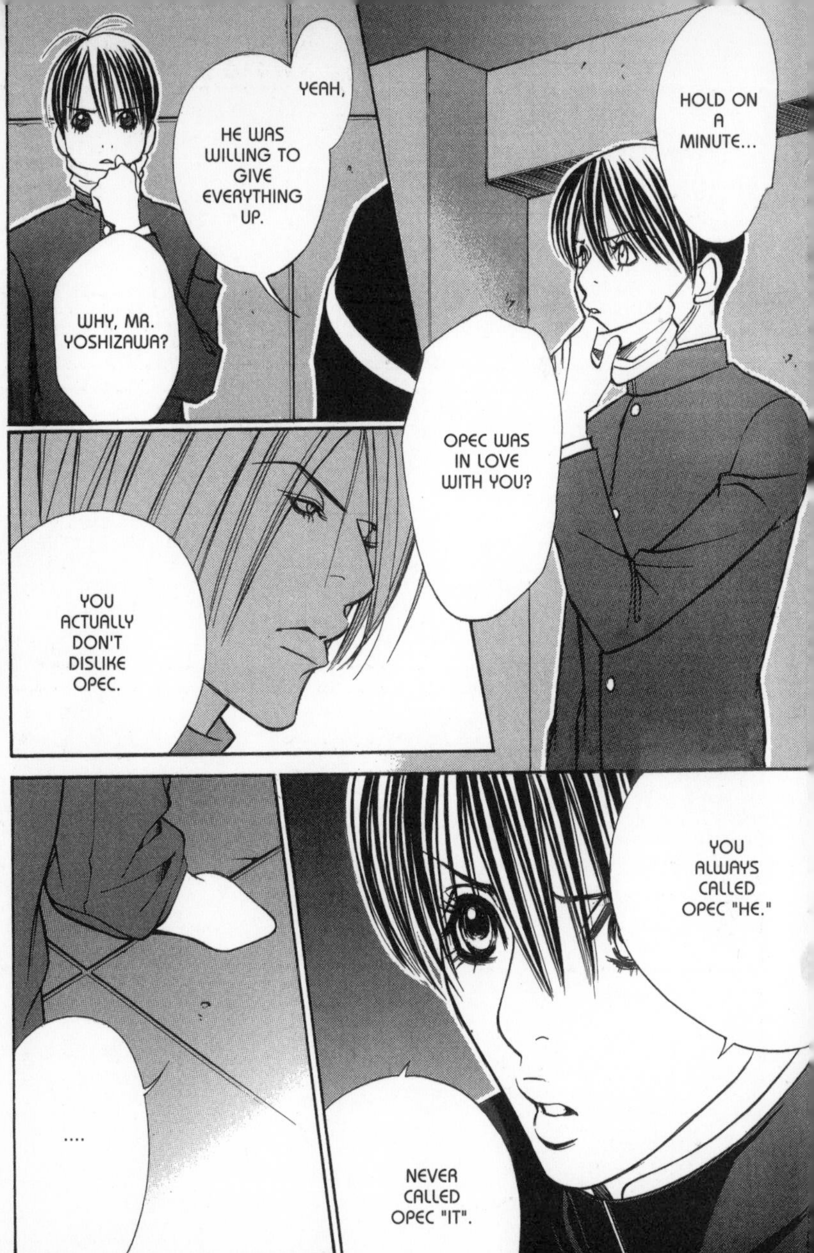
HOLD ON A MINUTE...
OPEC WAS IN LOVE WITH YOU?
YEAH,
HE WAS WILLING TO GIVE EVERYTHING UP.
WHY, MR. YOSHIZAWA?
YOU ACTUALLY DON'T DISLIKE OPEC.
YOU ALWAYS CALLED OPEC "HE."
NEVER CALLED OPEC "IT".
....

〈 IIDA-SAN CREATED THIS FOR ME 〉

MYSTERIOUS GUY MR. VENUS

HIS BUDDHIST SYMBOLS ARE TOO CUTE! USING THE LATEST TECHNOLOGY, HE CONTROLS A POWERFUL TROOP OF MIDDLE-AGED MEN. HE'S ALSO THE HEAD OF A HUGE PROSTITUTION RING. HE HAS A GRUDGE AGAINST CHERRY DRIVE BECAUSE THEY'VE INTERFERED WITH HIS WORK, BUT HE ALSO LUSTS AFTER MAMEZOU AND IIDA.

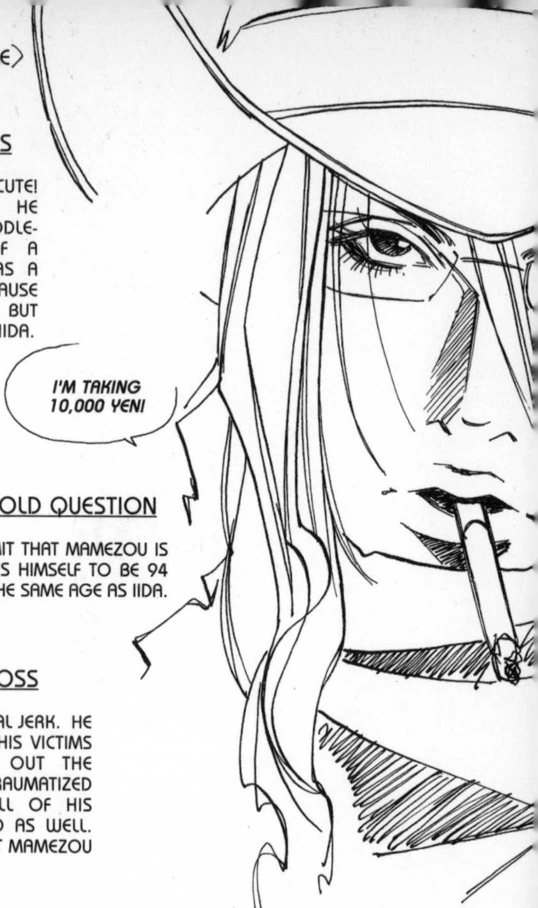
I'M TAKING 10,000 YEN!

SECRET BEHIND THE 94 YEAR-OLD QUESTION

ONE DAY, KENNY-BOY WILL FINALLY ADMIT THAT MAMEZOU IS MENTALLY INSANE. MAMEZOU BELIEVES HIMSELF TO BE 94 YEARS OLD, BUT HE'S ACTUALLY ABOUT THE SAME AGE AS IIDA.

KENNY-BOY'S MEMORY LOSS

WAY BACK WHEN, HE USED TO BE A REAL JERK. HE USED TO USE WOMEN, AND ONE OF HIS VICTIMS WANTED REVENGE. IIDA CARRIED OUT THE REVENGE REQUEST. KENNY WAS SO TRAUMATIZED AFTERWARDS THAT HE FORGOT ALL OF HIS MEMORY. HIS PERSONALITY CHANGED AS WELL. HOWEVER, THERE'S ALSO RUMOR THAT MAMEZOU ORDERED KENNY-BOY'S LOBOTOMY...

I THINK 10,000 YEN FOR THIS IS TOO STEEP...

story adviser — GUMI MAJYO

assistants — FURURIN
SU-SAN
MIDORI-CHAN

special thanx — PAPA-MAMA
SHINDO-SAMA
AND YOU